GROWTH AND CYCLES
IN
THE JAPANESE ECONOMY

BY

MIYOHEI SHINOHARA

ECONOMIC RESEARCH SERIES
No. 5
THE INSTITUTE OF ECONOMIC RESEARCH
HITOTSUBASHI UNIVERSITY

KINOKUNIYA BOOKSTORE CO., LTD.
Tokyo, Japan

PREFACE

The high rate of growth of the Japanese economy is now a well-known fact, not only in relation to the postwar period, but also to the prewar period. In this book, we intend first to ascertain this rate of growth statistically, and then to explore the various factors which are responsible for its high level, although we are not certain we shall cover all such factors. On the contrary, we have used available data to try to pry out some rather new hypotheses, even if we do not mention all the conditioning factors.

So far, some authorities have mentioned the high saving ratio, and others the secular mild inflation which permitted forced saving through an income redistribution favorable to capital accumulation. Still others emphasize the role of the introduction of compulsory education in the early Meiji period, paving the road for later economic development. Entrepreneurship also seems to be an important area of study, but we do not intend to discuss it specifically.

If we were to restrict our concern to the postwar growth of the economy, we should mention, as has Saburo Okita, the role of the extreme reduction in the proportion of defense expenditures in the government budget, emancipating funds for private capital formation. Moreover, in the postwar rehabilitation process, land reform in agriculture reduced the share of the land-owner's rent, and the greater power of labor unions increased labor's relative share of the natioal income, both playing an important role in widening the domestic market. Particularly important has been the introduction of new technology at an unprecedented rate since 1956, which technology is also closely tied to the structural change in household expenditure, *i.e.*, the rapid introduction of consumer durables, such as television, refrigerator, and electric washers.

However, in this book, we attempt to analyze the following factors :

1. Postwar recovery factors : the finding for example of an inverse correlation between the rates of decline (*e.g.* 1948/1938) and the rates of increase (*e.g.* 1954/1948) in industrial production and exports of various countries.

2. Export growth potentials : a study of the role of secular deterioration of the terms of trade in the prewar period in increasing exports, and an attempt at an international comparison of the degree of undervaluation of exchange rates through composing an international (cross-section) index of industrial production and comparing it with the dollar values of industrial incomes of various countries.

3. The effect of the concentration of capital in big firms upon the dual structure and the high rate of growth. In this analysis, we propose a hypothesis not only concerning the high rate of growth, but also concerning the causes of the dual structure.

4. The existence of the so-called Kuznets Cycle (a cycle in the growth rate of about 20 year period), through which we may become aware of the dynamic mechanism of cyclical growth.

Let us explain briefly the last factor. In the upswing of the long cycle, Japanese firms always expand their investment at an extraordinary tempo, thus bringing about a steep rise in the investment-*GNP* ratio. This entails a balance of payments difficulty as well as overcapacity in the end, leading to a situation in which wage-cut, price deflation, and even a sharp deterioration in the terms of trade must ensue. Investment boom—overcapacity—price deflation—deterioration of terms of trade—strengthening of export growth potential ; such was the sequence making up the long swings, we have seen twice in the prewar period. In other words, we see a process of rapid economic growth through explosive investment behavior and downward price adjustment. It seems to be important to recognize the role of such a disequilibrating mechanism in causing the exceptionally high rate of growth, for without this unstable mechanism we could not have attained such a rapid development.

No one will deny that the motive power of economic growth lies in the capital accumulation. In the 10-year Income Doubling Plan of the Ikeda Cabinet, investment in a private producer durables is supposed to increase to ¥3.6 trillion in 1970, but in the first year of the Plan, 1961, it had already surpassed the 1970 target amount. Moreover, in the past, from 1955 to 1961, this item showed an increase of about 5 times, which is a rate hardly to be expected even in the socialist countries. In Japan, we have had several economic plans so far, but it is very striking that in each case the plans' targets were extremely underestimated, as compared with the actual outcome. This seems to depend upon the fact that once a plan was announced, firms always behave assuming that the plan's target is a minimum line below which the firms could not but be defeated in the cutthroat competition with other firms. Therefore, firms try to expand their investment beyond the target prescribed by the plan in order to extend their market share.

This is a mechanism by which a reckless increase in investment is realized, and the extraordinary rate of growth is attained as a consequence. In this sense, one of the secrets of Japan's high rate of postwar growth may lie in the Economic Plans themselves, and in the sensitive responses of firm's investment behavior to these Plans.

There has been a so-called "Growth Controversy" about the possibility of a continuous 10% national product growth rate. Osamu Shimomura, an economic consultant of Premier Ikeda, raised the issue, and a large number of economists became involved in the controversy. In view of the importance of this problem, we took it up mainly from an academic point of view, and made some critical analyses relative to Shimomura's prediction.

The next problem in which we have interest is the business cycle in the postwar period. First, exploring the various aspects or peculiarities of postwar cycle phenomena, we found (a) a greater downward rigidity of investment in plant and equipment than in the prewar period, (b) that the cycles are more evident in the proportional composition of *GNP* than in the level of various economic variables, (c) that the cycles are more prominent in the rate of increase in industrial production, imports, *etc.* than in their levels, and (d), that the role of inventory investment is very important in the postwar cycles and in the difficulties in the balance of payments. Second, although it is a common sense that we cannot find the so-called "Juglar" cycle in the postwar economic series, we found about a ten year cycle in the ratio of producer's durables to *GNP* (based on the national income statistics). It is not still clear whether or not this cycle is illusory, but it seems to be an interesting phenomenon. Third, we find the striking fact that the inventory cycle of smaller firms leads that of large firms, and interpret this phenomenon as an influence of the dual structure (particularly the concentration of capital in big firms) upon the short-run business cycle.

The problems of growth and cycles are the main topics discussed in this book, but we have taken this opportunity to include a few other papers relating to the consumption function, the multiplier in a world of changing prices and the production function. This section of the book is a mixture of theoretical as well as empirical analyses, and does not always have any bearing on the subject matter of first and second parts. Moreover, the paper on the empirical analysis of the production function in the prewar manufacturing is not satisfactory and needs some revision or development, but we have decided to include it here as it is.

This book does not represent a consistently organized work, but is a collection of various articles already published in foreign or Japanese economic journals, although some amendments have been made in each paper.

The author acknowledges, with thanks, the permission granted by publishers of the following foreign journals to reprint with amendment papers included in this volume:

1. "The Structure of Saving and the Consumption Function in Postwar Japan", *Journal of Political Economy*, Dec. 1959.
2. "Relative Production Levels of Industrial Countries and their Growth Potentials", *Weltwirtschaftliches Archiv*, Band 86 Heft 1, 1961.
3. "Some Causes and Consequences of Japanese Economic Growth", *Malayan Economic Review*, April 1961.
4. "The Multiplier and the Marginal Propensity to Import", *American Economic Review*, September, 1957.

PREFACE

Further, the author would like to express his thanks for the help, of the Ford Foundation in translating papers (1) and (2), and also for the assistance of a number of foreign economists, particularly Harry Oshima and Arlon R. Tussing in the correction of my English. Studies in some papers were made under a grant from the Rockefeller Foundation. Without these aids, my book would not appear.

This book is in some respects an English version of the author's recent book published in Japanese the title of which is the same (*Nihonkeizai no Seicho to Junkan*, Sobunsha 1961) but owing to troubles of translation, the author could not but omit some part of it and even some of the statistical appendix. This book further differs from the Japanese edition in the fact that it includes the material of Part Three which did not appear in the Japanese edition.

January 1962

MIYOHEI SHINOHARA

CONTENTS

PART III   OTHER RELATED TOPICS

PART I

GROWTH

CHAPTER 1

SOME CAUSES AND CONSEQUENCES OF ECONOMIC GROWTH IN JAPAN

1. Introduction

The economic development of Japan since the Meiji Restoration in the nineteenth century has always attracted the attention of economists and planners. In particular, her rapid postwar recovery has excited the envy of those nations which are still in the underdeveloped stages, and in Japan itself the phenomenal rate of growth has often been regarded as an economic miracle. Few attempts, however, have been made to analyse the background and the various underlying factors behind this economic expansion, and where such studies have been attempted they have often been fragmentary and unsystematic.

This chapter does not attempt to present a comprehensive analysis of the causes and consequences of Japan's economic growth. The analysis here is confined to a detailed study of two aspects of this growth: first, the postwar recovery factor and, second, capital concentration in the large corporations and its relation to growth and the dual economy, with the main focus on the postwar economic process. Particular reference will not be made to the important role of the export growth potential in achieving rapid domestic expansion, which studies are presented in Chapter 2 and 3.

2. A Comparison of Postwar International Growth Rates

Before embarking on an analysis of Japan's high rate of growth, it will be useful to make a comparison of growth rates in the economies of various countries. Using United Nations data, we show

3

in Table 1 the gross national product (or gross domestic product) growth rates in various countries for 1951–57, and in Table 2 the growth rates of industrial production in various countries for 1948– 53 and 1953–58. In Table 1, we find that for fifteen selected countries, the gross national product growth rate of Japan is the highest and surpasses even that of West Germany, which has also been exceptionally high. The countries listed in Table 1 are capitalist countries; the socialist nations have been excluded because of differences in the concept of national income. However, in Table 2 we have computed the industrial growth rates of 36 countries in terms of indexes of industrial production. These include not only the capitalist but also the socialist countries, and both the advanced and the underdeveloped countries. Again, among the industrialized capitalist countries, Japan's growth rate of industrial production is the highest for 1948–53 as well as for 1953–58. Its industrial growth rate is comparable with the growth rates of the socialist countries, including the Soviet Union.

Of course, among the underdeveloped countries included in Table 2, some countries such as Pakistan exhibit higher growth rates. The explanation is that in such an underdeveloped stage the establishment of a single modern factory will often give a misleading

Table 1. Annual Gross National Product Growth Rates in Various Countries, 1951–57

	%		%
Japan	7.76	Puerto Rico	4.06
West Germany	7.50	Sweden	3.80
Greece	6.82	Luxemburg	2.98
Italy	5.35	United States	2.93
Netherlands	5.25	United Kingdom	2.45
France	4.64	Ireland	1.50
Canada	4.21	Argentina	1.45
Portugal	4.12		

Notes : When gross domestic product at constant prices is available, *GDP* is given instead of real *GNP*.
Source : United Nations, *Yearbook of National Accounts Statistics*, 1958.

Table 2. Annual Growth Rates of Industrial Production in Various Countries, 1943-53 And 1953-58

Industrialised Capitalist Countries	1948-53	1953-58
	%	%
Japan	22.67	10.93
West Germany	20.72	8.46
Austria	13.12	8.45
Italy	10.03	7.43
Netherlands	10.03	4.73
Ireland	7.40	0.98
Norway	6.50	4.39
Canada	5.92	3.37
Finland	5.65	5.32
France	5.65	7.86
United States	5.65	0.00
New Zealand	4.56	4.73
Sweden	2.36	3.37
Belgium	2.12	2.83
Luxemburg	2.12	3.89

Underdeveloped Countries	1948-53	1953-58
	%	%
Pakistan	25.17 *	13.63
Taiwan	20.11	8.30
Philippines	14.10 **	11.20
Greece	13.97	8.50
Peru	10.03	9.97 †
Brazil	7.64	6.65 ††
Chile	7.40	0.40
Algeria	6.50	8.73
Venezuela	6.50	12.60
Mexico	3.80	8.01
India	2.82	5.71
Arabia	2.61 ***	6.75 ††
Guatemala	1.91	6.95
Argentina	-0.99	3.80

Socialist Countries	1948-53	1953-58
	%	%
Hungary	24.08	4.06
Rumania	23.36	4.54
East Germany	17.28 *	8.46
Czechoslovakia	13.97	8.52
U.S.S.R.	13.14 *	11.76 ††
Bulgaria	6.50	8.73
Yugoslavia	4.06	13.58

Notes: (a) * 1950-53; ** 1949-53; *** 1951-53.
(b) † 1953-56; †† 1953-57.

Source: United Nations, *Patterns of Industrial Growth, 1938-1958*, New York, 1960.

figure of industrial expansion, while there is no corresponding improvement in real *per capita* income.

Apart from such considerations, the Japanese postwar expansion is still astonishing, and it could not have been anticipated that Japan would be able to accomplish such a remarkable economic recovery and progress within fifteen short years. So far, the targets of every long term economic plan have been underestimated, an indication of her high growth potential and unexpected vitality.

This should not be considered only a postwar phenomenon. Since the Meiji Restoration, the real national income growth rate has ranged between 4% and 5%, and although this is low compared with that in the postwar period, it still exceeded the growth rates of various other countries in the prewar period, as shown in Table 3.

Table. 3. Annual Real National Income Growth Rates in Various Countries, 1860–1913 And 1913–38

	1860–1913	1913–38		1860–1913	1913–38
	%	%		%	%
United States	4.3	2.0	Netherlands	2.3	2.1
Australia	3.7	2.1	Belgium	2.2	1.0
United Kingdom	2.4	1.0	Switzerland	2.6	1.6
			Sweden	2.0	1.9
France	1.1	1.1	Norway	2.3	1.9
Germany	3.0	1.3	Japan	4.1 *	4.5
Denmark	2.8	2.1			

Note : * 1878–1913.

Sources : (a) R. W. Goldsmith, " Financial Structure and Economic Growth in Advanced Countries," in *Capital Formation and Economic Growth*, Princeton, 1955, p. 115.

(b) The figures for Japan are based on data in Ohkawa and associates, *The Growth Rate of the Japanese Economy since 1878*, Kinokuniya, 1957.

These figures merely emphasize the long-run growth potential of the Japanese economy. Thus, we must not be misled by the view that Japan's exceptionally high growth rate is due only to the postwar recovery factor, for secular factors are also involved, as well as short-run postwar factors. However, we will first discuss postwar reconstruction and recovery factors, and then proceed to the examination of secular factors.

3. Postwar Recovery Factor in Japan

Even though Japan's plant and equipment were damaged in the war, certain economic assets remained undamaged, such as the labor force, levels of skill, education and technology. Moreover, there remained a great deal of unused equipment after the war which became usuable with the input of raw material and fuel—the bottlenecks of the period. Therefore, we could logically expect that in those countries in which production declined most sharply immediately after the war, recovery would be most rapid, and *vice versa*. In other words, we can find an inverse correlation in the various countries between the rates of decline in industrial production from the prewar to the immediate postwar level and the rates of recovery from the immediate postwar level.

The chart on page 8 presents the above correlation for 23 countries.[1] Excluding the six socialist countries (Rumania, Poland, Soviet Union, Czechoslovakia, Hungary and Yugoslavia), and the United States and Canada, there is a fairly clear inverse correlation between the rates of decline and the rates of recovery in industrial production. Those countries in which production declined most drastically, as in Japan and West Germany, also show the most rapid recovery after the war, whereas countries in which production declined least or even increased during the war years show the lowest rates of increase in the following period. Sweden, United Kingdom, Belgium, Luxemburg and New Zealand belong to this latter group.

The six socialist countries are exceptions to this empirical rule but this is understandable in view of the authoritarian planning in these

1) The chart is a correlation between the change in industrial production in various countries in 1948 (expressed as a ratio of industrial production in 1938=1) and 1956 (expressed as a ratio of industrial production in 1948=1). A position to the left of 1 on the horizontal axis indicates that the industrial production in 1948 did not come up to the 1938 level.

Fig. 1.   The Relation between the Decline and the Recovery of Industrial
Production in Various Countries

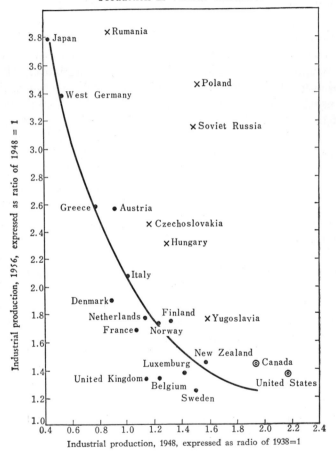

Source :   United Nations, *Statistical Yearbook*, 1959.

countries to accelerate economic growth. This is why the socialist
countries on the chart are scattered to the right of the downward-
sloping curve.[2] Canada and the United States also seem to be
exceptions, and this may be on account of the fact that these countries
did not suffer any damage to their industrial plants and were in fact
supplying Europe during the war, with a consequent expansion of
their industrial capacity.

The above empirical rule is valid not only for changes in industrial
production and real national product, but also for changes in exports
as shown in Table 4.[3] With the exception of France, Canada and

Table 4. The Relation between the Decline and Recovery of Exports
in Various Countries

	Changes in exports (Earlier year=1)	
	1948 / 1937–39	1953–55 / 1947
Japan	0.08	6.80
Germany	0.20	5.55
Netherlands	0.63	3.29
Denmark	0.67	2.27
Ireland	0.72	1.80
Norway	0.78	1.59
Italy	0.79	1.67
France	0.89	2.44
Belgium-Luxemburg	0.91	1.62
Turkey	1.00	1.62
Portugal	1.01	1.55
New Zealand	1.23	1.06
Malaya	1.36	1.15
Canada	1.90	1.15
United States	1.93	1.22

Source: United Nations, *Statistical Yearbook*, 1959.

2) This curve has been drawn freehand.
3) Table 4 shows the change in exports in various countries in 1948 (expressed
as a ratio of exports in 1937–39=1) and 1953–55 (expressed as a ratio of exports
in 1948=1).

the United States, the inverse correlation of decline and recovery in exports of various countries in the two respective periods is shown to be close.

Casual consideration would suggest that in the postwar recovery phase, the marginal fixed capital-output ratio would be lower than in the later stages, since there would be greater unused capacity in the immediate postwar years and in order to increase output not as much fixed investment would be needed as in the later period.

It may be convenient for our analysis to divide the postwar ex-

Table 5. Changes in the Ratio of Producers' Durables to Gross National Product in Japan, 1946–59

Fiscal year	Private $\frac{PD}{GNP}$	Total $\frac{PD}{GNP}$
	%	%
1946	7.8	13.4
1947	7.2	15.1
1948	7.9	14.9
1949	8.6	15.4
1950	9.9	16.0
1951	11.2	17.7
1952	11.6	18.8
1953	11.3	20.2
1954	10.2	18.3
1955	9.4	16.9
1956	14.7	22.0
1957	16.6	24.9
1958	15.8	24.5
1959	17.3	25.8

Notes: (a) Producers' durables in Japanese national income statistics include business construction, such as factories, buildings and dams, in addition to machinery and equipment.
   (b) Total producers' durables include both private and public producers' durables.
   (c) The fiscal year in Japan is from April 1 to March 31.
Source: Economic Planning Agency, *Kokuminshotoku Hakusho* (National Income Report), 1960.

pansion process into three stages: 1946–51, 1951–56 and 1956–59. The reason for this breakdown is explained in Table 5. In the first stage, 1946–51, the ratio of private producers' durables to gross national product was about 8%; it rose to 11% in 1951–56 and 16% in 1956–59. This increase was not a gradual process but took place by way of two distinct steps, thus dividing the entire postwar development into three stages. This division can also be seen in the total producers' durables-gross national product ratio; this is approximately 15% in the first, 19% in the second, and 24% in the third stage.

The period 1946–51 is of a purely postwar recovery nature. Although a deflationary policy was temporarily enforced in 1949 through the implementation of the Dodge Plan,[4] the entire period was characterized by normal postwar recovery, intermingled with a hyper-inflation which lasted to the end of the Korean Incident in 1951. During this period, industrial production rose sharply owing to the concentrated investment in key industries of the funds of the Reconstruction Finance Bank and the Counterpart Fund derived from American aid to Japan,[5] the granting of price subsidies to basic commodities, and the priority given to key industries in the allocation of electricity, coal and steel. As the rate of capacity utilization, that is, the ratio of output to existing capacity, was low in this period, nearly all industries could raise production levels without requiring much equipment investment, as long as the supplies of basic raw materials (especially imported materials), fuels and electricity were available.

The second period began with the mild recession after the Korean Incident, but production soon recovered and this recovery continued through the boom of 1953 to the so-called " Jimmu boom " in 1956.[6] On account of the outbreak of the Korean war, the utilization rate of equipment was tremendously accelerated. In manufacturing industries, it increased from 53.1% in March 1950 to 73.2% in March

4) This was an economic stabilisation plan recommended by Mr. J. Dodge, an economic adviser to the Occupation authorities.
5) This is the currency fund derived from the sale of United States aid goods.
6) Emperor Jimmu was the legendary founder of Japan.

1951.   The utilization rate was 74.3% in March 1953 and 83.0% in March 1956.   In other words, it continued to increase but at a declining rate as compared with the experience of the first stage. The rise in special procurement demand[7] after the start of the Korean Incident temporarily took the place of an endogenous increase of exports, but its subsequent decline compelled Japanese manufacturers to increase equipment investment and introduce new technology in order to strengthen the competitive power of their exports.   This was part of the reason for the increase in the producers' durables-gross national product ratio in the second period.

This ratio continued to increase in the third stage, 1956–59.   This period can be considered epochmaking, for a great many changes took place, not only in the method of production but also in the mode of life.   Comparing 1959 witn 1955, the index of production of manufacturing and mining rose by four-fifths while the production of electrical machinery increased by 4.6 times.   The production index of consumer durables also increased by 4.4 times.   The increase in the production of television sets, 21 times, electric washing machines, 2.6 times, and refrigerators, 18 times, are examples of output trends of some leading commodities.   It is very probable that in this dynamic stage the ratio of producers' durables to gross national product will continue to rise to new levels.

It will be particularly interesting, against the economic background described above, to estimate the marginal fixed capital-output ratio corresponding to the above three stages.   If we denote real producers' durables a₃ PD and real gross national product as GNP, then the marginal fixed capital-output ratio is $PD/\Delta GNP$.   This has a fixed relationship with the growth rate of GNP which can be indicated by the following identity

$$\frac{PD}{GNP} \bigg/ \frac{\Delta GNP}{GNP} \equiv \frac{PD}{\Delta GNP}$$

In other words, the ratio derived from dividing PD/GNP by the growth rate ($\Delta GNP/GNP$) is identically equal to the marginal fixed

7)   This is United States military expenditure in Japan for the procurement of Japanese goods and services.

capital-output ratio, as given in Table 6.

It is clear from Table 6 that the marginal fixed capital-output ratio, represented by either $\frac{a}{c}$ or $\frac{b}{c}$, rose very rapidly, comparing the first period with the second, but the increase in the third stage was relatively small. In the first stage the coefficient was very low, reflecting mainly the existence of surplus capacity immediately after the war; accordingly, the low level of the marginal fixed capital-output ratio indicates that the economy was still in the reconstruction and recovery phase. In the second stage, the $PD/\Delta GNP$ ratio increased, indicating that the unit investment requirements increased. On the other hand, the further rise in the third stage was caused (as already discussed) by the unprecedented technological revolution which took place within a very short period.

That the first stage belongs to the postwar recovery phase is evident, but what about the second and third stages? The 1957 White Paper stated that Japan had already passed the postwar recovery period. If we restrict our analysis to the rate of utilization of capacity, this statement would be valid. Some economists went so far as to assert that we were in the midst of " take-off ", on the way to joining the fraternity of advanced countries. If the present rate of growth continues for the next ten years, it is expected that

Table 6. Changes in the Marginal Fixed Capital-Output Ratio in Japan, 1946–59

	Private $\dfrac{PD}{GNP}$ (a)	Total $\dfrac{PD}{GNP}$ (b)	GNP growth rate (c)	Marginal fixed capital-output ratio	
				$\left[\dfrac{a}{c}\right]$	$\left[\dfrac{b}{c}\right]$
	%	%	%		
1946–51	8.8	15.4	11.2	0.79	1.38
1951–56	11.4	19.0	7.6	1.50	2.50
1956–59	16.1	24.3	9.0	1.79	2.70

Note: The GNP growth rate is computed by fitting a linear logarithmic equation for each period.

Source: Economic Planning Agency, *Kokuminshotoku Hakusho* (National Income Report), 1960.

13

Japan will catch up with the present *per capita* income levels in European countries. However, if we look at the problem from a different angle, even the present stage of technological innovation can be considered a kind of postwar phenomenon. During the war, the introduction of new technology had been suppressed but the development of ability, education, skills, and know-how continued to advance. The gap between the actual state of technology and the potential power to employ the new technology had been widened, on the one hand, as had also the gap between Japanese technology and that of other industrialised countries, on the other. The technological progress in recent years can be said to have narrowed the gap considerably, and if this gap is further narrowed in the future, then one might presume that the rate of Japan's economic growth would be slowed down.

However, this assumption does not take into consideration the fact that the high rate of growth of the Japanese economy is attributable not only to such short-run factors but also to secular factors. There is also an urgent need to explore the secular mainsprings of her rapid growth.

4. Growth, Capital Concentration and the Dual Economy

We shall take up here one of the secular factors, capital concentration and the dual structure of the economy. Other secular factors, such as the competitive power of exports, will be discussed in Chapter 2 and 3.

The term ' dual economy ' is often used to designate an economy in which modern (or capitalistic) large firms co-exist with pre-modern (or pre-capitalistic) medium and small firms, and in which there prevails enormous wage or income differentials not found in more advanced countries; there is also a polarization of output and employment in the very large and the very small firms respectively. In Japan this kind of dual structure did not exist in the Meiji period (1868–1912); wage differentials by size of firms were not as pronounced then as at the present time, as can be seen in Table 7.

14

Table 7. Wages of Total and Male Workers in Manufacturing Firms in Japan,
1909 and 1914

Unit : sen.   100 sen = 1 yen

	Size of firm by number of employees						
	5 −9	10 −29	30 −49	50 −99	100 −499	500 −999	1,000 and above
Average daily wage							
1909—All	34.2	33.2	31.7	32.5	34.0	32.5	34.4
Male	43.0	46.0	47.7	49.4	50.5	49.4	53.5
1914—All	39.5	37.0	34.6	35.4	35.9	39.3	43.4
Male	47.2	50.2	51.3	53.8	55.5	57.0	65.5

Source :   Estimates by M. Umemura and A. Nakamura based on data in Noshomu-
sho, *Kojotokeisohyo* (Summary of Factory Statistics) ; also available in
Showadojinkai, ed., *Wagakuni Chinginkozo no Shitekikosatsu* (Historical
Analysis of Japanese Wage Structure), p. 471.

Further, the concentration of output in the large firms was not as conspicuous.

The extensive wage differentials which developed from the middle of the Taisho period (1912–25) to the beginning of the Showa period (1925–) are shown in Table 8.   These wage differentials have been carried over almost intact into the postwar period.   The gap was temporarily narrowed in the immediate postwar years, 1946–48, on account of the hyperinflation and drastically reduced living standards.   However, apart from this temporary phenomenon, the sharp wage differentials of the early Showa period remain, as can be seen in Table 9.

In Table 10, wage and productivity differentials by size of firm in Japan are compared with those in the United States and the United Kingdom.   We can see that in the latter two more advanced countries the wage and productivity differentials are much smaller than in Japan.   Such a phenomenon, of course, may not be peculiar to Japan, for the recent Censuses of Manufactures of Ceylon and India also suggest the existence of fairly steep wage and productivity differentials as a result of the vigorous industrialization programs undertaken

15

Table 8. Wages of All Workers in Manufacturing Firms in Tokyo and Yokohama, 1932

Unit: yen

	Size of firm by amount of invested capital (in yen)									
	1 −99	100 −499	500 −999	1,000 −1,999	2,000 −4,999	5,000 −9,999	10,000 −49,999	50,000 −99,999	100,000 −499,999	500,000 and above
Average annual earnings										
1932—Tokyo	178.7	185.8	206.4	232.8	281.2	352.1	486.6	570.6	624.6	793.9
Yokohama	121.1	158.5	178.4	241.3	297.3	373.5	445.4	560.7	671.7	771.5

Source: Estimates by A. Nakamura based on data in *Kogyochosasho* (Survey of Manufactures), 1932; also available in Showadojinkai, ed., *op. cit.*

16

Table 9. Wages of All Workers in Manufacturing Firms in Japan, 1952–59

	Size of firm by number of employees						
	1,000 and above	4 −9	10 −29	30 −99	100 −199	200 −499	500−
1952	100.0	40.6	46.3	53.2	64.5	75.7	88.0
1953	100.0	41.7	46.8	54.4	63.5	73.8	85.3
1954	100.0	42.5	47.1	54.1	63.5	73.7	86.6
1955	100.0	39.9	44.2	50.7	59.1	69.4	79.2
1956	100.0	30.8	39.2	47.3	55.8	66.5	76.9
1957	100.0	29.8	38.8	47.3	55.5	65.3	76.1
1958	100.0	—	—	47.7	54.2	65.1	75.1
1959	100.0	—	—	50.1	56.7	66.5	76.8

Average wage in firms with 1,000 employees and above = 100

Note: The average monthly wage in firms with 1,000 employees and above increased by nearly 60% in this period from 17,400 yen in 1952 to 27,700 yen in 1959.

Source: Ministry of International Trade and Industry, *Kogyotokeihyo* (Census of Manufactures), 1952–57, and its Preliminary Summaries for 1958–59.

in those countries. However, were it not for the promotion of industrialization through foreign aid, the dual structure in underdeveloped countries would not be so conspicuous, and the situation then would probably have resembled somewhat that of the early Meiji period in Japan.

Can we, then, construct a hypothesis to explain the economy's dual structure, or as Professor K. Ohkawa prefers to call it, the "differential employment structure"? It is generally believed that the labor market is not homogeneous in Japan and that it is typically divided into two spheres, one the labor market for the large firms and the other for the small firms. In the labor market for the large firms, the demand for labor is principally for the new graduates from schools and not for experienced job seekers. In this labor market, workers once hired are more or less employed permanently (known in Japan as ' life-time commitment '), and their wage or salary level is in proportion to the length of employment. In general, these workers are never dismissed. Moreover, the active labor unions

17

Table 10. Wages and Productivity per Worker in Manufacturing Firms in Japan,
United Kingdom and United States
(Average wage and productivity in firms with 1,000 employees and above = 100)

Size of firm by number of employees	Wage differentials			Productivity differentials (Value added per employee)		
	Japan (1957)	United Kingdom (1949)	United States (1947)	Japan (1957)	United Kingdom (1949)	United States (1947)
1,000 and above	100	100	100	100	100	100
1–3 (1–9)	36	—	65*	17	—	108*
4–9 (5–9)	40	—	73*	23	—	90*
10–19 (11–24)	44	84*	79	30	90*	89
20–49 (25–49)	48	83*	84	36	92*	93
50–99	52	84	86	46	94	91
100–199 (100–249)	56	85	86	53	96	102*
200–499 (250–499)	66	86	88*	68	97	104*
500–999	76	89	90	85	98	105

Note :   * Indicates that the figures refer to the size of firms shown in parentheses.
Sources : Japan—Smaller Enterprise Agency, *Chushokigyo Kihonchosa* (Basic
Survey on Small Enterprise), 1957; United Kingdom and United
States—respective Censuses of Manufactures.

in the large firms act as bulwarks, preventing the breakthrough of
cheap labor from the other labor market. Since this labor market
is never invaded by trespassers from the pool of disguised unemployment, the system of pegging wages and salaries to length of service,
therefore, is firmly established and is not easily shaken.

On the other hand, in the labor market for the small firms, the
new employee is not necessarily the new graduate; he may come
from other firms, possibly bankrupt firms, through some personal
connections or other placement methods. The pressure of over-
population in this labor market is very strong, so the wage curve in
relation to length of service is not as steep as in the large firms. This
is confirmed by the statistical observation that the smaller the enterprise, the lower the wage level. Thus, the hypothesis which explains
the existence of steep wage differentials depends on the analysis of the
institutional aspects of the Japanese labor market which is typically

separated into two spheres, and in which labor mobility for regular employees exists only from large firms to small firms, but not in reverse.[8]

However, wages are determined not only by conditions in the labor market, but also by those prevailing in the other markets, such as, the capital and the product markets. In the product market, the prices of the competitive products of the smaller-scale enterprises have a greater downward flexibility in recessions, which to some extent increases the wage gap between large and small firms in a recession, since wages in the small firms will be affected by the decline in prices. This may partially account for the fact that in the period following World War I (1920–31) when prices continued to decline, the wage gap was considerably widened, as can be seen in Table 8.

However, the role of the capital market seems to be more important. Given the sharp wage differentials, what makes it feasible for the large firms to pay higher wages? The answer probably lies in the higher productivity per worker in the large firms. Then, why are there such sharp productivity differentials between large and small firms? Productivity is a function of capital intensity, that is, capital input per unit of labor employed. Hence, the productivity differentials now in question can be traced back to differentials in capital intensity between firms. The final problem remains: what caused the capital-intensity differentials between firms to be so large?

Given such relationships, we conclude that the large capital intensity differentials (which are not found in advanced countries) may be due to the concentration of investment funds in the relatively large businesses. Before the war, our Zaibatsu[9] banks concentrated their loans and investments in the Zaibatsu enterprises within the same group or hierarchy. After the war, the Zaibatsu combinations

---

8) With this qualification, that large firms do employ the so-called "Rinji-ko" (or temporary employees) for lower wages, under the condition that they may be dismissed whenever the management deems it desirable. In Japan, the "Rinji-ko" group increases during the upswings of the business cycles, and sharply declines in the recessions.

9) This can be literally translated as the 'money clique'. It is a generic term

were forcibly dissolved by the Occupation authorities, but after the conclusion of the peace negotiations they have been gradually restored to their original position. Thus, capital concentration in the large firms has not disappeared after the war. On the contrary, this tendency has been accentuated by the priority given in the allocation of public funds and the Counterpart Fund derived from American aid to Japan to large firms in the basic key industries, that is, coal, shipping, iron and steel and chemicals.

In addition, the recent developments caused by the technological revolution have made it necessary to revamp the business structure so as to build up a new hierarchy of corporations (often called the " Combinat "), whereby corporations in different industries, say, the chemical industry and the iron and steel industry, have been combined regionally, technically and financially in an integrated system. Such a movement may have broken the rigidity of the old Zaibatsu system to some extent and made for greater fluidity in the business world, but in general the new stage of the technological revolution has raised the capital-output ratio considerably. For instance, in the iron and steel industry, the introduction of the strip-mill has meant an increase in fixed capital investment per unit of output, and the transport of heavy equipment has necessitated the establishment of capital-intensive ancillary facilities, such as harbor facilities. In response to these developments, the concentration of capital in the larger firms may have been increased.

Such capital concentration may have accentuated the dual structure, but what has been its effect on economic growth? *Prima facie*, since this capital concentration has meant an increase in the capital-output ratio in a labor abundant economy, it might be considered a misuse of national resources and hence detrimental to growth. However, the recent upsurge of the machine industry, especially the electrical machine industry, has been made possible only by the preceding expansion and renovation of the iron and steel industry. This is similar to the situation in the early stages of industrialization, when the initial social overhead investments, such as road construc-

to describe the very large vertically integrated trust corporations that dominated the Japanese economy before the Second World War.

tion, establishment of railroads and the construction of hydro-electric dams stimulated the later growth of various industries. If such overhead investments can be recognized as contributing to economic growth, then in the present case the development of basic capital-intensive industries, such as iron and steel, should also be looked upon as stimulants to accelerated growth. The problem is then not a choice between capital-intensive or labor-intensive industries, but how to make them complement each other. In this sense, the investment concentration in the large-scale firms, which will introduce new technology into these firms, would be growth-accelerating, rather than growth-deterrent, from the long-run point of view. And this seems to have been the Japanese experience.

Capital concentration has in this way stimulated industrial growth, but at the same time it has to a large extent been responsible for intensifying the dual structure, widening the gaps in capital intensity, productivity and wages between large and small firms. Thus capital concentration not only directly contributes to growth, it also increases the rate of growth indirectly through the creation of a dual economic structure. The existence of the dual economy makes it possible for the relatively large firms to employ cheap labor[10] in combination with highly advanced technological production methods. The combination of cheap labor and high-level technology tends to reduce costs and raise profits, thus leading to greater capital financing from internal funds, on the one hand, and a lowering of product prices, on the other, which in turn helps to expand the foreign market.

This is an interpretation based mainly on Japanese experience and may not be applicable to present underdeveloped economies. However, semi-developed countries, such as Japan, find it necesssary to import and adopt highly advanced technology in order to compete in the world export market. In order to catch up with the advanced countries, a semi-developed country must achieve a greater than average growth rate, compared with other countries. The only practicable method to achieve a higher growth rate is to push up

---

10) That is, relative to labour costs in more advanced countries.

the export growth rate beyond the world average. But the raising of the export growth rate in such an economy may be possible (and actually has been possible in the Japanese case) only through a combination of advanced technological know-how and cheap labor. Again, this may not be a solution for the present underdeveloped countries where other complex problems exist.

Thus capital concentration may have been one of the most important secular causes of Japan's economic growth. But a weakness in this hypothesis is that capital concentration is not a monopoly of Japan. It also exists in advanced countries and it may be argued that capital concentration alone does not appear a sufficient explanation for the sharp dual structure.

The answer to this argument is that in the present advanced economies there is a developed capital market for stocks and bonds, and a large part of the fixed investment is financed internally. Capital concentration in such an economy is thus a concentration through "direct financing." However, in Japan, not only in the prewar but also in the postwar period, the chief method of financing fixed investment is through bank loans. In this sense, the method of financing in Japan is sometimes referred to as "indirect financing", for the allocation of deposit funds to firms is now entrusted to the banks. The problem is that banks are governed by a conservative policy in the lending or investing of funds at their disposal and necessarily favor loans to large firms which carry less risk. Thus, in the advanced countries, the concentration of capital is often restricted to the narrow limits of owned capital. However, in Japan, capital concentration develops on the basis of a much larger pool of funds, and the proportion of funds concentrated in large firms is far greater in Japan than in the advanced countries. This concentration may have supplied the essential stimulus to economic expansion.

We have previously referred to the increasing producers' durables-gross national product ratio in the postwar period, shown in Table 5. This development appeared to have been essential for the extraordinarily rapid expansion in the postwar period. If this is so, the institutional framework through which the tremendous pool of funds collected in the commercial banks are piped to big business plays a crucial role in the rapid expansion. The credit created through the Bank of Japan is also relevant in this context since this credit supports the rapid rate of investment, and the important role of the so-called " overloans " (that is, the excessive dependence of commercial banks on the central bank) should also be recognized.

5. *A Note on the Pattern of Capital Formation in a Dual Economy*

As already noted, this chapter does not aim at a comprehensive analysis of the causes and consequences of Japan's economic growth. But we would like to discuss a special point that arises from our analysis. The problem is that if large firms have a decided advantage in obtaining investment funds from the banks, then how do small firms expand their output, paralleling the increase in production of the large firms? One theory concerning capital concentration suggests that as capital concentration proceeds, the proportion of small firms will gradually be reduced through unequal competition with the large firms. However, this has not been the experience in postwar Japan. Utilizing the Census of Manufactures, we can compute the ratio of expansion of manufacturers' shipments by size of establishment. The rates of increase in shipments for 1950–56 were 137% for firms with 4–29 employees, 164% for firms with 30–49 employees, 179% for firms with 50–99 employees, 170% for firms with 100–199 employees, and 174% for firms with over 200 employees. This suggests an almost simultaneous expansion of big, medium and small firms, and that one group has not developed exclusively at the expense of the others. (Rigorously speaking, the smallest group shows the lowest rate of increase, and becomes an exception to our exposition, but it is natural that the smallest group cannot but decrease their share in the economic development, so their rate of increase is exceptionally small) This may be on account of the fact that there is an intimate relationship between the large and small firms in Japan, for example, through sub-contracts and production of parts. Recently, the vertical hierarchy of big and medium-sized firms has also been strengthened. Therefore, the ex-

23

pansion of big business has meant a parallel expansion of small and medium-scale firms. Large firms find it profitable to use parts produced by cheap labor in the smaller firms; in other cases, the large firms produce primary products such as steel or cotton thread while the smaller firms manufacture secondary products such as machinery or clothing. The problem remains—how do small firms which are handicapped in borrowing from banks finance their necessary investment in order to keep pace with the big corporations.

The answer is suggested in Table 11, where the proportion of used fixed assets in total purchases of fixed assets are computed for 1954–59 from the Census of Manufactures. In the smallest firms, with 4–9 employees, this ratio ranges from 34% to 49%. As the value of the used machinery is computed on the basis of resale prices, it is expected that the valuation of used equipment is extremely low relative to their physical productivity. The investment in used fixed assets, in *physical terms*, would constitute a much larger per-

Table 11. The Proportion of Second-hand Fixed Assets in Total Purchases of Fixed Assets in Manufacturing Firms in Japan, 1954–59

Size of firms by number of employees	1954	1955	1956	1957	1958	1959
	%	%	%	%	%	%
4–	48.8	40.2	34.3	41.0	—	—
10–	44.1	40.8	29.9	35.0	—	—
20–	39.5	34.3	28.7	30.5	—	—
30–	35.0	28.9	26.1	26.4	26.5	20.5
50–	31.5	22.0	22.3	22.1	20.9	17.1
100–	23.0	16.3	16.8	15.2	13.8	12.8
200–	15.2	9.1	9.9	9.3	10.0	9.5
300–	13.9	10.1	9.1	7.4	7.6	7.6
500–	11.2	5.2	4.2	4.6	6.3	9.6
1,000 and above	4.6	4.1	4.9	3.3	3.1	4.1
Total	18.3	14.3	12.3	10.9	—	—

Source: The Ministry of International Trade and Industry, *Kogyotokeihyo*, (Census of Manufactures), 1954–57, and its Preliminary Summaries for 1958–59.

centage, perhaps as high as 80%, in these small firms. In the Japanese economy, used machines discarded by the large firms are not destined for the scrap heap; they find a ready demand for their services in the small firms. This is a vital aspect of capital accumulation in a dual economy.

6. Conclusion

We have dealt with, in some detail, two factors which have contributed to Japan's economic growth. The first is the postwar recovery factor, which is indicated by the close inverse correlation between the rates of decline and recovery in industrial production and exports in various countries. The second factor is a secular one, that is, capital concentration and the dual economy. Had Japan's rapid economic growth been accounted for by the postwar recovery factor alone, then a gradual slowing down of the growth rate can be expected. The second factor, however, is a long-term phenomenon which may well contribute to a maintenance of the high growth rate, insofar as the dual economy will remain an integral part of Japan's economic structure.

These factors, of course, are not a sufficient explanation of the high rate of growth, though they constitute two of the most important ingredients. Other contributory causes, such as the export growth potential, the high savings ratio, enterpreneurial behaviour, the industry of her people, and other economic as well as social factors have also played a vital role.

CHAPTER 2

RELATIVE PRODUCTION LEVELS OF
INDUSTRIAL COUNTRIES AND
THEIR GROWTH POTENTIALS

The main purpose of this paper is to construct an international (cross-section) index of industrial production in 1956 (with the United States=100) and to study it in relation to problems of growth. Although attempts have been made by Colin Clark, Milton Gilbert and Irving Kravis to make international comparisons of prices or real national income levels without recourse to exchange rates, the author does not know of any attempt to directly construct an inter-country index of industrial production. Such an index, I believe, would throw light on the " catching-up " problem faced by the less developed countries as well as on the growth potentials of the exports of each country.

1. Construction of an International Index of Industrial Production

As this is an initial attempt, the countries to be compared are limited to seven: the United States, the United Kingdom, West Germany, France, Italy, Sweden and Japan. The main basic data utilized were the United Nations', *Statistical Yearbooks*, from which 62 commodities were used. There are some commodities for which the unit of measurement differs between countries, but these were reduced to the common quantum unit through information obtained from experts. The individual commodity quantities are converted into index numbers with the United States=100, and consolidated into the following industrial categories: (1) Metals, (2) Machinery and construction, (3) Chemicals and ceramics, (4) Food, beverages and tobacco, (5) Textiles and leather, (6) Paper and pulp, (7) Electricity and gas, (8) Mining.

The reader may be puzzled by the second category " Machinery and construction," for no published index has yet combined machinery with construction. However, this was necessitated by the fact that there were very few items in the machinery industry. The United Nations, *Statistical Yearbook* enumerates only wireless receivers (radios), merchant vessels and motor vehicles. Therefore, we have attempted to estimate the machinery output from the *input* side, giving up the use of the above three items. Fortunately, the U.N. statistics give the volume of steel consumption which is one of the chief raw materials used in the production of machinery. However, since steel is not only used in machinery production but also in construction, we were forced to combine machinery and construction. Moreover, we must take into consideration the consumption of cement and lumber, besides that of steel, as major construction materials. The index for " machinery and construction " is thus constructed by taking the weighted average of the indexes of domestic consumption of steel, cement and lumber, using the values of consumption of these three as weights. In aggregating the index of " machinery and construction " thus computed into the total index of industrial production, we have used the sum of values added in the machinery industry and the construction industry as the weight. The resulting index of " machinery and construction " will be a rough representation of the physical level of equipment and construction investments in each country. Strictly speaking, however, consumer durables are included in machinery and the portion exported does not comprise domestic investment. But, if this is taken into account, our index of " machinery and construction " will be useful and convenient, numerically indicating machinery production and construction activity.

In aggregating the individual items, the following added value weights were generally used : Japan (1955 added values), the United States (1954 added values) and the United Kingdom (1951 added values). As we have adopted the weighting systems of the three countries, we can compute these three indexes, according to whatever system is used. For some commodities for which the value added figures were not available, we were obliged to apply the value added ratios of one country to the value of production of another country.

The results are shown in Tables 1–3. In addition to the three indexes, the geometric averages of Japan-U.K.; U.K.-U.S.A.; Japan-U.S.A. are also computed. Table 4 presents the six indexes computed, together with the industrial incomes of each country converted into dollar values by the exchange rates. As will be later discussed, the differences between the physical volumes of industrial production and the dollar values of industrial income are very considerable. In Table 5, the baisc data used for deriving industrial incomes are shown.

2. Analyses of Export Growth Potentials

As can be seen from Table 4, in some countries there are tremendous differences between industrial incomes in dollar terms and the physical volumes of industrial production. Of course, there are

Table 1. International Index of Industrial Production, 1956
(Weights, Japanese added values in 1955; U.S.A.=100)

Industry	Weights	U.K.	Japan	West Germany	Italy	France	Sweden
Metals	11.4	16.1	8.9	21.7	3.9	12.7	1.9
Machinery & construction	27.9	14.7	13.2	24.5	12.4	9.4	3.8
Chemicals & ceramics	17.8	18.4	18.6	31.1	13.6	16.3	2.7
Food, beverages & tobacco	11.8	30.4	15.5	63.2	25.3	36.0	6.0
Textiles & leather	14.4	42.3	50.0	32.9	25.8	26.1	3.7
Paper & pulp	3.4	9.5	11.4	10.6	3.6	7.5	13.6
Electricity & gas	6.7	25.0	11.1	13.8	9.6	12.8	4.6
Mining	6.7	40.1	25.9	27.4	8.0	13.1	3.8
Total	100.0	23.5	19.9	30.1	14.3	16.9	4.0

RELATIVE PRODUCTION LEVELS

Table 2. International Index of Industrial Production, 1956
(Weights, U.S. added values in 1954; U.S.A.=100)

Industry	Weights	U.K.	Japan	West Germany	Italy	France	Sweden
Metals	13.1	18.3	9.0	23.6	3.4	14.8	2.2
Machinery & construction	42.3	16.3	11.3	22.5	9.0	8.4	2.0
Chemicals & ceramics	10.8	17.3	9.4	18.6	8.2	12.2	1.6
Food, beverages & tobacco	11.3	23.1	8.2	28.2	9.0	20.9	2.9
Textiles & leather	8.8	30.1	32.7	23.8	18.4	15.5	2.4
Paper & pulp	3.5	8.4	8.9	8.8	2.8	6.0	9.6
Electricity & gas	1.2	37.1	10.7	27.6	9.1	14.8	3.7
Mining	8.9	9.4	2.8	6.3	0.8	4.0	5.2
Total	100.0	15.3	11.4	11.1	7.9	11.4	2.9

Table 3. International Index of Industrial Production, 1956
(Weights, U.K. added values in 1951; U.S.A.=100)

Industry	Weights	U.K.	Japan	West Germany	Italy	France	Sweden
Metals	8.2	17.4	10.6	21.1	5.3	12.3	2.2
Machinery & construction	36.3	16.4	11.4	22.7	9.2	8.5	3.0
Chemicals & ceramics	11.6	27.3	10.8	29.1	10.6	13.8	2.3
Food, beverages & tobacco	10.0	27.7	16.9	30.6	10.3	19.1	3.9
Textiles & leather	16.8	36.3	34.1	27.9	22.1	23.1	3.0
Paper & pulp	3.4	16.1	12.1	13.5	4.9	10.3	8.9
Electricity & gas	5.2	40.7	10.5	31.7	8.9	15.5	3.5
Mining	8.5	47.0	10.8	28.2	0.3	12.0	0.4
Total	100.0	26.1	15.5	25.6	10.3	13.7	3.0

Table 4.   Alternative Results of General Indexes of Industrial Production, 1956 (All industries)[a]

Country	Japan's	U.S.	U.K.	Geometric averages of			Industrial incomes converted into the dollar values by the exchange rates[b]	
	Weight			Japan-U.K.	U.K.-U.S.	Japan-U.S.		
	Index						million $	index
U.S.A.	100.0	100.0	100.0	100.0	100.0	100.0	135,246	100.0
U.K.	23.5	15.3	26.1	24.8	20.0	19.0	24,094	17.8
Japan	19.9	11.4	15.5	17.6	13.3	15.1	6,998	5.2
West Germany	30.1	21.1	25.6	27.8	23.2	25.2	17,815	13.2
Italy	14.3	7.9	10.3	12.1	9.0	10.6	8,131	6.0
France	16.9	11.4	13.7	14.9	12.5	13.9	16,965	12.5
Sweden	4.0	2.9	3.0	3.5	2.95	3.4	4,581	3.4

[a] Sources to Tables 4–5: U.S.A., U.K., Italy: U.N., *Yearbook of National Accounts Statistics*, N. S., II, New York, 1958.—West Germany: *Statistisches Jahrbuch für die Bundesrepublik Deutschland*, Stuttgart u. Köln, 1959.—Japan: *Kokumin Shotoku Hakusho* (National Income Report), Tokyo, 1958.—France, Sweden: U.N. figures on 1952 and 1951 respectively are extrapolated to 1956 by the "wholesale price index × index of industrial production," before conversion.

[b] The above results exclude electricity and gas, for in the case of Japanese national incomes statistics they are included in public utilities together with transportation and communications and are not separable.   Only in West Germany figures, mining includes *Energiewirtschaft*, so it includes a little more in comparison with the figures of other countries.

slight differences in the coverages of both statistics, *i.e.*, electricity and gas are not included in industrial incomes in dollar terms (except for West Germany), but they are included in the production indexes. However, the effect of their inclusion or exclusion on the final results seems to be negligible.   According to the Japanese weighting system, the relative levels of Japan to the United States is 19.9% in physical terms, whereas it is 5.2% in dollar terms.   This gap is somewhat reduced when the U.S. weight is used (11.4% *vs.* 5.2%).   At any rate the ranking of the gap of each country is Japan first, West Germany second, and Italy third, and the gaps of France and Sweden

Table 5. Industrial Income in Dollars Converted by the Exchange
Rates, 1956

Country	Unit	Manu-factur-ing	Mining	Construc-tion industry	Total	Industrial incomes converted to dollar (million $)[a]
U.S.A.	million $	109,901	6,265	19,080	135,246	135,246
U.K.	million £	6,846	671	1,088	8,605	24,098
Japan	billion yen	1,969	167	383	2,519	6,998
West Germany	million DM	55,935	8,553	10,315	74,821	17,815
Italy	billion lire	4,064	181	837	5,082	8,131
France	billion francs	5,109		829	5,938	16,965
Sweden	million krones	20,355		3,343	23,698	4,581

[a] See Table 4.

Table 6. The Ratios of Industrial Incomes in Dollars to Industrial Productions
(U.S.A.=100)

	U.K.	Japan	West Germany	Italy	France	Sweden
Japan's weight	75.8	26.1	43.8	42.6	77.9	84.9
U.S. weight	116.4	45.6	62.4	76.1	110.0	116.9
U.K. weight	68.2	33.5	51.4	58.3	91.5	113.0
Japan-U.K. weight	71.8	29.5	47.4	49.7	84.2	96.9
U.K.-U.S. weight	89.1	39.1	56.8	66.8	100.3	114.9
Japan-U.S. weight	93.7	34.4	52.4	56.6	89.9	100.0

are fairly small.   As is well known, comparisons by index numbers
involves such difficulties that the results would differ according to
different weighting systems used.   Therefore, the multiplicity or
relativity of the results obtained is inevitable.   However, when the
ratios of industrial incomes (in dollars) to the volumes of industrial
production are computed for the six countries in Table 6, we find
that Japan's income-production ratios are the lowest for each weighting system, and those of West Germany and Italy follow Japan's.
Thus, Table 6 shows that although Japan's or Germany's ratios are
comparatively low, this must not be attributed *merely* to the effect

of the difference in industrial structure.   Much more fundamentally, it seems to reflect the relatively greater undervaluation of exchange rates in the cases of Japan, West Germany and Italy.

The hypothesis which suggests iteslf at this stage is that the differences in the export growth rates among countries reflects the degree of undervaluation of exchange rates.   In other words, in those countries such as Japan and West Germany in which the income (in dollar)-production ratios are very low and the degree of undervaluation of exchange rates are therefore greater, the export growth rates will also be greater.   By applying the equation $log\ X_t = a + bt$ (X_t = the volume of exports, t = year) for 1953–58, we derive the annual growth rates of exports as follows : the United States (3.40%), the United Kingdom (3.66%), Japan (19.47%), West Germany (14.49 %), Italy (11.76%), France (5.54%), and Sweden (7.22%).   We begin with 1953 because if we go back to the immediate postwar years, the postwar recovery factor would be more dominant, and in some countries like Japan the special procurement demands of the occupation forces would have discouraged exports, particularly before 1953.

The hypothesis can be tested by drawing a graph which indicates a correlation between the two variables under discussion.   The results shown in Fig. 1 are very striking.   There is a fairly good correlation between the two.   As we used the Japan-UK.. weight series, the U.K. point scatters a little downward, but if we use the U.K.-U.S. weight series to the United Kingdom ($\times$ U.K. (2)) only, we obtain a much better correlation.   In West Germany, where the exchange rate has been undervalued, gold and foreign exchange holdings increased from $1,958 million (1953) to $6,321 million (1958).   This is a 3.2-fold increase.   In Italy, it increased from $952 million to $2,321 million or 2.4 times.   In Japan, it showed only a 1.35-fold increase for the same period.   However, Japan could have realized a comparatively greater growth rate of industrial production (12.74%) than West Germany and Italy (8.74% and 7.40%). Japan seems to have chosen the course of the higher domestic growth than the accumulation of foreign exchange.   In France, the domestic growth rate of industrial production (9.13%) was much higher than

Fig. 1. The Relation of the Undervaluation of Exchange Rates to the Export
Growth Rates[a]

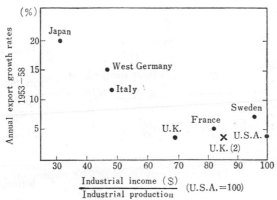

a As the income-production ratios, the series due to the Japan—U.K.
weight are used. But U.K (2) ×is due to the U.S.—U.K.weight.

Fig. 2. Comparisons of Industrial and Export Growth Rates, 1953–58

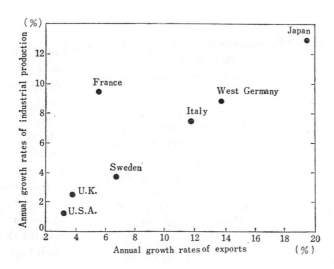

her export growth rate (5.54%) for this period, so the drastic decline in the foreign exchange holding of 44% had occurred from the end of 1955 to the end of 1958.

With France as an exception, a graph can also be drawn showing the close correlation between the growth rates of industrial production and those of exports (Fig. 2). It may be noted that in every country except France the export growth rates were always higher than the industrial growth rates. This seems to suggest that exports have been a major factor in postwar domestic expansion. Of course, other important factors accelerating growth can and should be mentioned, but export growth potentials should not be neglected in explaining the inter-country variations of domestic growth rates.

Thus, the differentials in the export growth rates between countries seem to be important in explaining the differences in industrial growth rates, but the former can, in turn, be explained very clearly (Fig. 1) by the intercountry variations in the degree of undervaluation of the exchange rates.

At this point, it may be objected that the definition of the undervaluation of the exchange rates is not too clear in my discussion. I believe that undervaluation may coexist with an equilibrium balance of payments. This may seem inconsistent to some readers as they may assume that the exchange rate can be undervalued only when the balance of payments is in surplus. However, the logic is as follows: Suppose that in one country there is an undervaluation of exchange rate and it is accompanied by an increase in exports. The resulting surplus in the balance of payments can be wiped out under the following circumstances: (1) an appreciation of exchange rates, (2) a rise of domestic prices, (3) a rise of domestic output, and (4) the accumulation of foreign exchange or gold. However, the first, an appreciation of exchange rate, cannot be realized without the permission of IMF at the inflexible exchange rate, and the second condition would not occur in an economy, like Japan's with a great deal of disguised unemployment and in which the increase of productive capacity due to the rapid rise of fixed investment tends to outpace the increase of effective demand. Actually in Japan, wholesale prices remained on about the same level for 1951–1958, though there have been fluctuations due to business cycles. Therefore, if we set aside the fourth condition for the time being, then the only possible way by which the surplus in the balance of payments can be wiped out is under the third condition, the rise of domestic output. If this occurs, the inbalance of the balance of payments can be filled up by the increase of imports entailed by the rise of domestic output or income. Then, as the first and the second conditions do not exist, the price relationship towards foreign countries remains unchanged. In other words, the price adjustment does not work, and only the income adjustment comes into being, thus the initial undervaluation of exchange rate does not disappear, though there exists an equilibrium in the balance of payments. In a world in which only the price adjustment operates, the surplus or deficit in the balance of payments may be an indicator of the undervaluation or overvaluation of the exchange rate, provided that there are no restrictions on foreign trade. However, in the actual world in which the both price and income adjustments obtain, the under- or overvaluation of exchange rate can coexist with an equilibrium in the balance of payments. Japan of 1951–58 may roughly exemplify this situation. The undervaluation of the exchange rate pushed up the exports, the domestic output, and the imports, and there was only a slight rise in the foreign exchange holdings. In brief, the export growth rate itself is an appropriate barometer indicating the undervaluation of the exchange rate in this case, as was shown in Fig. 1.

3. A Comparison by Industry

If we compute the added values in dollars by industry and compare them with the indexes of production by industry, we may have a rough criterion to determine which industry has a comparative advantage as far as the price structure is concerned. In Table 7, textile and leather production, for instance, in Japan and the United Kingdom are both around 30–40% in physical terms as compared with the United States, though there are some variations depending on which weighting system is employed. However, if we take the value

Table 7. Comparison between Added Values ($) and the Indexes of Production
by Industry, 1956[2]

Industry	Added values (million $ resp. %)			Indexes of production (U.S.A.=100)		
	U.S.A	U.K.	Japan	Weight	U.K.	Japan
Mtals	22,337 (100)	1,834 (8.2)	1,201 (5.4)	Japan U.S. U.K.	16.1 18.3 17.4	8.9 9.0 10.6
Chemicals & ceramics	21,868 (100)	2,428 (11.1)	1,518 (6.9)	Japan U.S. U.K.	18.4 17.3 27.3	18.6 9.4 10.8
Food beverages & tobacco	16,549 (100)	1,800 (10.9)	728 (4.4)	Japan U.S. U.K.	30.4 23.1 27.7	15.5 8.2 16.9
Textiles & leather	12,960 (100)	2,836 (21.9)	1,006 (7.8)	Japan U.S. U.K.	42.3 30.1 36.3	50.0 32.7 34.1
Paper, plup & printing	12,909 (100)	1,361 (10.5)	678 (5.3)	Japan U.S. U.K.	9.5 8.4 16.1	11.4 8.9 12.1
Mining	13,463 (100)	1,946 (14.5)	432 (3.2)	Japan U.S. U.K.	40.1 9.4 47.0	25.9 2.8 10.8

added by industry converted to dollars by exchange rates, then the
United Kingdom is 21.9% of the United States and Japan is only
7.8% of the latter.   This indicates the relative cheapness of textile
goods in Japan, given the present exchange rate.   The textile commodities of the United Kingdom are cheaper than those of the
United States, but those of Japan are much cheaper.

This shows why the textile industry is still large in postwar Japan

2)   Sources: Added values: U.S.A.: *Statistical Abstract of the United States*,
79th Ed., Washington, 1958; U.K.: *Annual Abstract of Statistics* No. 96,
London, 1959; Japan: *Kogyo Tokeihyo* (Census of Manufactures), Tokyo, 1956.—Mining (U.K. and Japan): U.N., *Statistical Yearbook*,
X, New York, 1958.—Indexes of production: Table 1–3.

despite the trend toward heavy industrialization.

It may be noted that in every industry production in physical terms is higher in Japan than the value added in dollar terms. As a matter of course, this may partly reflect the undervaluation of the exchange rate, but it cannot be the whole story. In Japan, the ratio of raw material costs to wage costs is higher in the various industries compared with other advanced countries. Therefore the value added ratio must also be smaller, *e.g.*, around 30% in Japan and 40% in the United States and the United Kingdom. The difference of the value added ratios between Japan and the United States may be still larger in some particular industries. However, this factor only will not account for total difference between the value added in dollar terms and production in physical terms. Still, the undervaluation of exchange rate would be an essential factor. However, in view of the relative character of index number, too much emphasis should not be laid on the absolute difference in production indices and the ratios of production and value added (in dollars). Nevertheless, the ranking of the various countries in the latter ratio is considered reliable for, in order to avoid bias, we used six different weighting systems, and thus made clear that the Japanese rank is the lowest in any weighting system.

In Table 7, we find that the index for mining was not successful. The largest difference is due to the difference in the weights used in the index of mining production. This seems to be because the weight of petroleum production is very large in the United States, whereas coal dominates in Japan and the United Kingdom. The extremely great distortion in the computation compels us to conclude that as far as the mining index is concerned international comparison is meaningless. It is thought that a comparison based on energy efficiency would yield better results.

4. Testing the " Machinery and Construction " Index by the Gilbert Estimate

One peculiarity in our index lies, as already explained, in the

" machinery and construction " index, for it is computed not on the basis of output but input. Therefore, it needs to be checked by some independent estimate. Fortunately, we have Milton Gilbert's elaborate comparisons of real national output of different countries, and his estimate of real gross fixed investment can be compared with our index of " machinery and construction." Of course, our index includes machinery exports, and consumer durables, but otherwise, the two series can be directly compared.

In Table 8, Gilbert's estimate and our's are comparable with respect to the U.S. weight. In this comparison, the difference of the two for the United Kingdom is only 1.0 point, that for West Germany is 2.4 points, and Italy's is only 0.3 points. A close agreement is indicated for these three countries and only in the case of

Table 8. Examination of " Machinery and Construction " Index[b]

Country	Gilbert's estimate (1955)			" Machinery and construction " index (1956)			Fixed investment[a] ($) in 1956, converted exchange rates	
	Geometric average	U.S.	European	Japan	U.S.	U.K.	million $	%
	Weight							
U.S.A.	100.0	100.0	100.0	100.0	100.0	100.0	74,028	100.0
U.K.	14.3	15.3	13.3	14.7	16.3	16.4	8,803	11.9
Japan	—	—	—	13.2	11.3	11.4	5,681	7.7
West Germany	18.3	20.1	16.6	24.5	22.5	22.7	10,548	17.1
Italy	8.5	9.3	7.9	12.4	9.0	9.2	4,874	6.6
France	11.6	12.2	10.9	9.4	8.4	8.5	9,599	13.0
Sweden	—	—	—	3.8	2.9	3.0	1,879	2.5

[a] Includes both private and public, and also both equipment and construction investments.

[b] Source : Gilbert estimate : Milton Gilbert and Associates, *Comparative National Products and Price Levels, A Study of Western Europe and the United States*, Publ. by the Organisation for European Economic Cooperation, Paris, 1958.—" Machinery and construction " index : Table 1–3.—Fixed investment in 1956 before conversion into $: U.N., *Yearbook of National Accounts Statistics*, N.S., II, 1958, except Japan (*Kokumin Shotoku Hakusho*, 1958) and West Germany (*Statistisches Jahrbuch für die Bundesrepublik Deutschland*, 1959).

France is there a big difference of 3.8 points (12.2 *vs.* 8.4). I did not examine the cause of the difference for France, but it is to be noted that excepting France both series coincide fairly well. In this sense, it can be expected that our " machinery and construction " index may also be used as a convenient index for equipment and construction investments in real terms, provided the proportion of exports and consumer durables in the machinery production is not so different between countries.

5. Comparison of Per Capita Levels of Industrial Production

The cross-section index of industrial production can be reduced to a per capita basis, whereby we may rank the industrial level or the degree of industrialization in various countries (Table 9). Again, we have trouble with a multiplicity of index numbers, but the general impression from this table is that, among the three indexes using the U.S., U.K., and Japan's weights, the lowest is that using the United States' weight, and the highest is that using Japan's weight. The index using the U.K. weight falls in the middle, with one exception with respect to the United Kingdom. The per capita industrial production of Japan, for example, is 37.1% of that of the United States according to Japan's weighting system, 28.9% of the United States according to the U.K. weighting system, and 21.3% of the United States according to the U.S. weighting system. This seems to suggest that the process of industrialization involved the problem of the transformation of industrial structure, in addition to that of raising the quantitative level, and the former gives rise to plural results in the index number expression.

It may be interesting to explore the per capita industrial growth rates required for a less developed country such as Japan to catch up with the level of advanced countries within the next ten or twenty years. Table 10 presents the required rates provided the present industrial levels of the advanced countries (U.S. and European countries) are constant within this period.

Converted by the exchange rates, Japan's per capita industrial

Table 9.   Relative Levels of Industrial Production Per Capita of Population,
1956

Country	Population		Per capita industrial production				
			U.S.	U.K.	Japan's	U.S.-U.K.	Japan-U.K.
	thousand	%	Weight			Geometric average	
U.S.A.	168,174	100.0	100.0	100.0	100.0	100.0	100.0
U.K	51,430	30.6	50.0	85.3	76.8	65.3	80.9
Japan	90.260	53.6	21.3	28.9	37.1	24.8	32.8
West Germany	50,786	30.2	69.9	84.8	99.7	77.0	92.0
Italy	48,279	28.7	27.5	35.9	49.8	31.4	42.3
France	43,648	26.0	43.8	52.7	65.0	48.0	58.5
Sweden	7,316	4.35	66.7	69.0	92.0	67.8	79.7

income level is 10% of that of the United States, and 33% of that of
the United Kingdom.   However, if we compute per capita relative
industrial output level by our index, then Japan is located around
25–32% of the United States, and 38–40% of the United Kingdom.
On the basis of the exchange rates, Japan's industrial level is considerably undervalued.   The growth rate of the Japanese economy
since 1868 has been noticeably higher compared with other countries.
Nevertheless, the per capita national income level (converted by
exchange rate) is said to be 11.7% of the United States' in 1957,
which can be compared with the levels of relatively underdeveloped
countries like Greece (13.7%), Mexico (11.0%) and Turkey (10.1%).
However, no foreigner who has had the experience of living or
traveling in Japan, will accept the classification of Japan as such an
underdeveloped country.

Therefore, in Table 10, the per capita annual growth rates required
to attain the present levels of advanced countries within next ten or
twenty years are computed, using our index of industrial production.
As indexes, we used the U.K.-U.S. geometric average and the
Japan-U.S. geometric average.   If this numerical result in Table
10 is correct, a per capita annual industrial growth rate of 12–15%
is needed for Japan to reach the present level of the United States,

Table 10. Per Capital Industrial Growth Rate Required to Catch Up With
the Present Level of Advanced Countries

Country	Per capita index of industrial production of advanced countries		Per capita annual growth rates to catch up with advanced countries (%) within			
	1956 Japan=100		10 years		20 years	
	U.K.-U.S.	Japan-U.S.	U.K.-U.S.	Japan-U.S.	U.K.-U.S.	Japan-U.S.
	Weight					
U.S.A	403.2	304.9	14.96	11.80	7.22	5.73
West Germany	310.5	280.5	12.00	10.86	5.83	5.30
U.K.	263.3	246.6	10.17	9.45	4.72	4.62
Sweden	273.4	343.0	10.58	9.29	5.16	4.54
France	193.6	178.4	6.83	5.96	3.36	2.94

and 9–12% to reach the present level of West Germany and the
United Kingdom, within the next ten years. If the period is extended to twenty years, the required industrial growth rates are
sharply reduced to 6–7% and 4.5–5.8% respectively.

There are conclusions derived from a mechanical calculation of
statistical figures. Many Japanese still suffer from an inferiority
complex with respect to their income levels compared with advanced
countries. However, Japan's very high growth rate and extremely
low income level (as expressed through conversion by exchange rate)
cannot be reconciled. Thus, our studies would be useful in breaking through this illusion as well as in exploring the possibility of
catching-up with the advanced countries.

Be that as it may, the above is based only on quantitative computation. In order for Japan to really catch up with the advanced
countries, there must be a change in the industrial structure toward
heavy industrialization. After the next ten years, a labor shortage
is expected owing to the rapid decline in the new supply of labor
force. Labor intensive methods of production will be forced to
give way to more capital intentsive methods. In similar way, the
" agricultural revolution " must keep pace with the " industrial

revolution " so that the industrial sector can draw additional supplies of labor from the rural areas.

However, in such situations where labor shortages are intensified, the industrial income ($)-industrial production ratio indicated in Fig. 1 will gradually rise, *i.e.*, the degree of the undervaluation of exchange rate will gradually be reduced, owing to the gradual rise in the wage level and with the vanishing dual structure. Other things being equal, this may reduce the export growth potential of Japan and her domestic growth rate. Therefore, a mere mechanical computation will not give the full story, and some policy concerning the transformation of industry, need to be established, in order to maintain high growth rate.

CHAPTER 3

ECONOMIC DEVELOPMENT AND
FOREIGN TRADE IN THE PREWAR PERIOD

1. Introduction

This chapter will attempt to explain the role of the rapidly expanding foreign trade in the striking Japanese economic development since the Meiji era (1867), and at the same time to analyze its various aspects, *e.g.*, the causes of high export growth rate, changes in the commodity composition of trade, the effect of changes in the terms of trade, *etc.* Especially important in the understanding of the above, is the fact that the Japanese export growth rate was among the highest in the world not only in the postwar period but also in the prewar. This raises an interesting problem: to what extent (relative to other factors) has the expansion of foreign trade been responsible for Japan's economic development and whether domestic demand or foreign demand has played the major role.[1] However, as will be discussed below, it is our opinion that the expansion of the export industry has had the leading part. This is one of our chief conclusions, obtained from the analysis in this paper, and to that extent the growth potential of our exports must be regarded as important in the understanding of the Japan's economic development.

2. International Comparisons of Export Growth Rates

Before going into factual analysis, it may be appropriate to explain one of our hypotheses. For a number of countries which show

1) W. W. Lockwood seems to emphasize the role of the increase in the domestic demand. See his *Economic Development of Japan, Growth and Structural Change, 1868–1938*, Oxford University Press, 1955, p. 369.

remarkably large rates of growth in industrial production or national output, rates of growth in exports are comparatively high. Of course, the question remains which was the cause and which the effect. However, it will be useful first to confirm the above correlation not only for prewar period but also for the postwar period.

Fig. 1 depicts the relation between the growth rates in exports of

Fig. 1. Relation of Annual Growth Rates in Exports to Those in Industrial Production in Various Countries, 1911–13 to 1926–29.

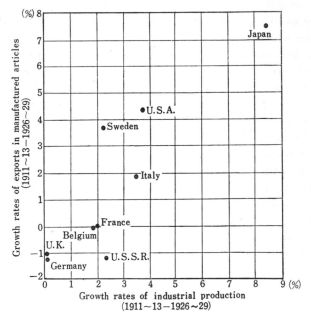

Source: Computed from the data in *Industrialization and Foreign Trade*, League of Nations 1945, except Japan's industrial growth rate which is computed from the Nagoya index of industrial production.

manufactured articles and industrial production among various countries for the period 1911–13 to 1926–29. This covers only about 15 prewar years, but in the prior period an increasingly larger part of production by smaller factories drops out from the production statistics. Also the index of production for a longer period may lose its economic meaning in so far as structural changes during the time are very great. Therefore we have adopted a shorter period as in Fig. 1. Moreover, the period from 1930 on includes the Great Depression, and if we were to take the 1930's as the years for comparison, it would be difficult to compute growth rates unbiased by the cycle. In Fig. 1, we find that those countries whose industrial growth rates were exceedingly high (Japan, U.S.A. and Sweden), had also the correspondingly greater rates of growth in exports, whereas the group of countries whose industrial growth rates were relatively small, such as France, Belgium, U.K. and Germany, had the export growth rates which were less than their respective industrial growth rates. In other words, the annual industrial growth rates of Japan, U.S.A., and Sweden for this period were 8.54%, 3.83% and 2.29%, respectively,[2] while their annual export growth rates were 7.57%, 4.40%, and 3.72%, respectively. These figures confirms very clearly the association of high growth rates in industrial production and exports. In case of U.S.A. and Sweden, the growth rate of exports is higher than industrial growth rate itself, but in Japan the former is a bit smaller than the latter (7.57% vs. 8.54%). This may seemingly contradict my hypothesis that exports had played a key role in Japan's industrial development. However, it is clear that in the Nagoya index of industrial production there is increasing omission of output of smaller-scale establishment, as we go farther back into the earlier period, so that the growth rate as shown in the industrial production index is somewhat overstated. Therefore, in Japan we can expect that the growth rates of industrial production and exports would not differ very much.

For the postwar period, I have also computed the growth rates in industrial production and exports for seven countries, by fitting linear logarithmic function to each of the series for 1953–58. From this comparison too, we see that Japan again showed the highest rate

2) The industrial growth rate for Sweden is not very high in this period, but if the period is extended to earlier years, a much higher growth rate is obtained. Although the foreign trade ratio in the United States follows a secular falling trend, it was fairly stable in this period.

Table 1. International Comparison of Export and Industrial Growth Rates,
for 1953–59

	Export growth rate	Industrial growth rate
Japan	19.47%	12.74%
W. Germany	14.49	8.74
Italy	11.76	7.40
France	(5.54)	(9.13)
Sweden	7.22	3.71
U.K	3.66	2.55
U.S.A.	3.40	1.30

Source: Computed from the United Nations, *Statistical Yearbook*, 1959.

of growth in industrial production as well as in exports in the postwar period. More interesting is the close rank association between the two growth rates and the uniformly higher growth rates in exports than in industrial production, except in the case of France.[3] After the war, the industrial growth rates in many countries exceeded those of the prewar period, so the larger growth rates in exports became, much more apparent, with the exception of France. In France, the industrial growth rate was larger than the export growth rate, but this brought a about the drastic decline (of 44%) in foreign exchange holding from the end of 1955 to the end of 1958.

From the foregoing, we can see that in an economy whose growth rate is exceedingly high the export growth rate is also supposed to be very high and the latter seems to have a leading, causative role in industrial development. Of course, the causes of the rapid export expansion must be explored, but as a first step in our analysis, it is necessary to confirm the close correlation between the two in the very rapidly growing economies. In other words, without a strikingly rapid advance in exports, the extraordinarily high domestic growth rate (from the standpoint of international comparison) does not occur, and therefore the rapidity of Japan's economic development should be considered with special attention to her high export

3) See Chapter 2, " Relative Production Levels of Industrial Countries and Their Growth Potentials ".

growth potentials.

3. Dependency on Exports

Even though the export growth rate is very high, its relative importance will not be great, if the country's dependence on exports is slight (By dependency is meant the proportion of exports to total output). On the contrary, Japan's dependence upon exports had been fairly high, especially in the textile industry before the war. As the proportion of textile industry in the total manufacturing output was 50.2% in 1909, 59.9% in 1919 and 33.9% in 1934, the prewar industrial growth of Japan can be considered to depend mainly on the increase of her textile exports. It is important to recognize here that this textile industry which comprised a large proportion of manufacturing before the war, had also been highly dependent on exports as the two tables indicate. Table 2 shows how high the proportion of raw silk exports (and tea) were relative to their production over a long period, and how rapidly the exports-output ratio of cotton fabrics increased, (up to the ratio of 55.9% for 1933–37). In the case of cotton yarn, the ratio suddenly jumped to around 40% between 1888 and 1897, and then decreased gradually to 2.5% for 1933–37, reflecting the substitution of cotton fabrics for cotton yarn in textile exports through further fabrication.

Table 3 shows the proportions of the main export commodities (tea, raw silk, cotton fabrics, and silk fabrics) in the export total. Although tea constituted about one-fourth of the total exports in the early Meiji period, it declined to about 3% at the end of the Meiji era (1908–12) and further to 0.5% in 1933–37. Raw silk, on the other hand, maintained very high proportions for a long period before the war, and for 1868–32 it ranged from 24% to 37.8%. Only in 1933–37 and afterwards, did its proportion drastically decreased. For 1868–97 and 1923–32, the ratio was over 30%, but for 1898–1922 it was around 24–28%. Instead, the proportion of silk fabrics was swollen in the latter period, and therefore the total share of raw silk plus silk fabrics seems to have been fairly constant for 1868–1932.

Table 2. Exports-Output Ratios in Selected Major Export Commodities, 1883–1937

	Raw silk			Tea			Cotton fabrics			Cotton yarn		
	Production (a)	Exports (b)	$\frac{b}{a}$	Production (a)	Exports (b)	$\frac{b}{a}$	Production (a)	Exports (b)	$\frac{b}{a}$	Production (a)	Exports (b)	$\frac{b}{a}$
	thousand kan	〃	%	thousand kin	〃	%	thousand yen	〃	%	bale	〃	%
1883-87	641	432	67.4	38,563	31,391	81.4		149				
1888-92	930	695	74.7	44,267	35,039	79.1	16,319	252	1.5	29,454	46	0.2
1893-97	1,422	827	58.2	51,368	35,719	69.5	33,490	2,005	6.0	97,337	40,392	41.5
1898-1902	1,761	1,030	58.5	46,708	32,761	70.1	49,991	4,738	9.5	601,129	237,126	39.4
1903-07	2,115	1,426	67.4	43,650	32,330	74.1	67,700	11,615	17.2	866,227	285,142	32.9
1908-12	3,169	2,278	71.9	51,755	30,485	58.9	126,505	19,638	15.5	1,104,014	286,859	26.0
1913-17	4,275	3,288	76.9	57,702	35,526	61.6	239,754	58,893	24.2	1,750,770	526,523	30.1
1918-22	6,124	4,194	68.5	61,423	23,071	37.6	730,823	256,023	35.0	1,916,244	328,618	17.1
1923-27	8,320	6,510	78.2	61,067	19,033	31.2	736,651	358,835	48.7	2,363,839	230,538	9.8
1928-32	11,203	8,482	75.7	65,281	18,557	28.4	594,825	304,896	51.3	2,629,344	64,000	2.4
1933-37	11,481	8,206	71.5	78,393	28,555	36.4	868,155	485,664	55.9	3,541,358	89,998	2.5

Sources: Production: The Ministry of Agriculture and Commerce, *Noshomutokeihyo* (Statistics on Agriculture and Commerce), and The Ministry of Commerce and Industry, *Shokoshotokeihyo* (Statistics on Commerce and Industry).

Exports: The Ministry of Finance, *Dainihongaikokuboekinempyo* (Annual Statistics on Foreign Trade in Japan).

Note: 1 kan=3.759 kg: 1 kin=600 g.

Table 3.　Share of Major Commodities in Total Exports, 1868–1937

	Total exports	Tea		Raw silk		Exports of						% of 5 items
						Cotton fabrics		Cotton yarn		Silk fabrics		
	thousand yen	″	%	″	%	″	%	″	%	″	%	″
1868–72	15,600	3,818	(24.5)	5,892	(37.8)	3.8	(0.02)			2	(0.01)	62.3
1873–77	22,125	5,720	(25.9)	8,152	(36.8)	10.8	(0.05)			4	(0.02)	62.8
1878–82	30,263	6,665	(22.0)	10,622	(35.1)	31.9	(0.1)			23	(0.08)	57.3
1883–87	41,714	6,822	(16.4)	15,365	(36.8)	149.5	(0.4)	″	%	66	(0.2)	53.8
1888–92	72,600	6,633	(9.1)	26,404	(36.4)	252.4	(0.3)	35	(0.005)	1,662	(2.3)	48.2
1893–97	124,010	7,748	(6.2)	39,970	(32.2)	2,005	(1.6)	3,914	(3.2)	7,994	(6.4)	49.6
1898–1902	219,153	9,017	(4.1)	60,172	(27.5)	4,739	(2.2)	22,119	(10.1)	20,490	(9.3)	53.2
1903–07	357,293	12,148	(3.4)	92,377	(25.9)	11,615	(3.3)	31,916	(8.9)	33,169	(9.3)	50.8
1908–12	444,841	13,339	(3.0)	128,099	(28.8)	19,639	(4.4)	38,324	(8.6)	31,305	(7.0)	51.8
1913–17	932,468	15,205	(1.6)	224,019	(24.0)	58,894	(6.3)	80,299	(8.6)	46,016	(4.9)	45.4
1918–22	1,779,931	16,823	(0.9)	492,125	(27.6)	256,023	(14.4)	124,043	(7.0)	129,258	(7.3)	57.2
1923–27	1,919,484	13,313	(0.7)	719,803	(37.5)	358,835	(18.7)	84,150	(4.4)	121,566	(6.3)	67.6
1928–32	1,629,480	9,734	(0.6)	533,629	(32.7)	304,897	(18.7)	19,548	(1.2)	88,626	(5.4)	58.6
1933–37	2,480,088	13,147	(0.5)	372,931	(15.0)	485,664	(19.6)	33,664	(1.4)	71,758	(2.9)	39.4

Source:　The Ministry of Finance, *Dainihon Gaikokuboekinempyo* (Annual Statistics on Foreign Trade in Japan).

49

The proportion of cotton fabrics, however, continually rose, but the proportion of cotton yarn reached a peak during 1898–1902, and then tended to decline.

It is to be noted that only five items compose about 50% of total exports for the 1868–1932 period and this proportion had been fairly stable, as indicated in the last column of Table 3. However, for 1933–37, the proportion of the five items declined to 39.4%. Evidently, this downward trend continued during the second World War. This was caused by the sharp increases in the exports of machinery and parts, canned foods and rayon yarn (See Fig. 2). Here, we see how Japanese exports had been oriented to light industry commodities before the war, how their dependence on foreign trade was high, and how the continual expansion of foreign trade was indispensable for the attainment of the accelerated domestic growth.

Fig. 2. Proportions of Selected Items in Total Exports, 1925–1944

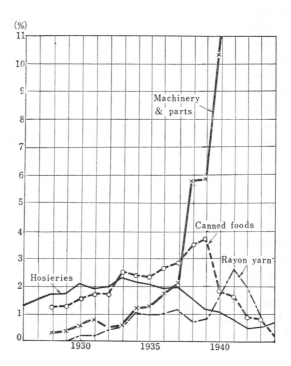

4. Phases of Economic Growth and the Balance of Payments

In explaining the various phases of Japan's prewar economic development with reference to her balance of payments, it may be convenient to divide the whole period into five, *i.e.*, 1) 1868–81; 2) 1882–1903; 3) 1904–14; 4) 1915–30; 5) 1931–44.[4]

The first period, 1868–81 begins just after the Meiji Restoration and runs up to the start of the Finance Minister Matsukata's deflationary policy.   Through the Meiji Restoration, Japan launched on capitalistic development by casting off the old feudalistic fetters and creating a unified country.   As Japan had no customs autonomy then and the tariff barrier was lowered to a level of above 5%, the impact upon the weak industries was shattering.   After the restoration, the local restrictions set up by the feudal clans were removed, and the domestic market was widened from clan units to nation-wide dimensions.   This stimulated those industries with comparative advantages, such as the raw silk or tea, on the one hand, and struck a destructive blow to those industries which had been protected by the clans, on the other, for example, the paper industry in Uwajima (Ehime Pref.), the cotton cloth industry in Himeji (Hyogo Pref.), the sugar industry in Sanuki (Takamatsu Pref.), and cotton cultivation in various areas were hard hit.   The liberalization of trade, however, consolidated the competitive power of tea and textile industries in foreign trade, paving the way for their subsequent, rapid development.

For 1868–81, the total of exports was ¥302 million and that of imports was ¥380 million, thus the import surplus amounted to ¥78 million, with the consequent exodus of gold and silver of ¥71 million.   This gold and silver had, of course, been accumulated during the feudalistic period, and these assets were used to finance the balance of payments deficits which in part were incurred to

---

4)   I have also attempted to explain our prewar economic development in terms of Long Waves (Kuznets cycle), in Chapter 4 " Growth and Long Swings in the Prewar Period ".

import foreign machinery, to invite foreign engineers, to support students studying abroad, *etc.* In this way, the gold and silver accumulated in the past contributed to start Japan's capitalist development.[5] Besides these, a flotation of foreign loans of £1 million was used for the construction of a railroad from Tokyo to Yokohama in 1870, and in 1873 another loan of £2.4 million was floated.

The economic expansion in the early Meiji period was directly financed by increasing the issue of paper currencies, but finally the deficits caused by the excess imports was made up by the gold and silver exports and by the flotation of foreign loans. Although economic growth through the above method could be sustained until around 1880, the intensified inflation after the outbreak of the Satsuma Rebellion (1877) exhausted the stock of gold and silver due to the persistent import surplus. Some deflationary measures became imperative at this stage.

In the second phase, 1882–1900: The galloping inflation and continuing outflow of gold and silver seems to have necessitated the enforcement of a deflationary policy by the Finance Minister Matsukata at the end of 1881. Matsukata firmly believed that the cause of rising prices was the increase of paper notes, and initiated a traditional deflationary policy. He attempted to curtail government expenditures and increase internal revenues by imposing new taxes, and hoped as a consequence to decrease substantially the paper notes in circulation.

Actually from the end of 1881 to the end of 1885, the notes in circulation decreased from ¥153.3 millions to Y118.5 million or by about 23%. Due to Matsukata's policies, the discrepancy in the values between silver coins and paper notes declined from 1.795 in April 1881 to 1.001 in December 1885, and prices fell tremendously. Farmers and small businesses were hard hit by this policy, but imports fell from ¥36.6 million in 1880 to ¥29.4 million in 1885, while exports increased from ¥28.4 million to ¥37.1 million for the same period. The balance of payments thus turned into a surplus there-

5) See, for example, K. Mitani, *Balance of Payments and Japan's Economic Growth* (in Japanese), 1957, pp. 79–83.

after and a sound basis for Japan's industrialization was laid.

The Japanese economy continued to industrialize at a rapid pace following the Matsukata deflation until around 1900's or 1910's when the growth rate of national output was temporarily retarded. During this period, Japan acquired ¥365 million in reparations from China after the settlement of the Sino-Japanese War of 1894–95. This was about one-fourth of the annual national income at that time and these reparations made possible the expansion of the army and navy, the extension of railroad, telegraph and telephone services, the establishment of the Yawata Iron Mill, as well as the adoption of the gold standard. A point which should be noted here is the role of reparations in raising the ceiling of the balance of payments. Compared with 1893 (just before the Sino-Japanese War), the increase of exports until 1897 was only 82%, but the increase of imports amounted to 2.5 times. Since 1896, the balance of payment was again unfavorable, and the total deficits for 1896–1903 came to about ¥354 million which was close to the amount of the reparations, ¥365 million; hence, it is evident that the reparations made possible the acceleration of growth by making up the deficit in the balance of payments.

The brisk activities in domestic construction and production, together with the impetus from the reparations and the decline in the relative price of silver under the silver standard, made the decade of the 1890's the " take-off " stage in Meiji economic development.

The third phase, 1904–14, can be considered a stage of retardation in growth. First, the boost given to exports (similar to the impact of an exchange devaluation) through the relative fall of the price of silver, disappeared with the adoption of the gold standard in 1897. Second, in view of the world-wide Kondratieff waves prices sagged and tended to bottom in this period. Third, the advance of such activities as railroads, cotton yarn production, *etc.* tapered off.

Moreover, the outbreak of the Russo-Japanese War (1904–5) entailed huge war expenditures, amounting to ¥1,716 million. The public debt issue during the war was ¥1,470 million, of which ¥800 million was floated as foreign loans. The excess in imports was ¥78 million in 1904 and ¥176 million in 1905. If invisible trade is further taken into account, the foreign species necessary for the prosecution of the Russo-Japanese War can be estimated to be ¥400 million. However, the specie holding at the end of 1903 was only ¥139 million. Thus, if foreign loans had not been forthcoming, it would have declined to zero. In addition to the weakness of exports, and the balance of payments as noted above, the expansion of the domestic economy contributed to the persisting menace of excess imports and financial crisis. Even after the 1907 crisis, the Katsura Cabinet, which was formed in 1908, was forced to adopt a retrenchment policy and to make every effort to strengthen economic stability.

The fourth phase, 1915–30, covers the outbreak of the 1st World War and its aftermath. As Japan had not directly participated in the war, she profited immensely as a bystander and her balance of payments were greatly improved. Through the increase of exports by 3.3 times and of imports by 2.8 times during 1914–18, the cumulative total of export surplus amounted to ¥1,408 million. While the belligerants had been involved in the war, Japan expanded her exports to Latin America, Africa, Asia, *etc.* However, the Japanese economy was in an unstable condition for a long time after the war. The boom lasted for only a short time after the war, collapsing in 1920 owing to the financial crisis caused by the increasing excess imports and monetary contraction. Even after the crisis, the economy was in a stagnant condition due to the comparatively high domestic price level, the excess imports and the efflux of gold. Nevertheless, easy financing for accumulation of inventories and spending for reconstruction after the Kanto earthquake (1923) continued. Thus, the volume of production increased mainly because of brisk construction activity, but prices continually tended to decline. In 1927, a financial crisis occurred as a consequence of the postwar easy money policy. In 1928, the Hamaguchi Cabinet announced that in January, 1930, it would lift the gold embargo which had been in effect since 1917. In preparation for this step, a policy of austerity was pursued. However, because this policy was enforced during the world depression and at the old par, there was a huge (¥700 million) specie outflow in 1930–31, and the attempt failed.

54

The following fifth phase, 1931–44, is very easy to explain. It was caused by an increase in military expenditures and by a sharp expansion of exports made possible through exchange devaluation in 1932. We will omit a summary of the situation here, as it is fairly well known.

5. Changes in the Commodity Composition of Trade

As explained above, the " take-off " in the Meiji industrialization seems to have occurred between 1882–1904. Almost in parallel with this development, the commodity composition of foreign trade underwent a transformation. In Table 4, we see on the one hand, that the proportion of raw materials in total exports declined from 23.2% of 1868–72 to 11.3% of 1898–1902, whereas its proportion in total imports increased from 4% to 31.4% for the same period. On the other

Table 4. Changes in the Commodity Composition of Foreign Trade, 1868–1956
(in percent of total)
Commodity Composition of Exports

	Food	Raw materials	Semi-manufactured raw materials	Finished manufactures	Miscellaneous
1868– 72	32.2	23.2	40.8	1.9	1.9
1898–1902	12.0	11.3	47.2	26.7	2.8
1933– 37	7.9	4.3	26.2	58.7	2.9
1953– 56	8.2	3.4	25.9	62.0	0.5

Commodity Composition of Imports

	Food	Raw materials	Semi-manufactured raw materials	Finished manufactures	Miscellaneous
1868– 72	29.0	4.1	20.2	44.5	2.2
1898–1902	22.9	31.4	16.3	28.0	1.3
1933– 37	7.9	60.0	20.1	11.3	0.7
1953– 56	26.7	50.4	10.7	12.1	0.1

Source : Computed from Nippon Tokei Kenkyusho (Japan Statistical Research Institute), *Nihonkeizai-Tokeishu* (Statistics on Japanese Economy), Tokyo, 1958.

hand, the exports of finished manufactures increased from 1.9% to 26.7%, but the imports of finished manufactures decreased from 44.5% to 28%. In other words, it is evident that during these thirty years the pattern of foreign trade underwent a drastic change. In 1868–72, Japan imported 44.5% of finished manufactures, 29% of food and exported 32.2% of food, 23.2% of raw materials and 40% of semi-manufactured raw materials. This is the typical pattern of foreign trade in a country producing primary products. However, in 1898–1902, Japan transformed her structure of foreign trade into a pattern of a so-called processing-nation, *i.e.*, importing raw materials and exporting finished manufactures. This change in the pattern of foreign trade was a necessary consequence of the rapid industrialization. As Japan became more industrialized, the proportion of finished manufactures exported rose, and the proportion imported declined.

In the early Meiji years (1868–72), the import of textile fabrics was 34.2%, the import of textile yarns was 18.3%, and the import of rice 18.3%. These three items totaled 70.8%. On the other hand, the exports of tea were then 24.5% and the exports of raw silk were 37.8%. The two came to 62.3%, indicating clearly the pattern of exporting highly specialized indigenous products. However, in 1898–1902, tea exports declined to 4.1%, and raw silk to 27.5%, while the exports of cotton yarn, increased to 10.1%, and those of cotton fabrics to 2.2%. The exports of silk fabrics became 9.3%. Foreign trade became more diversified and changed to a processing pattern. On the other hand, from 1868–72 to 1898–1902, the proportions of certain commodities in total imports changed as follows: cotton yarn (15.9% ot 2.2%), cotton fabrics (16.4% to 4.7%), and raw cotton (2.1% to 24.0%).

These relations are shown for the cotton textile industry in Fig. 3. This chart indicates that in the early phase of Japan's industrialization, the imports of cotton fabrics and cotton yarn comprised fairly large portions, but as industrialization proceeded, their proportions fell rapidly, and the imports of textile material—raw cotton principally—increased very sharply. Particularly interesting in this case is that the share of cotton yarn in total exports reached a peak in

1898–1902, after which it gradually fell. However, the proportion of cotton fabrics in total exports shows a very quick rise up to high plateau which began from 1923–27 on. These sequences in the dynamics of industrialization reflected in the commodity structure of foreign trade seem to be noteworthy.

Professor K. Akamatsu of Hitotsubashi University in 1937 confirmed his theory of " Gankokeitai " (wild-geese flying pattern), by applying it to the successive changes of imports, domestic production, and exports of cotton yarn, cotton fabrics, and cotton textile machinery.[6] Later, his analysis was extended to other industries. The meaning and essence of his analysis are as follows: Wild geese are said to come to Japan flying in inverse V-shapes, each of which overlaps to some extent, and Fig. 4 represents the pattern of industrial development like this.

First, consumer goods progress with sequence in the economic development as follows: imports → production → exports, and then, capital goods (the sequence is again similar) with some overlapping in these processes in consumer goods and capital goods. Since 1898–1902, the Japanese economy advanced tremendously and as Professor Akamatsu suggests, the economy gradually moved into a stage in which the share of capital good production became much larger.

Table 5 reveals that in the movement of investment goods the proportion of machinery imports reached a peak (11.3%) in 1893–97, and then leveled off around 7%, but that the imports of ores and metals rose to 16.4% in 1913–17 from the early low figure of 2.3% in 1868–72, and then declined (except the war period 1933–37.) Here again, we can see that the imports of finished machinery was gradually replaced by their domestic production, so the proportion of the raw material imports for the manufacture of machinery increased in the later period. Actually, in the Showa period (from 1926 on), the proportion of metal and machine industries increased

6) K. Akamatsu, " Synthetic Dialectics of Industrial Development in Japan ", *Journal of Nagoya Higher Commercial School*, July 1937 (in Jpanese). See also his article, "A Theory of Unbalanced Growth in the World Economy ", *Weltwirtschaftliches Archiv*, Band 86 Heft 2, 1961.

Fig. 3. The Share of Cotton Textiles in Foreign Trade, Sequencial Pattern, 1868–1937

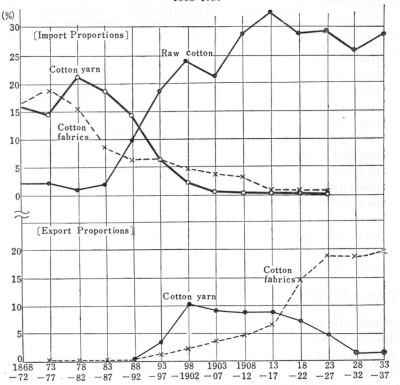

Source: The Ministry of Finance, *Dainihon Gaikokuboeki-nempyo* (Annual Statistics on Foreign Trade in Japan).

Fig. 4. Prof. Akamatsu's " Wild-Geese Flying Pattern " in Industrial Development

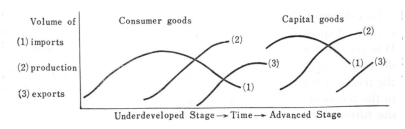

Table 5.   The Share of Investment Goods in Total Imports, 1868–1937

	Imports of machineries		Imports of ores and metals		Imports of fabricated metal products	
	thousand yen					
1868– 72	459	(2.2)%	522	(2.3)%	45	(0.20)%
1873– 77	1,354	(5.1)	1,231	(4.6)	268	(1.01)
1878– 82	1,219	(3.7)	1,962	(6.0)	448	(1.37)
1883– 87	2,066	(6.3)	1,729	(5.3)	1,180	(3.60)
1888– 92	5,755	(8.3)	3,344	(4.8)	2,791	(4.02)
1893– 97	16,428	(11.3)	8,232	(5.7)	5,824	(4.01)
1898–1902	19,145	(7.3)	19,093	(7.3)	8,119	(3.09)
1903– 07	30,355	(7.3)	38,049	(9.1)	11,264	(2.69)
1908– 12	37,382	(7.7)	48,655	(10.0)	15,352	(3.16)
1913– 17	35,715	(4.9)	120,074	(16.4)	11,344	(1.55)
1918– 22	133,570	(6.9)	287,306	(14.8)	40,832	(2.11)
1923– 27	163,739	(7.1)	201,990	(8.7)	32,701	(1.41)
1928– 32	130,734	(7.6)	171,884	(10.0)	15,666	(0.91)
1933– 37	160,894	(6.1)	440,192	(16.7)	9,897	(0.37)

Source: The Ministry of Finance, *ibid.*

enormously, not only as a natural course of economic growth but also due to the development of the war economy.   It is well known that, after the war, the share of heavy industry increased in total output as well as in exports, but we shall not discuss the postwar period in detail here.

6.   *Factors which raised Exports up to Around 1900*

In exploring the background of the rapid export expansion, it may be adequate to divide the whole period before the Second World War into two periods with about 1900 as the dividing line.   This division is supported by the fact that while we see no deterioration in the terms of trade before the 1900's, there were two severe declines in the terms of trade after that and, by the fact that the 1900's was the turning point when the Japanese economy changed its pattern of foreign trade from the exporting of indiginous products to a pattern of a processing nation. We may summarize the factors which accelerated exports for the 1868–1900 period as follows:

1. The liberalization of foreign trade with lowered tariffs under the unequal treaty immediately after the Meiji Restoration meant, a sifting-out process of the healthiest industries, and thus tea and raw silk became the selected commodities which had a relatively strong competitive power in foreign trade. Matsukata's deflationary policies also provided the Japanese economy with a sound starting point from which her exports could grow rapidly.

2. There were several propitious factors in the early export picture. One is that Japan had carried over great deal of gold and silver from the feudalistic period and could divert this to cover the continued deficits in the balance of payments. Another is that in 1876 the exports of raw silk more than doubled due to the spread of silk-worm diseases throughout Europe. The average of raw silk exports for 1873–75 was ¥5,978 thousand, but it jumped in 1876–79 to an average of ¥10,238 thousand. This was a sudden jump in an export item which had been relatively stagnant during 1868–75 although constituted a large share in the total exports of that time.

3. The third was the injection to the economy of the reparations acquired as consequence of the Sino-Japanese War (1894–95). The large amount of reparations not only made possible the construction of railroad and communication and the establishment of the steel industry, but also the raising of the balance-of-payments ceiling, thus contributing to the advance of industrialization, which in turn stimulated the establishment of the processing trade and the expansion of exports.

4. It is natural that raw silk played a leading role in the export growth up to 1900's, for its proportion in total exports had been the highest. In its initial stage, raw silk exports benefited from the silk-worm diseases in Europe, but the problem was how to continue increasing its export even after that. It is difficult to make an analysis of the qualitative improvement in Japanese raw silk. However, Fig. 5 which indicates the comparative developments in sericultural productivity in Japan, Italy and France may suffice to give a general

impression of the rapidity of the quantitative increase in productivity in Japanese sericulture as compared with her competitors. In addition to this, we should take into account the rapidity of quality improvement, unparalleled in any other country. Scientific management of sericulture, introduction of silk reeling machines, quality improvement in cocoons and raw silk, and the standardization of cocoons, together with cheap labor, increasingly strengthened the competitive position of Japanese raw silk exports.

The cheapness of wages and cost of production in Japan, com-

Fig 5.　Comparison of Productivity in the Sericulture of Japan, Italy and France, 1886–1940

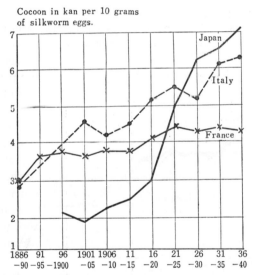

Source :　Nihonseni Kyogikai (Japan Textile Conference Association), *Nihonseni Sangyoshi* (History of Japan's Textile Industry), Tokyo 1958, Vol. 1, p. 73.

Note :　1)　Five year averages of cocoon per 10 grams of silkworm eggs.

2)　Original data : Japan : The Ministry of Agriculture and Forestry, *Sanshigyo Yoran* (General Survey of Silk Reeling Industry), 1939 and 1953 ; Italy and France : The Ministry of Agriculture and Commerce, *Sericulture in Italy and France* (in Japanese), Aug. 1916.

3)　1 kan＝3.759 kg.

61

Table 6. Comparison of Wages and Costs of Production in Sericulture in Japan, Italy and France in 1913-14

(Unit : yen)

	Japan	France	Italy
Daily wages in sericulture :			
Male	0.50	1.14	0.95
Female	0.28	0.56	0.43
Cost of production of co-coon per kans	*4.20	5.17	4.65
Sale prices of cocoon per kans	4.50	4.98	4.98

Source : Japan : *Noshomu Tokeihyo* (Statistics of Agriculture and Commerce); France and Italy : The Ministry of Agriculture and Commerce, " Silk Reeling Industry in Italy and France" (in Japanese), (Aug. 1916).

Note : * refers to 1916. In 1913, it was far less than ¥4.20, for the selling price of cocoon per kan was ¥5.36 in 1916. 1 kan=3.759 kg.

Fig. 6. Decline of Price of Silver Relative to Gold and the Exchange Rate, 1874–97

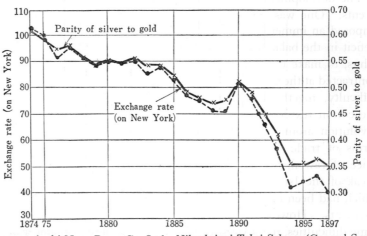

Source : Asahi News Paper Co. Ltd., *Nihonkeizai Tokei Sokwan* (General Summary of Japanese Statistics), 1930.

pared with Italy and France is indicated in Table 6.

5. A probable factor pushing up the rate of export growth may

be the secular decline in the price of silver compared to gold, which followed the continued drop in Japanese exchange rates—Japan had adopted the silver standard then—on those countries which was on the gold standard, such as U.K. or U.S.A. This effect appears similar to that of exchange devaluation which may stimulate exports if there is a lag in the adjustment of domestic prices. Fig 6 indicates clearly how secular decline of silver prices relative to gold is reflected almost perfectly in the exchange rates (on New York) for 1874–97 during which time Japan was on the silver standard. However, in such a process, it may be expected that a lag in the adjustment in the domestic prices would decidedly stimulate exports to the countries on the gold standard.

7. Deterioration of the Terms of Trade and Export Expansion after the 1900's

The development of foreign trade after the 1900's involves many events. One was the outbreak of the Russo-Japanese War, which imposed an immense drain on the Japanese economy and made the deficit in the balance of payments relatively chronic and persistent. Thus, to make up this deficit, large amounts of foreign loans were contracted at the end of the Meiji period but this balance of payments difficulty, together with the tendency towards overproduction in the cotton textile industry due to the completion of the industrial revolution around 1900's resulted in a severe deterioration in the terms of trade (*i.e.*, export price of finished commodities / import price of raw materials), by about 33% for 1903–1913. The outbreak of the 1st World War, however, was providential to Japan which had been harrassed by persistent difficulties in the balance of payments. However, after the war, Japan again fell back into the same difficulties, mainly due to the higher domestic prices during the war and the rise in domestic construction expenditure necessitated by the Kanto Earthquake (1923). Thus, after 1920 and up to 1931, wholesale prices dropped by 55.4% in adjustment to these troubles. In addition to this, the second sharp deterioration in the terms of trade, arose due to the exchange devaluation, at the end of 1931, the extent of which was greater than that of any other country.[7] The astonishing thing was that Japan's exports and production could maintain its rapid rate of expansion throughout the World Depression of the 1930's when almost all countries suffered declines in exports and production. Therefore, we will focus our analysis on the effect of the terms of trade on export expansion from the 1900's on, particularly in the 1930's.

To get a bird's-eye view, Fig. 7 is presented, showing how Japan's

Fig. 7.   The Terms of Trade, Japan *vs.* U. K., 1903–1937 (1913=100)

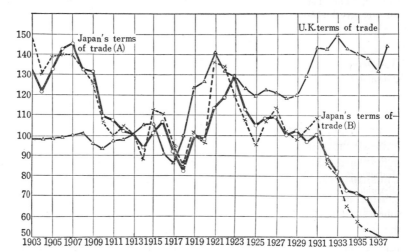

Source: U. K., 1914–19: W. Schlote, *British Overseas Trade from* 1900 *to the* 1930's, (English Translation, Oxford 1952, p. 155; 1903–13 and 20–38: C. P. Kindleberger, *Terms of Trade* 1956, p. 12; Japan: Oriental Economist Co., *Nihonboekiseiran* (The Foreign Trade of Japan: A Statistical Survey) 1935, but for 1931 onwards, the Yokohama Specie Bank index for (A) and the Kobe University of Commerce index for (B) were used. (A) index represents export price divided by import price and (B) index, export price of finished commodities divided by import price of raw materials.

7)   Concerning the extent of exchange devaluation in various countries, see S. E. Harris, *Exchange Depreciation*, Cambridge Mass. 1936, p. 422.

terms of trade followed a downward trend (although cyclical changes were violent), in contrast to the upward trend of the U.K. terms of trade. Japan and U.K. have a somewhat similar pattern of foreign trade, *i.e.*, importing raw materials, then their fabrication and export. Nevertheless, the movements in their terms of trade were quite the opposite. This seems to be responsible, at least partly, for the difference in the growth rates of exports in the two countries.

Table 7 and 8 show to what extent the changes in the terms of trade differed among various countries in the 1930's and different behavior

Table 7. The Terms of Trade in Various Countries, 1927, 1933, 1937 with 1927=100

	1933	1937		1933	1937
U.S.A.	137.8	128.9	Hungary	78.2	91.9
Germany	139.2	114.3	Canada	75.5	89.3
France	118.9	113.7	Chile	82.7	89.1
Finland	91.6	110.7	Yugo-Slavia	71.3	89.0
U.K.	122.3	107.3	Ireland	92.3	87.8
South Africa	84.3	101.2	Denmark	82.5	78.1
Norway	103.2	100.3	Italy	97.0	67.7
Latvia	61.6	94.1	Dutch East Indies	68.6	67.2
Estonia	79.0	71.8	Japan	81.9	60.5

Source: Colin clark, *Conditions of Economic Progress*, 1st edition, 1940, p. 456.

Table 8. Average Export Indexes in Various Countries, 1936–1938. 1929=100

	Price in gold	Quantum	Total value in gold
Germany	64	62	39
Switzerland	59	64	38
France	51	55	28
U.K.	50	78	39
U.S.A.	45	74	33
Italy	39	93	36
Japan	29	168	49

Source: W. A. Lewis, *Economic Survey, 1919–1939*, 1950, p. 122.

of export prices and quantities. Particularly important is the fact that Japan was the country which suffered the severest deterioration in the terms of trade, whose export prices declined most drastically, and whose volume of exports showed the greatest expansion in the very midst of the Great Depression when exports of many countries fell steeply.

In Japan, the export price in gold fell from 1929 to 1936–38 by 71%, on the one hand, and the quantity of exports increased in the same period by 68%, on the other. Taking into consideration the decline in world income during this period, we may guess that the elasticity of export demand with respect to the decline of export price was more than unity.

As already mentioned, the major items of Japanese exports consisted of textile goods in the prewar period. However, changes in the export demand of textile goods may depend on the movements in world income and also on the relative prices of the textile goods exported in the world market. It is not evident how high the growth rate of the world real income was, but it is said that the U.S. growth rate was around 3.5%, the European growth rate was less, and that of underdeveloped countries extremely small in the prewar period. Let us assume, therefore, that the average growth rate of world real income was about 2%, probably an overestimate, while the income elasticity of textile demand ranged from 1 to 1.5. Then the world growth rate in textile exports would be 2–3% ($2\% \times 1 \sim 1.5$). However, the Japanese growth rate in exports (which is mainly composed of textile goods) was 7–8%, far exceeding the export growth rate based on the above assumption that only the world income effect would have operated. The difference between 7–8% and 2–3% could easily be ascribed to the terms of trade effect. The sharp deterioration in the terms of trade which occurred during 1907–14 and during 1932–37, seems to have been crucial in maintaining an export growth rate higher than any other country's, even during the World Depression.

Of course, the advance of Japan's exports depended to a large extent also on imperialistic aggression, but if the exported commodities were not cheaply priced, the expansion in exports may not

66

have been sustained.   Even in the Indian cotton cloth market which Japanese imperialism could not directly affect, the percentage of imports supplied by U.K. declined from 97.1% (1913–14) to 47.3% (1935), while that supplied by Japan increased from 0.3% (1913–14) to 50.9% (1935).   In the South American cotton cloth market too, U.K.'s share decreased from 53.2% (1929) to 46.4% (1935) while Japan's share increased from 4.5% (1929) to 38.6% (1935). Also the share of U.S. and Italy declined in the same period from 42.3% to 15.0%.[8]   These figures clearly show how effective prices or the terms of trade were in promoting Japan's export expansion in the prewar period.[9]

The deterioration in the terms of trade in the 1930's was due to an exchange devaluation greater than any other country, but what of 1907–14?   The exchange rate to Western countries did not change very much, but that to Asian countries changed some.   Nevertheless, a sharp decline in the terms of trade occurred.   For 1907–14 both in U.K. and Japan, import prices generally increased.   But, in Japan, the export price of cotton yarn fell by 27.2%, cotton cloth price by 39.6% and raw silk price by 24.2%.   Therefore, it may be inferred that the increased productivity in the textile industry (especially in the cotton textile industry which had become a strong export industry around the 1900's) made possible a curtailment in prices of textile commodities.   In that sense, increased productivity seems to have been a cause of the deterioration in the terms of trade for 1907–14, in contrast to the 1930's when the terms of trade fell due to the drastic exchange devaluation and to the export drive.   However, it is well-known that in this period overproduction in the cotton textile industry began to set in, and the period of the curtailment of operation by cartel agreement, which started in 1899, lasted until 1914, a period of 5 years and 11 months.   By comparing the export

8)   ILO, *The World Textile Industry, Economic and Social Problems* (Studies and Report Series B. No. 27), Geneva, 1937, p. 124–5.
9)   According to the study of Shozaburo Fujino, Hitotsubashi University, the elasticity of substitution between Japan and British cotton cloth in the China market was−8.147 (1924–31), and−11.092 (1932–36).   See his " Market Structure and Business Cycles " (in Japanese) in S. Tsuru and K. Ohkawa, eds., *Nihonkeizai no Bunseki*, Vol. 2 (Analysis of the Japanese Economy), 1955.

price with the domestic wholesale price, we can arrive at the conclusion that the export price of cotton cloth fell far more than its
domestic price. Therefore, the increased productivity, together
with the export drive, is supposed to have severely aggravated the
terms of trade.

8. Some Consequences of the Decline in the Terms of Trade

In order to ascertain the effects of the aggravation in the terms of
trade, the total behavior of the terms of trade is broken down into
sectoral terms of trade, e.g., the ratio of export price of cotton yarn
to import price of raw cotton, the ratio of export price of cotton
cloth to import price of raw cotton, the ratio of export price of raw
silk to total import price, etc. Thus, Fig. 8 is shown. We see from
this graph that the terms of trade for raw silk dropped (from about
150 to 40) most drastically, but the terms of trade between cotton
cloth and raw cotton also followed a downward trend (from about
140 to 70). However, in the case of the terms of trade between cotton yarn and raw cotton, it tends to rise. This break-down makes
clear the following points. First, the combination of the two opposite
tendencies, i.e., the terms of trade turning favorable for the cotton
yarn-raw cotton relation and the terms of trade turning unfavorable
for the cotton cloth-raw cotton relation, suggests that the big cotton

Fig. 8. The Sectoral Terms of Trade, 1903–1937

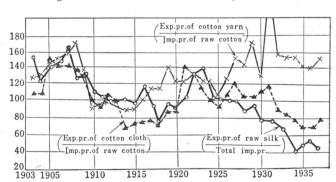

spinning corporation could shift the disadvantage entailed by the increase of relative prices in raw materials (raw cotton) to the smaller-scale weaving factories, by utilizing their monopolistic position. By observing the graph, we see that the relatively high price relation for cotton yarn as compared with cotton cloth continued from 1914 on to 1921, but after the temporal cessation of the above relation, it again showed a widening gap from about 1927 onward. As the proportion of cotton cloth in total exports was increasing and that of cotton yarn declining very rapidly in this period, we should attach much more importance upon the cotton cloth-raw cotton relation, than the cotton yarn-raw cotton relation.

Next is raw silk's terms of trade. Though raw silk proportion in total exports is gradually declining (29.9% in 1913, 35.8% in 1926 and 14.6% in 1937), it continued to be important. In the case of silk-reeling firms, their scale was larger than the weaving firms but far smaller than the cotton spinning corporation. Hence, their monopolistic positions were weak. Moreover, as the raw silk exports were concentrated to the United States, the influence of U.S. business cycle on the price fluctuation in the raw silk was powerful. The makers of raw silk were numerous, small and competitive household firms, whose trade marks varied considerably from firm to firm and among which price agreements through cartels could not be enforced adequately. Therefore, changes in price of raw silk were always determined by the U.S. business cycle, and the price of cocoon was largely derived from the price of raw silk. As the value-added margin of raw silk was slim, the cocoon price corresponded to about 80–90% of the raw silk price. Furthermore, as the monopolistic position of silk-reelers was weak, the relative price between cocoon and raw silk was fairly stable. Thus, once the raw silk price started to decline relative to general prices, the price decline would be shifted to sericulture, a sector of agriculture.

In the case of the cotton textile industry, the rise of raw material prices caused by the deterioration of the terms of trade was shifted from the big cotton spinners to the smaller-scale weaving firms by their oligopolistic pricing power. In the case of the silk reeling industry, the deterioration of terms of trade was transferred to a large-number of small sericulturists. It is important to note the existence of a cushion,—small scale weavers and sericulturalists behind the dramatic expansion of Japan's exports. It is also interesting to see that, although prices fluctuated violently, Japan's exports could rise on a straight line, thanks to the existence of a cushion. This can be called a cushion, for there were no strong trade unions with the power to resist or other combinations by which their interests were asserted. It seems to me that what made possible the sharp deterioration in the terms of trade was the existence of a market structure in which the weak sectors absorbed any pressure caused by the deterioration. If, on the contrary, we assume the existence of strong unions or combinations of workers and farmers, then the prewar deterioration of the terms of trade could not have been so tremendous.

Another consequence of the change in the terms of trade should be mentioned. In Japan, the value-added ratio in manufacturing can be computed from 1929 onwards directly from the Census of Manufactures. After the end of 1931, when the exchanges were devalued, the value-added ratios in manufacturing as a whole and in the textile industry dropped from 35.3% and 26.9% in 1932 to 27.6% and 14.9% in 1937, respectively. The percentage rates of decline were 22% and 45%, respectively, owing to the rise of the relative prices of raw materials brought about by the exchange devaluation. This drop of the value-added ratio was extremely noticeable, specially with reference to the textile industry. From 1932 to 1937 the production index in the textile industry increased by 31%, the value of production by 92%, but value-added by only 6%. With a 23% increase in the cost of living index the real income produced in that industry declined by 14%. It is because of the noticeable effect of the aggravation of terms of trade upon the divergence of output and value-added that real income declined by 14%, even though production increased by 31% in the textile industry.

We must add a few words here. So far, we have discussed the probable consequences of the deteriorated terms of trade in particular sectors of the domestic economy. But this is not the same as saying that foreign trade gave Japan only disadvantages. On the contrary, it may be expected that the continued expansion of exports through the decline of the terms of trade could increase employment and output through its multiplier effect as well as through the increase of imported raw materials, thus contributing to the striking tempo in domestic economic growth. Further, it must be demonstrated by some econometric technique that the decline in the terms of trade can have a positive influence upon exports as well as the balance of payments. But this problem is beyond the scope of this Chapter.[10] There is one other problem, namely, that although my hypothesis is applicable for the prewar period, it may not be relevant to the expansion of exports in the postwar period when the terms of trade indicate no up-or downward trend. According to the official index, the terms of trade became favorable only by 10% compared with the base period, 1934–36. Therefore, it is important to see that the prewar low level of the terms of trade has remained almost unchanged in the post-war period, making this factor one of the favorable conditions in stimulating exports.

9. The Role of Wages and Wage Structure in Exports

In the prewar period, the Japanese cotton spinning industry was excellent in various respects. First, it had excellent sources for purchasing raw cotton and good factory management. Second, it had wonderful capability in the processing techniques, such as the mixing of raw cottons mentioned above. Third, labor was extremely cheap. Fourth, especially after the exchange devaluation of 1932, its penetration into the world market was accelerated.

It would be useful here to present Table 9 which compares internationally the efficiency wage (wage bill per unit of output). This table was prepared by the Fuji Cotton Spinning Company for the period of the 1930's. The efficiency wage was lowest in Japan,

10) On this point, see Chapter 4 " Growth and the Long Swing in the Prewar Period ", p. 82. According to my computation, the price elasticity of exports was 1.0563 and that of imports 0.19149 for 1924–37, so the sum of the two price elasticities exceeds unity, satisfying the so-called " Lerner's Condition ". This shows that the exchange devaluation would improve the balance of payments.

except for China where Japanese factories were in operation. In India, it was markedly high on account of her low labor efficiency. In view of the level of technique, the United States is most prominent and Japan might not be as good, as is shown in the figures of workers required per 1000 spindles. However, a very low money wage rate enabled Japanese cotton textiles to assume hegemony over the world market.

Of course, the wage rate was low as compared with other countries, but we must not overlook the peculiar wage structure in prewar Japan. The wages in light industries, especially in the textile industry, indicated a large differential from those in heavy industries.

In Table 10, the wages in various industries in the United States (1945) and Japan (1950 and 1933) are compared. As the wage structure in the United States is not expected to undergo any drastic change, even such a casual comparison would make clear the sharp

Table 9. Costs of Fabrication of No. 40 Cotton Yarn in Various Countries, 1930's (all cost in yen)

	(a) Weekly wages per man	(b) Person required per 1000 spindles	(c) Weekly wages per man, per 1000 spindles (a×b=c)	(d) Weekly output per 1000 spindles (bales)	c/d Cost of fabrication per bale	Index of c/d with Japan = 100
United States	¥35.0	3.4	¥119.0	2.4	¥49.6	376
India	5.5	15.0	82.5	2.4	34.4	260
Netherlands	14.0	5.5	77.0	2.3	33.5	254
United Kingdom	18.0	4.0	72.0	2.3	31.4	238
Switzerland	14.0	5.0	70.0	2.3	30.4	230
France	12.0	5.5	66.0	2.4	27.5	208
Germany	13.0	4.5	58.0	2.3	25.4	192
Italy	11.0	5.5	60.5	2.4	25.2	191
Czechoslovakia	10.0	5.5	55.0	2.3	23.9	181
China	3.7	8.9	32.9	2.8	11.8	89
Japan	5.8	6.1	35.5	2.7	13.2	100

Source: Estimates by Fuji Cotton Spinning Company.

Table 10. A Comparison of Interindustry Wage Structures of Japan and the United States

	Hourly wages in USA (1954)[a]	Monthly wages in Japan (1950)[b]	Hourly wages in (1933)[c]
	U.S.cent	yen	sen
Shipbuilding	137.0	11,403	24.9 (private) 25.8 (government)
Petroleum refining	127.6	14,245	16.9
Automobiles	125.6	10,715	32.1
Rolling Stock	122.4	10,569	25.6 (private) 29.9 (government) 33.8 (municipal)
Airplanes	121.8		27.2 (private) 23.0 (government)
Machinery	114.0	8,801	
Printing	114.0	9,780	20.1 (private) 19.6 (government)
Rubber	112.5	8,887	12.8
Nonferrous metals	106.8	10,994	
Aluminum	106.5	11,661	
Electric machinery	105.3	8,929	20.4
Machine tools	99.2	6,136	
Chemicals	98.9	10,405	14.0 (total)[d]
Plate glass	95.0	9,105	16.6
Flour milling	94.2	10,768	18.2
Paper	88.3	10,851	12.3 (private)
Food processing	88.1	7,410	15.7 (total)[d]
Furniture	87.0	5,897	16.7
Bakery products	86.7	5,400	⎧ 8.5 (apparel, private)
Apparel and knitted goods	85.7	4,935	⎨ 18.6 (apparel, government)
			⎩ 9.5 (hosiery)
Boots and shoes	82.3		
Canned food	80.8	5,973	8.4
Hosiery	80.8	4,342	
Dairy products	78.2	9,773	
Tabacco	76.4		20.9
Silk, *etc.*	74.4		4.4
Textile goods	75.7	5,570	7.2 (total)[d]
Cotton yarn and cloth	68.4	6,700	7.8

[a] from Lebergott, " Wage Structures ", *Review of Economic Statistics*, November 1947.

[b] from *Kogyotokeihyo* (Census of Manufactures), 1950.

[c] from *Rodotokei Jitchi Chosahokoku* (Report of a Survey on Labor Statistics), 1933.

[d] Japanese figures represent broader categories than those for the USA.

73

contrast in the interindustry wage structure between the two countries.

If we compare Japan (1933) and the United States (1945), the difference is that the ratio of wages between the highest and lowest industries was about 7 in Japan (1933) and about 2 in the United States. This contrast can be more sharply depicted if we construct a chart in which both are correlated. (However, in 1950 this differential in Japan was narrowed to 3.3 owing to the relative increase of wages in light industries). This large differential in the interindustry wage structure, coupled with the given productivity differential, rendered possible a comparative advantage in the textile industry. To my way of thinking, this is an important point in the understanding of Japanese economic growth. It affords a key to an understanding of why exports of textiles expanded so much, and why their production occupied such a large percentage of total manufacturing production.

10. Conclusions

Although our discussion has not taken up every aspect of the role of foreign trade in Japan in economic development, we now summarize our results.

1) Not only in the postwar period but also in the prewar period, the Japanese export growth rate ranks among the highest in the world. In view of the close correlation between industrial and export growth rates, high export growth may have played a leading part in the striking industrial growth in countries like Japan, and Sweden.

2) In the period before the 1900's various factors operated in increasing our foreign trade, i.e., the secular decline in the relative price of silver under the silver standard, the acquisition of reparations from China due to the Sino-Japanese War, some chance factors, such as the legacy from the past of silver and gold, the silkworm diseases in Europe which stimulated raw silk exports, etc.

3) After the 1900's the drastic deterioration in the terms of trade (in the 1910's and in the 1930's) may have contributed to export

expansion, in the case of the 1930's despite the world-wide great depression.

4) When the terms of trade were aggravated sharply, the value-added ratio was reduced, causing a widening of the gap between output and value added. Moreover, there was a mechanism through which the income gap between big and smaller firms was intensified, namely, by shifting the price rise in imported raw materials to the smaller firms through oligopolistic pricing. The sericulturalists were also a cushion in the sense that a price decline of raw silk was transferred to them. However, in spite of this, the export expansion through the deteriorated terms of trade contributed to the domestic economic expansion through the multiplier effect as well as through increasing introduction of imported raw materials.

5) Behind the rapid expansion of textile exports, we see a combination of advanced technology and cheap labor. Thus, wages per unit of output in the cotton spinning industry were among the lowest in the world. Moreover, the interindustry wage differential between heavy and light industry was extraordinarily widened compared with other countries and this is one of the major causes for the prevalence of a comparative advantage in the textile industry.

6) The commodity composition of foreign trade has gradually shifted towards the processing trades since that early Meiji period, and the 1900's was a turning point in the sense that cotton textiles began to be exported instead of being imported.

CHAPTER 4

GROWTH AND LONG SWINGS IN THE PREWAR PERIOD*

1. The Problem

According to income estimates by Y. Yamada and K. Ohkawa, the long-term growth rate of real national income in Japan was around 4–5% per annum during the prewar period.[1] Evaluations of this growth rate have been concerned mainly with the average rate over a long-period, say fifty years, rather than its fluctuation. This is because of the convictions of analysts that the long-term income estimates have statistical weaknesses which, though not an obstacle to evaluation of the long-run growth rate, make it difficult to evaluate the short-run or long-run cycles of real income. Another difficulty is that, in deriving a real income series, the wholesale price index was often used as a deflator. However, its oscillations are particularly sharp compared with an estimated price index for final commodities. Therefore, real income sometimes rises in depression and declines in boom when the wholesale price index is used. Moreover, the number of items used in constructing the index is less for the prewar period than for the postwar period, another factor making for sharp oscillations of the deflator.

Nevertheless, it is possible to break through this data bottleneck

---

* Just at the time this paper was published in Japanese, I had the opportunity of reading Prof. K. Ohkawa's paper (unpublished), " The Pattern of Japanese Long-term Economic Growth ", written at Berkeley. In that paper, he develops some ideas on the long swing of the Japanese economy, but it is quite different from mine in terms of measurement, hypothesis and construction.

1) Yuzo Yamada, *Nihon Kokumin Shotoku Suikei Shiryo* (A Comprehensive Survey of National Income Data in Japan), Tokyo, 1951 ; Kazushi Ohkawa and others, *The Growth Rate of the Japanese Economy since 1878*, Tokyo, 1957.

and ascertain the long-cycles of the real income growth rate, although it is still difficult to clarify short-run cycles. Fortunately, Saburo Yamada has recently provided a long-term cost-of-living index estimate, so a weighted average of the wholesale price index and the cost-of-living index can be used as an alternative price deflator.

Thus, the problem is to (1) define and analyze the long swings of the real income growth rate, checking them by various reference series, (2) study the variation in the growth rate between the "take off" stage before 1900 and the period after 1900, industry by industry, and (3) consider the role of expansion of foreign trade in Japanese economic development, particularly with reference to secular deterioration in the terms of trade.

2. Long Swings in Prewar Japan

The so-called "Kondratieff Waves" relate mainly to the long waves of the wholesale price index the duration of which ranges from thirty to sixty years. However, the long swings computed here are somewhat different. They are the cycles of the real income growth rate. In this sense, the Japanese counterpart of the "Kuznets cycle "[2] will be determined. In the United States, the length of the Kuznets cycle is around twenty years. Is this also true in the case of prewar Japan?

As a national income deflator, the weighted average of the wholesale price index and the cost-of-living index, with the relative weights of 3 : 7 was used. In view of the composition of national expenditure, one might like to give more weight to the wholesale price index, but its bias in the direction of crude and semi-manufactured raw materials, and the small number of commodity items used led to adoption of the above weighted average, here. As the money national income series, Ohkawa's estimate was used.

The computational process and the sources for basic data are indicated in Table 1. Growth rates for five year averages of real

2) S. Kuznets, "Long-term Changes in the National Income of the United States of America since 1870", *Income and Wealth*, Series II.

Table1. Cycles of the Rates of Change in Income and Prices

A, C, F, I=Unit : ¥ million

	A Money national income	B Cost of living index	C $\frac{A}{B}$	D Annual rate of increase of C	E Wholesale price index	F $\frac{A}{E}$	G Annual rate of increase of F	H Aggregate** deflator $[\frac{B\times0.7}{+E\times0.3}]$	I $\frac{A}{H}$	J Annual rate of increase of I	K Annual rate of increase of A	L Annual rate of increase of E
1878–82	667	*26.69	2,499	%	41.7	1,600	%	31.02	2,150	%	%	%
1883–87	607	24.41	2,487	-0.10	31.6	1,921	3.80	26.41	2,298	1.34	-1.87	-5.40
1888–92	809	25.99	3,113	4.59	37.1	2,181	2.59	29.22	2,769	3.80	5.91	3.26
1893–97	1,203	32.18	3,754	3.81	41.7	2,897	5.84	34.83	3,468	4.61	8.58	3.36
1998–1902	1,978	42.83	4,618	4.23	53.1	3,725	5.16	45.64	4,334	4.56	10.36	4.95
1903–07	2,522	51.21	4,925	1.30	63.7	3,959	1.23	54.63	4,617	1.27	4.95	3.71
1908–12	2,366	56.20	5,989	3.99	68.5	4,914	4.42	59.53	5,654	4.14	5.94	1.64
1913–17	4,593	60.61	7,586	4.84	81.2	5,663	2.88	66.40	6,925	4.14	6.44	3.46
1918–22	11,385	116.64	9,761	5.17	150.4	7,570	5.98	126.02	9,034	5.46	19.88	13.12
1923–27	12,946	117.80	10,990	2.40	139.6	9,274	4.14	123.53	10,476	3.00	2.60	-1.94
1928–32	12,132	100.93	12,020	1.81	100.0	12,132	5.52	100.00	12,132	2.98	-1.29	-6.46
1933–37	16,161	101.24	15,963	5.84	107.4	15,047	4.40	102.44	15,776	5.40	5.90	1.44
1938–42	34,547	176.99	19,519	4.10	184.6	18,715	4.46	178.13	19,394	4.22	16.41	11.43

Sources : Money national income : Ohkawa and others, *The Growth Rate of the Japanese Economy since 1878*;
Cost-of-living index : Saburo Yamada, " Long-term Cost-of-Living Index from the Early Period of
the Meiji Era to World War II ", (mimeographed in Japanese, Rockefeller Project B. 36 of the Inst. of
Econ. Research, Hitotsubashi University).

Notes : * S. Yamada does not give a cost-of-living index figure for 1858. Thus, it is estimated from the change
in the wholesale price index from 1878 to 1879.

** As S. Yamada's index (B) is 1934–36=100, and the wholesale price index (E) is 1928–32=100, the
geometric average of the two was computed after the former was converted to a 1928–32 base.

income were computed. This might not eliminate the influence of shorter (say, Juglar's) cycles, but the cycles derived are almost free from such influence. Moreover, compared with a tentative computation using ten year averages, the temporal location of cycles is much more determinate. For this table, three kinds of real income growth rates were computed using three different deflators: the wholesale price index, ths cost-of-living index and the aggregate deflator.

The three kinds of real income growth rates are depicted in the upper part of Fig. 1. In spite of the fact that, in the case of the growth rate deflated by the wholesale price index, the trough of the 1930's disappears, in terms of the other two growth rates, the existence of such a trough is very clear. Thus, the existence of a long swing, the duration of which is between 20 and 25 years is ascertained.

As shown in the lower part of Fig. 1, the rates of change in the volume of exports and government construction roughly parallel the growth rate of real income until the 1900's. Thereafter, how-

Fig. 1. Growth and Long Swings

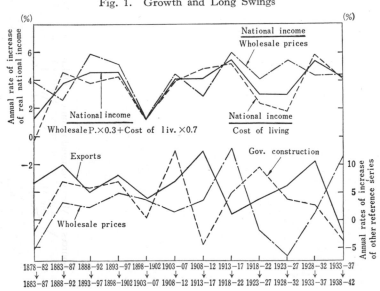

Fig. 2. Long Swings of the Rates of Increase in Money-term Magnitudes

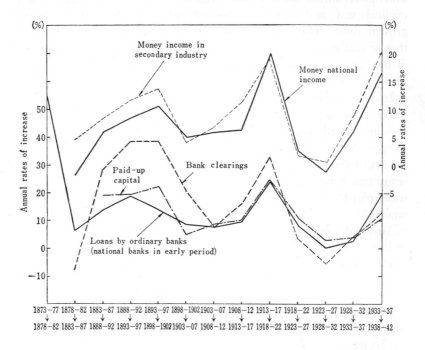

Fig. 3. Long Swing of the Rate of Increase of Money Supply

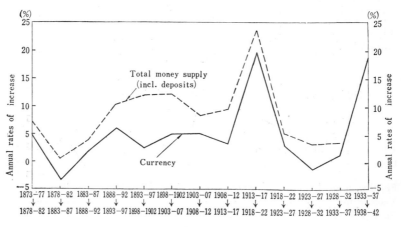

ever, government construction behaves in a rather inverse (contra-cyclical) way, and exports do not precisely coincide with the income growth rate. The rate of change in wholesale prices is similar to that of real income, except that the former's trough lags behind that of the latter in the second downswing in the early 1900's. There-fore, the long swing patterns of other series must also be examined.

In Fig. 2, the long swings of the rates of change in five other series, *in money terms*, are depicted. As these are in money terms, they are sharply pointed in the World War I period, when price rose steeply. With this exception, their patterns of long swings are similar to that of the real income growth rate. The second trough in some series lags behind that in the real income growth rate, but the second trough in the long swing of paid-up capital coincides with it very nicely.

Although some doubt remains concerning the location of the second trough (1903–07 or 1908–12), from the behavior of the rates of change of such series as bank clearing, loans, and paid-up capital, the existence of a Kuznets cycle (20 to 25 years) is roughly establish-ed.

Incidentally, Fig. 3 indicates the cycle of the rate of change in money supply. This almost corresponds with the rate of change in wholesale prices shown in Fig. 1. In this case, total money supply is defined broadly, including time deposits, and involves " Han-satsu " (notes issued by the feudal clans) in the early Meiji period. This series is from Shozaburo Fujino's[3] estimate, which has been converted from the original annual figures to 5 year averages.

3. *Explanation of the Long Swing*

According to Figs. 1–3, the first trough of the long swing is around 1883–87. This includes the years 1881–86, when a drastic defla-tionary policy was enforced by Finance Minister Masayoshi Matsu-

---

3) Shozaburo Fujino, "Estimates of Money Supply, Marshallian k, and Income Velocity for 1874–1940," (Capital Accumulation Studies, 16 of the Institute of Statistical Research), mimeographed (in Japanese).

kata to wipe out an excess of paper notes issued during the preceding civil war (the " Satsuma Rebellion ").

It is clear that, before 1883–87, the growth rate was higher, for the rate of increase of bank loans (Fig. 2) was much higher and the rate of increase of money supply (Fig. 3) was also higher for 1873 - 82. Also, developments during this period confirm this view. First, in 1870, a flotation of foreign loans of £1 million was used for the construction of railroads from Tokyo to Yokohama and Osaka to Kobe. In 1881, the railroads were extended to a total length of 138 miles. Second, during this period, various government factories were established, paving the way for industrialization. These included the Tomioka Silk Reeling Mill in 1872, the Senju Woolen Mill in 1876, the Aichi Spinning Mill and Hiroshima Spinning Mill in 1881, the Fukagawa Cement Factory in 1875, and the Shinagawa Glass Factory in 1876. Third, the " Satsuma Rebellion " broke out in 1877, which, together with the beginning of industrialization, caused a hyperinflation which accelerated the mushroom growth of small scale firms.

During the period 1881–86, Finance Minister Matsukata succeeded in reducing the amount of paper notes in circulation by about ¥40 million by curtailing government expenditure and increasing tax revenues. Because the total amount of government and bank notes in circulation in 1881 was about ¥153 million, this meant a 26% reduction. Due to a 30% decline in wholesale prices and a 50% decrease in the price of rice, farmers and small scale firms suffered greatly during this period. This period was the first trough of the long swing in Japan. As a result of Matsukata's deflationary policies, many small scale firms were liquidated, the interest rate declined and the accumulation and concentration of capital were accelerated. Further, exports were greatly stimulated and the excess of imports were wiped out. Thus, the upswing in the long cycle began from the end of this period and continued until the early 1900's when the second trough in the long cycle occurred. The first so-called capitalistic crisis in Japan occurred in 1890, but it did not affect the shape of the upswing in the growth rate.

The period from the end of Matsukata's policy of deflation to the early 1900's constituted the so-called "take-off" stage, in which there was rapid increase in the tempo of Japanese industrialization. First, there was a tremendous expansion of the railroad network, and growth in electric power output and shipping. From 1881, when the Japan Railroad Company was established, until 1891, the number of railroad companies receiving franchises increased to 150, and the length of lines operated by private railroads in 1892 totaled 1,322 miles, more than double the 557 miles of government railroads in the same year. After 1892, when the Railroad Act was passed, the Government also launched upon a railroad expansion, national lines in operation totaling 1,500 miles in 1905, though some of this increase was due to government purchase of private lines. Thus, private railroad construction and expansion of national railroads were important causes of rapid expansion in this period.

Since the establishment of the Tokyo Electric Co. in 1887, the use of electricity remarkably increased, and spread throughout the country (electric power: 1,500 kw in 1890, 80,239 kw in 1903). After the appearance of the Osaka Shosen Kaisha (O.S.K.) in 1884 and the Nippon Yusen Kaisha (N.Y.K.) in 1885, shipping extended its routes to foreign countries and the number of ships increased each year. Under the protection of a subsidy and other government favors as a result of the Shipbuilding Act and the Navigation Promotion Act, the three large ocean lanes (the European, American and Australian) were opened.

Second, before Japan adopted the gold standard in 1897, it had been on a silver standard. The world-wide tendency toward decline in the price of silver, had the same effect upon exchange rates between Japan and countries under the gold standard as continual exchange devaluation. This resulted in rapid expansion of exports.

Third, Japan acquired the sum of ¥365 million in reparations from China after the Sino-Japanese War of 1894–95. This was about one fourth of the national income at that time, and financed expansion of the army and navy; establishment of the Yawata Iron Mill; extension of railroad, telegraph and telephone services; and government monopoly enterprises, as well as the adoption of the anticipated gold standard. It was also during these years that the Hypothec

Bank of Japan, the Industrial Bank of Japan, the Bank of Taiwan, and other special banks appeared on the scene. Thus, the huge amount of reparations should be regarded as having played a most important supporting role in the "take-off" stage during the Meiji era.

After the above mentioned upswing, there was a second trough in the early 1900's for which the following were important causes. First, economic activity during this period seems to have followed a kinked curve. The advance of such activities as railroads, and cotton thread production tapered off about this time. Second, in view of the Kondratieff waves in the world-wide sense, the declining tendency of prices reached bottom in this period. Third, by adopting the gold standard, Japan lost the stimulating effect upon exports of the secular, relative decline of the price of silver. This, for some time, made domestic prices high relative to those of countries on a silver standard. Thus, exports of cotton goods to China, for example, were depressed. As a result, despite the Japanese tendency toward expansion during the Russo-Japanese War (1904–5), there were several crises and a persistent import surplus after 1897. After the Russo-Japanese War, the Government attempted to solve these difficulties by floating foreign loans of about ¥800 million, as well as by heavy taxation. Even after the crisis of 1907, the Katsura Cabinet, which was formed in 1908, was forced to adopt a retrenchment policy and to make effort to strengthen economic stability.

In Fig. 1, the second trough of the long swing of the real income growth rate is around 1903–07. The same holds true for real government construction, volume of exports and paid-up capital. However, the next period, 1908–12, is the trough for wholesale prices, bank clearings, and money supply. This indicates that prices and finance remained depressed despite expansion of the economy. Domestic investment and exports increased in 1908–12, raising the volume of production. The accompanying deficit in the balance of payments was supported by flotation of foreign loans amounting to about ¥2 billion. Of this amounts ¥800 million was used for Russo-Japanese War expenditures, the remainder for expansion of industry. These loans interrupted a decline in prices to some extent

84

and raised the growth rate. However, after 1910, the outflow of gold and silver reached enormous proportions, leading to monetary contraction and a great decline in prices in 1914.

The succeeding upswing of the long cycle was caused by the outbreak of World War I and, as shown in Fig. 1, the downswing ended in 1928–32, during the great world depression. Although 1928–32 becomes the third trough according to Fig. 1, the annual real income growth rate declines from 4–5% to about 3% in 1923–27, and the third downswing is much longer than the second.

The reasons the 1920's witnessed the third downswing of the long cycle were stated already in Chapter 3 " Economic Development and Foreign Trade ", so we will not repeat their exposition. The following upswing is very easy to explain. It was caused by an increase in military expenditures and by a sharp expansion of exports made possible through exchange devaluation in 1932.

To summarize : in the long swing as viewed from the stand-point of the real income growth rate cycle, the upswing has always occurred during a period of war. On the one hand, the acquisition of reparations after the Sino-Japanese War and the immense accumulation of foreign exchange during World War I, led the economy into prosperity, lifting the level of foreign trade. On the other hand, in the trough of the long swing, there have always been severe monetary contractions—e.g., the Matsukata deflation, the adoption of the gold standard, the lifting of the gold embargo—in association with balance of payments difficulties. As a consequence, the terms of trade were seriously and adversely affected—a 31% decrease in the terms of trade for 1907–13 and a 40% decrease for 1931–37.

It would be nonsensical to attempt to establish some cyclical law to which the economy is subject in the long swing. Rather, the aim here is to determine the main factors which caused fluctuations in the process of rapid economic expansion since the Meiji era,—the secular prosperities and the three big liquidation processes. Most striking in this analysis are the roles of war and monetary contraction in the development of the Japanese economy.

As is generally noted, the Japanese economy exhibited a high secular growth potential, but it was also highly susceptible to wide fluctuations (in the sense of fluctuations in the growth rate). The troughs of the long swing should also be noted as structural turning points. The " take-off " process started after the first trough. It is generally recognized that Japan's industrial revolution, centering on the cotton textile industry, was established about the time of the second trough in the early (1900's). From the third trough (during the world depression), the importance of heavy industry drastically increased. Thus the process of economic growth cannot be expressed simply by a straight line or exponential curve. Although care should be exercised in applying such a purely mechanical device, the fact that the Japanese economy had a long swing of 20–25 years duration should be taken into consideration in any future projection of economic growth.

4. Internal Structure of the Long Swing

The long swing of the real income growth rate has been discussed. Next, the growth rates of industrial production and various individual commodities will be examined. Fig. 4, presents comparison of the growth rates of industrial production in the U.S.A., U.K., Germany and Japan.

Contrary to our expectation, the industrial production growth rate cycle for Japan is not so clear as the real income growth rate cycle. It should also be noted that, in the case of Japan, there is a difference between the arithmetic average and the geometric average index of industrial production, which affects the computation of industrial growth rate. In the original index of industrial production estimated by the Nagoya Commercial College, the geometric average method was used. The arithmetic average was computed by the author using individual industries (*e.g.*, metals, chemicals, textiles, *etc.*), not commodities, as the basis. In both cases, the industrial growth rate turns upward just when the real income growth rate is in its second trough. The reason for this will be explained when an analysis by industry is given.

Fig. 4 shows that, while the industrial growth rates of the United

Fig. 4. International Comparison of Industrial Growth Rates

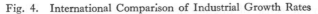
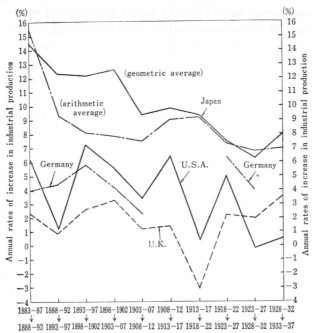

States and U.K. rise and fall, embodying the influence of a Juglar cycle, the industrial growth rate of Japan seems to be quite free from such influence, regardless of whether the arithmetic average or the geometric average is used.   This might be because, in Japan, where the upward trend was very sharp, the influence of a Juglar cycle upon the five-year average rates of increase of industrial production and real income was much weaker than in other advanced countries.

The unexpected difference in the growth rate, depending on whether the arithmetic average or the geometric average is used, can be explained as follows.   When the geometric average is used, individual series of production are averaged after they have been reduced to logarithms.   Thus, a commodity or industry with a relatively higher rate of increase has a relatively greater effect on the total index of production in this method.   However, when the arith-

87

metric average is used, only the absolute size of changes is relevant.

In Fig. 5, the rate of growth of production in various industries is shown, using the Nagoya index. Although the growth rates of food-processing, textile, and chemical industries behave as expected, metal industry output shows a remarkably high rate of increase in 1903–07, when the second trough in the long swing of the real income growth rate occurs. This was due mainly to the Russo-Japanese War. To a lesser extent, the machinery industry was

Fig. 5.   Changes in Industrial Growth Rates By Subsector

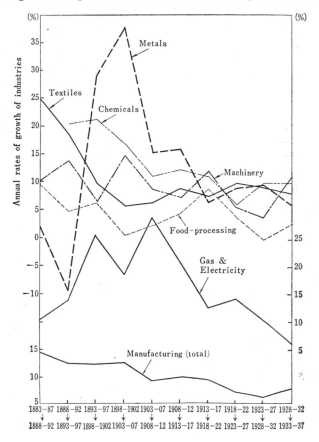

subject to the same influence. When the geometric average index is used, this influence is sensitively reflected in the total index.

These relationships can be examined in detail by commodity; the outputs, exports and imports of cotton goods, silk, pig iron and steel are shown in Figs. 6–8.

In Fig. 6, the second trough (1903–07) of the long cycle in the rates of increase of silk and cocoon production (or exports) precisely coincides with that of the real income growth rate. However, there is no recovery after the world depression of the 1930's, because the proportion of silk in total exports drastically declined, silk having

Fig. 6. Long Swing in the Silk Reeling Industry

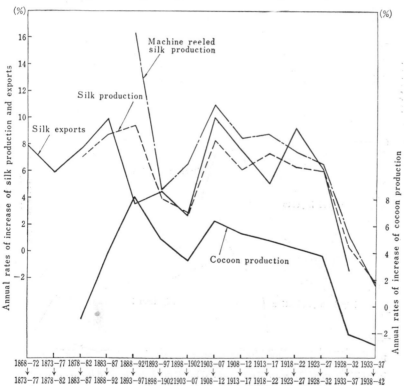

Fig. 7. Long Swing in the Cotton Textile Industry

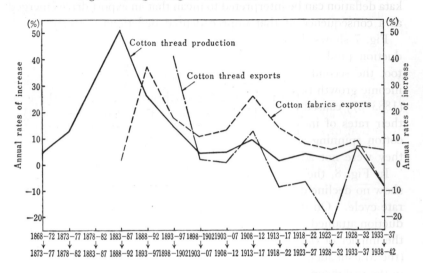

Fig. 8. Long Swing in the Iron and Steel Industry

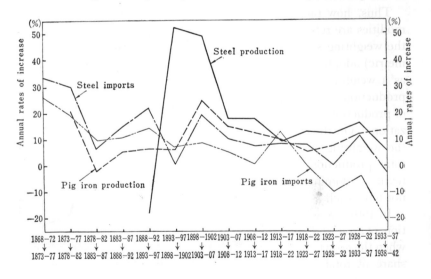

been replaced by synthetic textiles in foreign markets. At the same time, that the growth rate of silk exports increased during the Matsukata deflation can be interpreted to mean that an export drive emerged as a consequence of that unprecedented deflationary policy.

Fig. 7 shows the cycles in the growth rates of cotton thread production (and exports) and cotton fabrics exports. In this chart, too, the second and third troughs coincide with those of the real income growth rate. However, in the first trough of the long swing (1883–87) caused by the Matsukata deflation, there is no decline in their rates of increase. The reason for this may be that, because cotton spinning and weaving were then young, growing industries, they were not adversely affected by such forces.

In Fig. 8, the rates of increase of pig iron and steel production show no decline during the second trough in the real income growth rate cycle. On the contrary, 1903–07 was a period when steel production attained a spectacular rate of increase (52 % per annum) under the impact of the Russo-Japanese War. However, the first trough (the Matsukata deflation) and the third trough (the world depression) in the real income growth rate cycle are clearly reflected in the cycles of the growth rates in pig iron production and imports.

Thus, how rates of increase in the production of individual commodities are reflected in the total index of production depends upon the weighting system and the averaging method (arithmetic or geometric) adopted. The more recent the industrial composition used as a weighting system, the more sharply the growth or change in production of, say, the metal industry is reflected in the total index of production, if there has been a tendency towards heavy industrialization. On the other hand, under the same assumption, the earlier the weighting system adopted, the smaller the rate of increase in total production, because the proportion of food-processing and textiles is dominant and a sharp increase in, say, steel production does not have such a great effect upon the total index of production.

In 1904–05, when the Russo-Japanese War took place, the proportion of iron and steel output in total production was still small, so when the growth rate of textile output, which formed the predominant share of total production, declines, the index of total production naturally reflects this decline. Therefore, the rate of increase of industrial production based upon the Nagoya index (in which 1930 weights are used) does not correctly reflect cyclical behavior. Moreover, a downward trend of its growth rate would probably be expressed too excessively. If the weight given to light industry were increased, the decline in the industrial growth rate would be smaller. At any rate, it is interesting that the metal-machinery industries and textile-food-chemical industries have mutually oppositite effects on the index of total production.

5. Growth Rates by Industry in Different Stages

It seems that there was no upward or downward trend in the real income growth rate, in the prewar period. However, it can be expected that the growth rates of manufacturing and other basic industries would be considerably greater in the earlier phases of industrialization, and would slow down only in the later stages. The reason this tendency is not reflected in the real income growth rate is that, in the earlier stage, the proportion of rapidly expanding industries was still very small. Therefore, it is necessary to examine growth rates and patterns in greater detail.

Table 2 gives annual output growth rates computed from individual commodity production series which are available for a comparatively long period. These rates were computed for an earlier and a later period (mainly 1868–72~1903–07 and 1903–07~1938–42, respectively). Figures for 1868–72 are not available for some of the commodities. In those cases, annual growth rates were computed by comparing the earliest obtainable 5-year averages with the 1903–07 figure. 1903–07 and 1937–42 were generally compared in computing annual growth rates in the later period, but for a few commodities, lack of data made it necessary to use the 1933–37 average.

Table 2 shows that the higher the growth rate of an industry or commodity in the earlier period, the lower it is in the later period. Tea, sake, wheat flour and pig iron are the few exceptions. For cotton thread and electricity, which have the highest rates of increase

Table 2.   Growth Rates by Industry in Two Periods

	Earlier period (A)	Later period (B)	(B—A)
The index of	%	%	%
Industrial production	12.92	8.33	−4.59
Textiles	14.26	7.91	−6.35
Machinery	11.22	7.92	−3.30
Chemicals	19.49	9.87	−9.62
Metals	13.21	10.36	−2.85
Gas, Electricity	16.84	15.11	−1.73
Silk	6.31	5.80	−0.51
(machine-reeled silk)	8.75	7.20	−1.55
Cocoons	3.78	3.75	−0.03
Cotton thread	22.07	4.80	−17.27
Spinning machines (mule plus ring)	18.78	6.92	−11.86
Rayon thread	—	57.39	—
Rayon cloth	—	25.27	—
Paper (Western)	15.39	8.08	−7.31
Tea	0.60	1.97	+1.37
Beer	16.92	7.32	−9.60
Sake	−1.51	0.74	+2.25
Wheat flour	2.87	4.69	+1.82
Cement	(18.05)	10.19	−7.86
Pig iron	9.89	10.54	+0.65
Steel	23.33	14.50	−8.83
Coal	11.69	4.20	−7.49
Electric Power	(30.14)	15.53	−14.61
Rice	2.03	0.91	−1.12
Barley & Wheat	2.17	0.52	−1.65

Notes: 1) With the exception of a few commodities, A period is 1868–72 to 1903–07, and B period is 1903–07 to 1938–42.
2) In the case of cement (A period), production figures for the entire country are not available, so total cement production by the Asano Cement Co. and the Onoda Cement Co. for 1883–87 was compared with that for 1903–07.
3) Electric power production figures are available only from 1903, but an estimate for 1890 was used in computing the A period growth rate (mentioned in *Nihon Keizai Soran*, p. 863).
4) The Nagoya index was used as an index of industrial production.

in the earlier period, there was a drastic slowing down in the later period. It seems that the "take-loff" stage of industrialization was completed around the early 1900's, entailing general kinks in the growth curves of various commodities.

The hypothesis that the higher the growth rate of a commodity in the earlier period, the lower it is in the later period is tested in Fig. 9. The decline of growth rates (B–A in Table 2) is measured on the vertical axis, and growth rates in the earlier period are measured on the horizontal axis. The hypothesis tests almost perfectly. It may be called as the "law of equalization of growth rates of industries". It should be noted that pig iron, steel and electricity are located on the lower curve of the graph, indicating the tendency of heavy industrialization which interrupted them to fall along the upper line fitted by a free hand in the Figure.

Fig. 9. Tendency of Growth Rates of Industries to Equalize

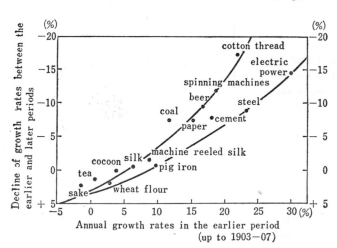

6. Growth Rates of Other Items

The rapid expansion of Japan's economy seems to depend to a great extent upon the very high rate of growth in exports over a long period. Although the export growth rate declines from the earlier period (7.32%) to the later period (6.69%), as can be seen from Table 3, the long-term growth rate of exports is very high compared with that of other countries. The growth rate of imports declines from 7.98% to 4.76% for the same periods, so the degree of slow-down is larger for imports than for exports. This difference is largely explained by the drastic deterioration in the terms of trade given by the Oriental Economist combined with that of the Yoko-hama Specie Bank: 145.1 (1907), 100.0 (1913), 100.0 (1919), 104.4 (1925), 95.4 (1930), 60.8 (1937). Table 3 also indicates the growth rate of exports of silk, cotton thread and cotton fabrics, as a reference.

An important factor which consolidated the basis of the earlier industrialization was investment in social overhead capital. The growth rates for miles of railroad in operation and other transporta-

Table 3. Growth Rates of Foreign Trade, Transportation and Communication

	Earlier period (A)	Later period (B)	(A—B)
	%	%	%
Index of total volume of exports	7.32	6.69	−0.63
Index of total volume of imports	7.98	4.76	−3.22
Exports of silk	6.24	6.60	−0.18
Exports of cotton thread	20.34	−3.54	−23.88
Exports of cotton fabrics	16.38	12.51	−3.77
Miles of railroad in operation	16.82	3.95	−12.87
Total tonnage of steamboats	11.72	5.10	−6.17
Acceptance of ordinary postal matter	13.60	4.76	−8.84
Number of carriages	20.03	3.44	−16.59
Number of carts	8.35	0.43	−7.92
Number of " Rikisha "	1.07	−6.84	−7.91
Number of automobiles	—	28.10	+28.10
Number of bicycles	21.35	15.38	−6.15

Notes: A period: 1868–72 to 1903–07 ; B period: 1903–07 to 1938–42. How-ever, for cotton thread exports in the earlier period, 1903–07 was com-pared with 1890–92, and for cotton fabrics exports, 1903–07 was com-pared with 1883–87. For miles of railroad in operation in the later period, 1933–37 was compared with 1903–07.

tion indicators, are shown in Table 3. In general, these have an extremely high rates of growth. For example, that for miles of railroad in operation in the earlier period was 16.82% per annum (it declined to 3.95% in the later period).

The older means of transportation such as " Rikisha ", carts and carriages, were replaced to a great extent by the automobile in the later period, although some of them have notably high growth rates in the earilier period. The number of carriages, for instance, showed an annual growth rate of 20.0% in the earlier period. The extremely rapid expansion of transportation facilities and electric power characterized early Japanese industrialization until the early 1900's. Their growth rates increase as they are traced to the earlier period, as shown in Fig. 10. The important role of transportation in the early stage of the Meiji economic development can be recognized from this.

Fig. 10.　Changes in Growth Rates of Transportation and Electric Power

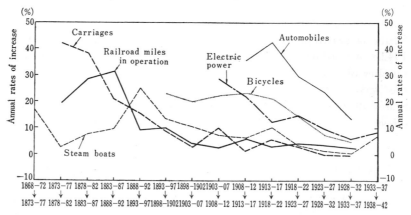

One subject remaining to be discussed is the role played by education. Recently, it has been recognized that low levels of education and technical skill are sometimes intractable bottlenecks to economic development in underdeveloped countries. As a result, there have been attempts to re-evaluate the role of education in the early industrialization of the advanced and semi-advanced countries. The author concurs in the opinion of a foreign economist, Colin Clark, who pointed out that the early adoption of compulsory education (1879) by the Meiji government laid the foundation for the rapid growth potential of the later Japanese economy. This chapter does not attempt an overall analysis of the role of education, but only indicates some computational results relating to it.

In the United States, the proportion of the total population enrolled as pupils and students (elementary schools to universities) was 22.6% in 1900, 24.2% in 1930, and 21.1% in 1952. This may be looked upon as a numerical barometer of the level of education in an advanced country. Compared with this, Table 4 shows that the percentage of the population attending schools in Japan reached 24% in 1938–42, indicating the rapidity with which it attained the level of advanced countries in about 70 years. Particularly, it should be noted that, in 1923–27, the percentage was already 19.32%. Of course, such a numerical comparison does not show the quality of education, but it is important as a preliminary reference.

Fig. 11 compares the average annual rates of increase in the number of pupils and students by school category in Japan and the United States using two periods, and Fig. 12 depicts this rate in Japan, 1873–1942. According to Fig. 11, the annual rates of increase in the number of pupils and students by school category in Japan during the period 1903–07~1933–37 are similar to those in the United States during the period 1900–1930. Fig. 12 is particularly interesting because the long swing in the rate of increase of students

Table 4. Percentage of Population Attending Schools

	Total population	Pupils and students		Students in middle schools		Student in higher schools, colleges, and universities	
	thousand	thousand	%	thousand	%	thousand	%
1878–82	36,911	2,589	(7.01)	22.5	(0.06)	7.5	(0.020)
1893–97	41,894	3,815	(9.11)	47.4	(0.11)	15.6	(0.037)
1908–12	49,728	7,413	(14.91)	511.7	(1.03)	47.6	(0.096)
1923–27	59,827	11,561	(19.32)	1,886.4	(3.15)	130.5	(0.218)
1938–42	71,678	17,208	(24.01)	4,226.4	(5.90)	232.9	(0.325)

in higher schools, colleges and universities lags five to ten years behind that of the real income growth rate. Therefore, it is clear that long-term changes in the number of students enrolled in higher education have been strongly influenced by the long swing of the real income growth rate.

Fig. 11. Comparison of the Rates of Increase of Pupils and Students in Japan and the United States

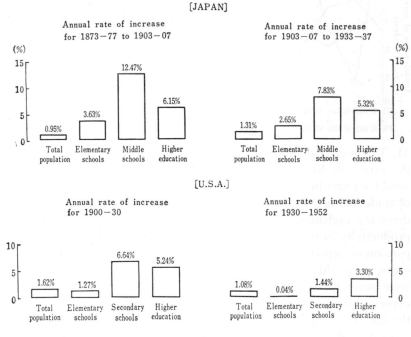

7. The Terms of Trade and the Growth Rates of Exports and Imports Classified by Items of Commodities

It is this writer's hypothesis that rapid growth of the Japanese economy in the prewar period was strongly supported by the secular deterioration in the terms of trade from the end of the Meiji era. This hypothesis has been the target of strong criticism by K. Kojima,

Fig. 12.   Long-term Changes in Rates of Increase of Pupils and Students

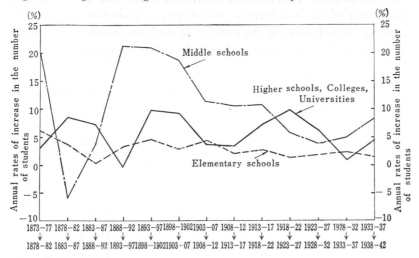

M. Tatemoto and others.[4]   However, the writer still believes that the extremely high rate of growth of exports in the prewar period would not have been possible, if such drastic deterioration in the terms of trade had not occurred, whether this came about through export drive (or exchange devaluation) or the sharp rise of comparative productivity in the export industry.   In other words, the rapid expansion of exports could not have taken place only as a result of increase in world income.   Even in the 1930's when world exports were severely stricken by the great depression, Japanese exports experienced a spectacular expansion.   Thus, the strong push through the terms-of-trade effect upon exports should be reconsidered.   Of course, this is merely a " strategic " emphasis of a point which has been neglected in explaining the development of Japan's

---

[4] Recently, the articles concerning this controversy were compiled in a book: K. Kojima (ed.), *Ronso: Keizai Seicho to Nihon Boeki* (The Controversy over Economic Growth and Foreign Trade in Japan), Tokyo, 1960.   See also an article in English by K. Kojima, " Japanese Foreign Trade and Economic Growth: With Special Reference to the Terms of Trade ", *Annals of the Hitotsubashi Academy*, April 1958.   However, I do not believe that my thesis is presented in his paper as I originally formulated it.

exports and production. This thesis will be bolstered by adding a new analysis in this paper.

The foreign trade index given in the Oriental Economist, which hitherto has been the only long-term index available, lacks detailed breakdown. Therefore, Mr. Katsumi Yamada, my colleague, has computed a new index beginning in 1900, from which time a drastic decline of terms of trade occurred. The analysis made here depends largely upon the new data he presents. Computation of the rates of growth in exports and imports of various commodities from 1903–07 to 1933–37 shown in Table 5 was made on the basis of his figures.

Considerable differences in the export and import growth rates of various commodities can be seen in Table 5. These differences can be explained to a large degree by the differences in changes in the terms of trade. Fig. 13 (A) shows that there is an interesting inverse correlation between export growth rates and changes in the terms of trade classified by commodity during the period 1903–07 to 1933–37. The greater the deterioration in the terms of trade, the higher export growth rate, and vice versa. In Fig. 13 (B), import growth rates and changes in the terms of trade for various commodities are compared. In contrast to the case of export growth rates, a positive correlation is obtained. For those commodities with favorable changes in the terms of trade, import growth rates are also higher. Thus, export and import growth rates are presumed to have been highly elastic to changes in the terms of trade by commodity.

Fig. 14 (A) and (B) measure changes in export and import prices, respectively, instead of changes in terms of trade on the horizontal axis. As a result, in Fig. (A), in which export growth rates are measured on the vertical axis, there is no clear correlation between the two. However, in Fig. (B), there is a fairly nice correlation. The reason for this is as follows. In explaining the influence of export prices, the behavior of foreign export prices is also relevant, so variations in domestic prices alone are inadequate to explain differences among export growth rates of various commodities. In explaining the effect of import prices, only changes in foreign prices are relevant, provided domestic prices are given. The fact that imported goods are often not produced domestically is, at the same

GROWTH AND LONG SWINGS

Table 5. Annual Growth Rates of Exports and Imports by Commodity
—1903–07 to 1933–37—

	Growth rates of imports	Growth rates of exports
	%	%
Total	4.76	6.69
1. Animals and plants	−3.63	4.37
2. Food, beverages and tobacco	1.14	5.03
2.1 Cereals and seeds	⎫	6.31
2.2 Vegetables and fruits	1.13	3.33
2.3 Other foods	⎭	5.49
2.4 Liquors and tobacco	2.13	0.11
3. Thread, fabrics and apparel	4.17	7.47
3.1 Thread and cotton cloth	5.22	5.75
3.2 Fabrics	−7.08	10.36
3.3 Other cloth goods	−6.05	5.68
3.4 Apparel	−8.16	9.36
4. Leather, bones and hair	2.97	5.44
5. Oils, fats and chemicals	7.75	5.45
5.1 Oils and fats	5.82	7.08
5.2 Inorganic chemicals	7.69	⎫
5.3 Organic chemicals	12.10	4.34
5.4 Dyestuffs and cosmetics	−0.53	11.81
6. Nonmetallic minerals, metals and metal products	7.51	5.66
6.1 Nonmetallic minerals and their products	9.72	0.46
6.2 Glass and clay products	−0.04	7.61
6.3 Iron ore and other ores	13.59	⎫
6.4 Iron and steel	4.88	4.75
6.5 Nonferrous metals	7.75	⎭
6.6 Metal products	3.71	12.24
7. Machinery	3.41	4.30
8. Timber and wood products	11.14	4.04
9. Others		
9.1 Miscellaneous products	3.89	4.52
9.2 Paper and paper products	0.67	7.23

Sources: 1) Katsumi Yamada, "Prewar Foreign Trade Index" (General Report, B. 25) and (Report by Commodities, B. 37), mimeographed, in Japanese. These are a part of the research of the Inst. of Ecom. Research of Hitotsubashi University supported by the Rockefeller

Foundation.

2) In the K. Yamada index, the price index is derived on the basis of 1928–30 weights. The quantity index is derived by deflating the value index by the price index.

Fig. 13. The Relationship between Terms of Trade and Export and Import Growth Rates by Commodity

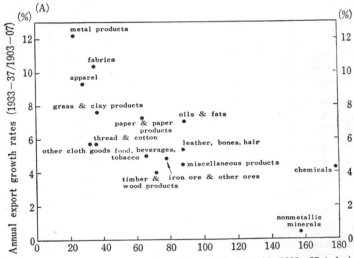

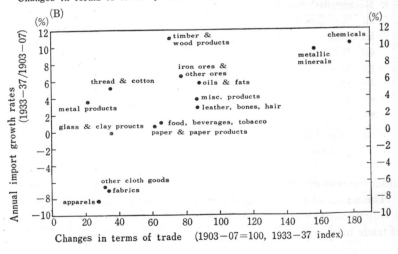

Fig. 14. The Relationship between Export and Import Prices
and Their Growth Rates by Commodities

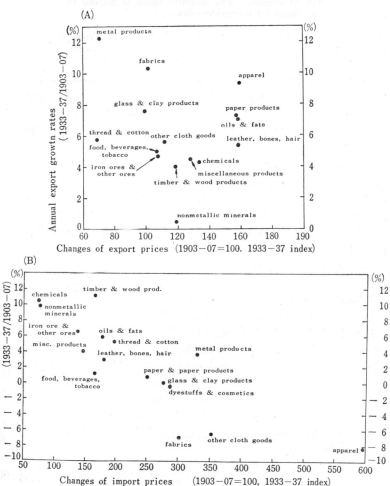

(A)

Annual export growth rates (1933−37/1903−07)

metal products

fabrics

apparel

glass & clay products

paper products

oils & fats

thread & cotton   other cloth goods   leather, bones, hair

food, beverages, tobacco

iron ores & other ores   chemicals

miscellaneous products

timber & wood products

nonmetallic minerals

Changes of export prices (1903−07=100. 1933−37 index)

(B)

Annual import growth rates (1933−37/1903−07)

chemicals   timber & wood prod.

nonmetallic minerals

iron ore & other ores   oils & fats

misc. products   thread & cotton

leather, bones, hair   metal products

paper & paper products

food, beverages, tobacco   glass & clay products

dyestuffs & cosmetics

fabrics   other cloth goods

apparel

Changes of import prices   (1903−07=100, 1933−37 index)

time, the reason a good correlation is obtained in the case of Fig. (B).

The terms of trade effect in the case of exports and imports of individual commodities has been shown above. Then, do the terms
of trade have any bearing on variations in total exports and imports?

Fig. 15 gives the annual growth rates of exports and imports, on the one hand, and the five-year average rate of change in the terms of trade, on the other. Excluding the two periods, 1883–87 to 1888–92 and 1928–32 to 1933–37, the cyclical fluctuations of the import growth rate and changes in the terms of trade are perfectly parallel. The first exceptional period in which the variables are inversely related (1883–87 to 1888–92), can be interpreted as one in which imports, suppressed by the Matsukata deflation, reacted sharply when the deflation ended. The inverse correlation during the period 1928–32 to 1933–37 can also be easily understood as a consequence of the beginning of a war economy.

Except for two periods, there is an inverse relationship between the export growth rate and changes in terms of trade. In one of the periods, 1908–12 to 1913–17, a favorable change in the terms of trade could coexist with the rise of exports because of the influence of World War I. The second exception, 1918–22 to 1923–27, was a period of post-war reconstruction in European countries, so favorable terms of trade and a rise in the export growth rate could again coexist.

The above analysis of the effect of the terms of trade with respect to aggregate magnitudes as well as individual commodities, supports this writer's hypothesis concerning the role of the terms of trade. Of course, Fig. 15 completely neglects the income effect, and merely compares price-quantity relationships. In this regard, some computations of export and import functions made during the author's controversy with Masahiro Tatemoto are presented.

Denoting exports by x, world real income by y_w, and the terms of trade by π, Mr. Tatemoto has computed the following export function for 1924–37.

$$\left. \begin{array}{c} log \ x = 4.4547 - 1.5754 \ log \ \pi + 0.3629 \ log \ y_w \\ R = 0.974 \end{array} \right\} \cdots (1)$$

The author computed the function using relative export prices (compared with world prices), p_x/p_w, instead of the terms of trade.

$$\left. \begin{array}{c} log \ x = 1.7981 - 1.0563 \ log \ (p_x/p_w) + 1.1750 \ log \ y_w \\ R = 0.9689 \end{array} \right\} \cdots (2)$$

Fig. 15. Total Export and Import Growth Rates and Changes
in the Terms of Trade

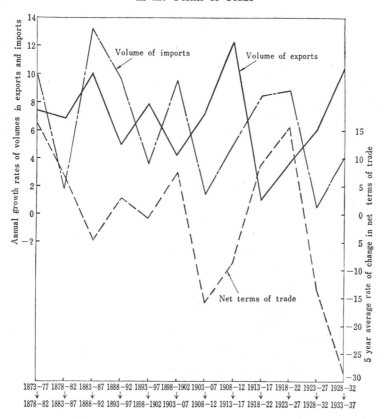

It is interesting that price elasticity in the export function in both computations is very high, exceeding unity, although the income elasticity in (1) seems too small.

On the other hand, the import function computed by the author for the same period, in which real domestic income is money national income deflated by the cost-of-living index, is as follows. Denoting imports by m, domestic real income by y, and relative import prices by (p_m/p),

$$log\ m = 1.06101 - 0.19149\ log\ (p_m/p) + 0.67145\ log\ y_w$$
$$R = 0.9121$$
$$m = 575.760 - 0.19910\ (p_m/p) + 0.67183\ y$$
$$R = 0.9730$$

$\left.\vphantom{\begin{array}{c}1\\2\\3\\4\end{array}}\right\}\cdots(3)$

In this import function, price elasticity is about 0.2, much smaller than in the export function.

The sum of the two price elasticities (1.575 or 1.056+0.191 or 0.199) exceeds unity, satisfying the so-called " Lerner's condition ". Therefore, deterioration in the terms of trade would be effective in adjusting the balance of payments in deficit. The potential deficit which would have occurred under constant terms of trade as the result of a higher income growth rate relative to other countries, would be wiped out by deterioration of the terms in trade, provided the sum of the two price elasticities exceeds unity.

It is interesting that the terms of trade deteriorate just after the long swing in the real income growth rate reaches a trough. They deteriorated by 31% in 1907–13, and by 40% in 1931–37. To repeat, the change to the gold standard, the occurrence of a trough in the world Kondratieff cycle and other factors mentioned in discussing the long swing characterized the second trough of the long swing in Japan. These factors together with the rise in comparative productivity of the cotton textile industry (as an export industry) through the industrial revolution in the early 1900's, had a strong bearing upon the succeeding deterioration of the terms of trade. The second deterioration in the terms of trade also occurred after a trough (the third) of the long swing, as a result of the unprecedented exchange devaluation in 1932.

8. Mechanism of the High Rate of Growth through a Peculiar Pattern of the Long Swing

So far, we have engaged in the measurement aspect of the long swing in Japan, but here we are going to pose some tentative hypotheses concerning the relation between the high rate of growth and the actual movement of the long swing.

Apart from the causes of the long swing, it may be of interest to observe that the long swing in the prewar Japan had the following peculiarity; in its upswing investmet in plant and equipment increased tremendously, so that the investment-*GNP* ratio increased. However, at the peak, we always see a balance of payments difficulty, overcapacity, curtailed operation, wage cuts, and price deflation, as an adjustment to the excessive investment. In the end, there was a drastic deterioration in the terms of trade, that is, a deterioration of about 40% in 1903–13 and about the same amount in 1931–37. Therefore we can formulate the pattern of the long swing experienced twice in the prewar period as in Fig. 16.

Fig. 16. Pattern of the Long Swing in Prewar Japan

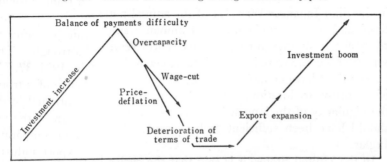

It has often been noticed that in the cotton spinning industry investment in plant and equipment increased even amidst the depression, when curtailed operation was maintained through a cartel agreement. The investment behavior of Japanese enterpreneurs was so reckless and aggressive that the adjustment of overcapacity could not be made except through reductions in wages, prices and the terms of trade. As the expansion had already been pushed beyond the ceiling of the balance of payments, overcapacity could not be overcome by the expansion of domestic market. The only way out of this difficulty under the rigid monetary system of the gold standard was the expansion of exports through price deflation.

Thus, the Japan's high rate of growth was attained only through such a disequilibrating process as a sequence of excessive investment, overcapacity, price deflation and the aggravation of the terms of trade. This is a high rate of growth by means of an unstable oscillation of investment and prices, and not as smooth-going a process as is formulated in modern economic growth theory.[5] If such a disequilibrating process did not exist, and if investment behavior were conservative, and monetary and fiscal policy too restrictive toward expansion, then Japan's growth rate might not have been as high. In this sense, it should be called a process of an unstable high rate of growth, not of stable high rate of growth.

One problem will remain: Why the boom in plant and equipment investment was not adjusted within the Juglar cycle of ten years duration? In relation to this problem, we should take into consideration great " outside shocks " like the acquisition of reparations in the Sino-Japanese War (1/4 of the annual national income at that time) and the accumulation of an immense amount of foreign currency as a bystander during the first World War. If such an outside source of income were injected into an economy, then the investment boom might have enough buoyancy to expand itself into longer cycle of twenty-year duration. It is difficult, of course, to substantiate the regularity of the long swing, but two such great outside shocks should have been sufficient to have caused longer cycles than the Juglar.

In the United States, it is said that the cycles in the migration of capital and labor composed twenty-year waves which were reflected not only in the railroadization cycles but also in the cycles of the real *GNP* growth rate. Such a migration can also be interpreted as the result of great outside shock, and to that extent we find a similarity in the causes of the long swing. In postwar Japan, we see a steep rise in the private producer's durables-*GNP* ratio from about 7% in the immediate postwar period to about 23% in 1961, and this seems to be an upswing phase of long swing. In this case, we have

5) The author owes this point to the excellent insight of Professor G. C. Allen developed in his paper " Factors of Japanese Economic Development " (mimeographed) submitted to the study group on the Economic History of East and South-East Asia, (11–20 July, 1961) held at the University of London. We would like to combine his view with our long swing analysis.

no counterpart to the migration or the immense amount of reparation. However, it seems to me that the widened gap of technology between advanced countries and Japan spurred the Japanese firms to introduce foreign know-how at an unprecedented speed, so that we had an age of extremely rapid technological innovation and investment at an accelerated rate never experienced before. In such a case, the external injection might have been the introduction of foreign technology on an immense scale.

Whether this postwar long upswing will continue or not is a difficult question, but if we measure twenty years simply from the prewar depth in 1930, then 1950 will become the postwar trough. This is too mechanical an arithmetical procedure and will prove acceptable to no one. Actually, the postwar trough in production was 1945–46, but let us ignore that, for the period 1946–50 may have been a purely postwar rehabilitation process. Now, twenty years after 1950 will be 1970. If this simple mechanical arithmetic were valid, our economy should reach to trough in 1970 after experiencing less than 5 years prosperity. This too mechanical operation, however, may have some substantial justification, for from about 1970 on, the Japanese economy will have to suffer from a severe labor shortage due to a radical decrease in the supply of new labor force. Moreover, the technology gap which was tremendously large in the immediate postwar years will not be so large around 1970, so that the speed of the introduction of new technology will have to slow.

Such speculation, of course, may be completely ineffective, if some epoch-making innovation should appear on the scene. However, the analysis of the long swing seems to give us a hint that if some strong shock were given, the economy could continue to follow the curve of a long swing, the duration of which is about twenty years.

CHAPTER 5

THE POSTWAR 'GROWTH CONTROVERSY'

1. Shimomura's View

When the investment boom of 1956–57 collapsed because of the deficit in the balance of payments and the tight money policy, many economists in Japan believed that the spectacular postwar growth would slow down decidedly because of overproduction following the heavy investment of the boom years. This expectation was based upon the experience that the prewar growth rate of national income was 4–5%, while the growth rate in 1951–57 exceeded 7%. So, as soon as the postwar rehabilitation period should come to an end, the extraordinary rate of growth would give way to the prewar secular rate, which was regarded as normal. Not only academic economists (Marxian as well as modern) but also the writer of the Economic Planning Agency's 1957 White Paper, took the 76% increase in private fixed investment in 1955–56 very seriously, regarding it as overinvestment, and believed that the overcapacity expected to follow would bring about a kink in the postwar growth curve.

At first sight, the continuation indefinitely of the rapid postwar growth after the recovery factors disappeared could not have been anticipated. The author of the White Paper, the late Mr. Yonosuke Goto, in 1955, used the catch-phrase " No more post-war period "; if that were true, the growth rate of the economy should have slowed. However, after 1956, the Japanese economy actually continued to expand with even a higher growth rate than before. This is the reason why Dr. Osamu Shimomura's[1] assertion that the potential

1) Shimomura was an economist in the Ministry of Finance when the controversy occurred, but in 1960, moved to the board of executives of the Japan Development Bank.

110

of the Japanese economy is and has been much higher than the accepted view, has now been the object of fierce controversy among Japanese economists. Shimomura has declared out that a growth rate of about 10% may be possible in terms of real national income, but that the too stringent monetary policy which has been followed was one of the main causes making the actual growth rate less than the potential. In the earlier period, little serious attention was paid to this view, which was regarded even as eccentric. But since the investment boom of 1956–57, the growth rate has become much higher, and Shimomura's view and analysis have attracted increasing attention and keen interest.

Shimomura's view has changed to some extent during the controversy, but it will be convenient here to start with his initial opinion. He assumed that the Japanese economy before 1956 had been a capacity-deficient economy, while the economy after 1957 became a capacity-abundant economy. In other words, before 1956, total demand was in excess of actual capacity, and the economy was in a " high-pressure " state. After 1957, the Japanese economy entered a new stage in which capacity became abundant compared with total demand. His policy view was, therefore, opposed to the accepted idea that the tight money policy was necessary to overcome the balance of payments difficulty and the excessive investment boom. He speculated that after 1957 there would appear more than enough equipment and that the apparent increase in 1956–57 of the imports-*GNP* ratio would be quite temporary, due to the speculative piling-up of stocks of imported raw materials partly because of the boom and partly because of the Suez incident in 1957. This temporary increase in the import ratio would have decreased automatically, so that the tight money policy which clearly deterred economic growth was absolutely unnecessary, according to his view.

As the actual situation was one of equipment abundance, the balance of payments difficulty was only temporary and could be met by any short-run financing from foreign sources, he insisted that we should have taken more active fiscal and monetary measures to accelerate growth. The tight money policy has merely suppressed the growth potential, and if the potentiality were to be left free from

111

such monetary stringency, the Japanese economy could grow at an annual rate of about 10%. Such is his view, but how does he arrive at a 10% growth rate?

His analysis proceeds from two sides, one the capacity-increasing coefficient of private investment in producer durables,[2] and another the ratio of imports to *GNP*. He found for 1950–56 that the investment in producer durables in one year corresponded closely to the increase in *GNP* in the next year. In other words, denoting investment in private producer's durables by *PD*, his derived result was $\Delta GNP_t/PD_{t-1}=1$. When the cumulative total of private investment in producer durables for 1950–55 is compared with the increase of *GNP* in 1950–56, the ratio $[GNP_{56}\text{-}GNP_{50}] / \sum_{50}^{55}PD=1$. In this case, ΔGNP and $\sum PD$ were measured in current prices, and this fact is a defect in the formulation of Shimomura's analysis, later becoming an object of attack by debaters. At any rate, if $\Delta GNP/PD$ is around 1, producer durables of ¥100 million will entail an increase of capacity by the same amount in the next year. However, from 1956 on, investment in private producer durables in one year began to produce a rise of *GNP* in the next year by less than the same amount. For example, investment in private producer durables in the fiscal year 1956 was ¥1,369 billion, but the increase in *GNP* from 1956 to 57 was only ¥790 billion. The same relation has prevailed for 1957–58 too. From this, Shimomura formed a judgment that in spite of the fact that the capacity-increasing coefficient is around unity, the increase in total demand became lower than that of capacity, and the Japanese economy now entered a new stage in which "low pressure" prevailed. If the economy is of a "high pressure" nature, then a tight money policy may have some significance, but as the economy has moved into a new stage

2) Private producer durables here stand for machinery and equipment, factories, business buildings, dams, *etc.* Therefore it is a wider concept than the producer durable equipment in the national income accounting of other countries, *e.g.*, the United States, in that it includes some construction activities. Shimomura excludes the public producer's durables mainly because he attempts to measure the direct effect of the private *PD* upon the capacity. Social overhead capital was considered as not having any definite relation to capacity.

112

of "low pressure", tight money policy would decidedly lose its *raison d'etre*. According to his assumption, as $\dfrac{GNP_t-GNP_{t-1}}{PD_{t-1}}=1$, then $GNP_t-GNP_{t-1}=PD_{t-1}$. Therefore, if this relation is divided by GNP_{t-1}, then we get,

$$\frac{GNP_t-GNP_{t-1}}{GNP_{t-1}} = \frac{PD_{t-1}}{GNP_{t-1}}$$

This means that the ratio PD_{t-1}/GNP_{t-1} is equal to the growth rate of GNP. However, as he was concerned with the capacity effect of PD, the movement in GNP should implicitly parallel the changes in capacity and this relation should be called as the equation of the growth rate of capacity. For instance, in the fiscal year 1957, GNP was about ¥10 trillion, and investment in private producer durables was ¥1.68 trillion, so the maximum growth rate of GNP is apparently 16.8% per annum (1.68/10). However, as GNP would be less than the national capacity, and investment in producer durables, ¥16.8 million, naturally involves replacement investment, the capacity growth rate would be lower than 16.8% and close to, but at least more than 10%. This is a conclusion he derived on the assumption of the unity capacity coefficient of private investment in producer durables, concerning the rate of growth of capacity.

The second prop in his theory is the imports-GNP ratio. From 1951 onward, this ratio has fluctuated with the business cycle, but its trend has maintained almost the same level around 9%. Therefore, Shimomura guessed that even if the import ratio might rise in the upswing with the accumulation of inventory in imported raw materials, it would be destined to soon decline in the downswing; so we should not be misled by a temporary increase in the import ratio and consider it as a long-run trend. The White Paper of 1957 emphasized that the rising trend of the import ratio in the 1956 boom was not temporary but of a semi-secular nature, due to the rapid rise in investment in producer durables (which might have a higher dependence upon imported raw materials) necessitated by the technological revolution and heavy industrialization since 1956. Since the rise of the import ratio was considered as semi-secular, it was a logical consequence that the author of the White Paper imagined the curtailment of the growth rate as inevitable in order to cut down increasing imports and wipe out the deficit in the balance of payments. Against this judgment, Shimomura regards the cycle in the import ratio as a consequence of inventory fluctuation.

As he then believed that exports would increase by an annual rate of about $300 million on the average, the Japanese economy should have an ability to in crease imports each year by about ¥100 billion. Moreover, the average (and marginal) propensity to import is less than 10%, excluding the effect of inventory changes. If we assume now that it is 10%, the capability to increase imports by $300 million (=about ¥100 billion) would make it feasible to increase the domestic effective demand by ¥1,000 billion ($300 million÷10%=$3 billion =about ¥1,000 billion). As the *GNP* in 1957 was around ¥10 trillion, this means a possibility of a 10% rate of growth (¥1 trillion ÷¥10 trillion). In other words, the rate of growth which would guarantee the equilibrium of balance of payments is 10%, according to Shimomura.

On the one hand, the capacity growth rate is far greater than 10%, and on the other, the equilibrium balance-of-payments rate of growth is also around 10%. Therefore, Shimomura concluded that the Japanese economy would have sufficient ability to expand at a growth rate of 10%. Not only capacity, but also the domestic effective demand could expand at a 10% rate of growth, without either a general price-rise or balance-of-payments difficulties. Such is his view, and he strongly rejected the tight money policy which has often been executed by the Bank of Japan. He maintained that monetary policy should back up the economic growth positively, and in order to sustain the rapidity of growth, the so-called *over-loan* (excessive dependence of the commercial banks on the Bank of Japan) is rather to be accepted, although his opinion goes against the general view that the " over-loan " is an evil.

2. *Inventory Controversy*

Before the so-called " Growth Controversy ", we had the " Inventory Controversy " between Shimomura and the late Mr. Goto (the author of the White Paper) in relation to the evaluation of the role and measurement of inventory accumulation of imported raw materials during the fiscal year 1956. As the Inventory Controversy heralded the Growth Controversy, and the former became an integral part of the latter, it seems to be essential for us to start with the Inventory Controversy.

In brief, Shimomura estimated the accumulation of inventory in imported raw materials in the fiscal year 1956 as amounting to $500–600 million, while Goto and the rest of the White Paper group at that time estimated it as amounting to no more than $200–300 million. At the beginning of the controversy, (originally, the articles were published mainly in the journal *Kinyuzaiseijijo* (Monetary and Fiscal Affairs) beginning in February 1957), import figures on raw materials were preliminary. One side in the debate could not but use preliminary estimates based on import credit statistics, as far as the period Dec. 1956–March 1957 was concerned, whereas the other side could use definite figures in the discussion. Therefore, in order to make clear the divergent points between them, it is not adequate to quote the original preliminary figures here. At the final stage of the Inventory Controversy, Mr. T. Takemura and H. Kanamori made a table which compares the two estimates, from which it may be convenient to start our discussions here.

In Table 1, we reproduce their comparisons. By looking down from (a) to (k), the reader may understand how the estimates of inventory accumulation were made. In brief, by applying the elasticity of consumption of imported raw materials with respect to manufacturing production to the predicted increase in manufacturing production, we estimate the future consumption of imported raw materials. By comparing the latter with the actual imports of raw materials, we find the inventory accumulation of imported raw materials as the difference between two. Of course,

Table 1. Two Estimates Concerning the Accumulation of Inventories of Imported Raw Materials in the Fiscal Year 1956

	Shimomura	Takemura Kanamori	Remarks
(a) Increase in the index of manufacturing production	21%	24.4%	Shimomura's is a computation based on the preliminary report.
(b) Elasticity of consumption of imported raw materials with respect to mfg. prod.	1.3	1.3	
(c) Increase in consumption of imported raw materials $c=a\times b$	27%	31.7%	
(d) Increase in import prices	4—8%	4—8%	
(e) Increase in the amount of consumption of imported raw materials $e=(1+c)\times(1+d)-1$	32—37%	37—42%	
(f) Amount of imports of raw materials in f.y. 1955	$1,500 mil.	$1,500 mil.	
(g) Inventory increase of imp. raw materials in f.y. 1955	$100 mil.	$50 mil.	Shimomura first estimated this as $100 mil., but later changed it to $50mil.
(h) Value of current imports of raw materials in f.y. 1955 $h=f-g$	$1,400 mil.	$1,450 mil.	
(i) Increase in current imports of raw materials in f.y. 1956 $i=h\times e$	$448—518 mil.	$537—609 mil.	
(j) Actual value of imports of raw materials in f.y. 1956	$2,510 mil.	$2,315 mil.	One difference is due to inclusion or exclusion of semi-manufactured raw materials, in addition to crude raw materials.
(k) Imports for inventory accumulation $k=j-(h+i)$	$662—592 mil.	$328—256 mil.	

Source : Takemura and Kanamori, " Inventory Changes and the Balance of Payments " (in Japanese), *Analyst*, Nov. 1957. This is reprinted in the book, O. Shimomura, *Keizaiseicho Jitsugen no Tameni* (For the Acceleration of Economic Growth), 1958, Tokyo, pp. 297–307.

Note : The rate of increase in the import price, 4–8%, represents divergent results due to the differences in the method of computation; the Laspeyres or the Paarsche.

these are transformed into money terms in the process from (a) to (k).

The difference in the final estimates between the two in Table 1, *i.e.*, \$662–592 million *vs.* \$328–256 million can be analyzed as follows:

1) The difference in the increase rate of the manufacturing production (for 1955–56) is due to the adoption of either the preliminary or the final report. Therefore, Shimomura will accept a change in (a) to 24.4%. If so, the rate of increase in the value of consumption of imported raw materials (e) will be the same, computed as based on the same elasticity of consumption in imported raw material consumption (b) and the same rate of increase of the prices of imports (d). Further, since the value of imports of raw materials in 1955 is also common, all the figures from (a) to (f) will be the same.

2) We must notice another difference in the actual value of the raw material imports in the fiscal year 1956 (j), *i.e.*, \$2,510 million *vs.* \$2,315 million. As this difference (\$195 million) accounts for 58% of the total difference (\$335 million), it must be taken seriously. However, it is at first sight strange that there exists a difference at all in so objective a value as the actual imports of raw materials.

3) The third is the difference in the estimate of increase in inventories of imported raw materials (g).

Thus, it appears to be very easy to judge the "Inventory Controversy", so far as its measurement aspect is concerned. Provided that the increase rate in manufacturing production is 24.4%, and that there are only the two differences in (j) and (g), the final difference will be reduced from \$335 million to \$264 million. So, Table 1 is analyzed as follows:

Difference in estimate of imports for inventory accumulation in f.y. 1956	\$335 million (100%)	1. Due to the difference in the increase rate of manuf. production	\$70 million (21%)
		2. Due to the difference in estimate of inventory increase of imp. raw materials in f.y. 1955	\$70 million (21%)
		3. Difference in the actual value of imports of raw materials in f. y. 1956	\$195 million (58%)

117

The sources of the difference of opinion in relation to the 1956 inventory increase thus become evident. One of the sources (1) becomes lost, and (2) and (3), particularly the latter, are important in the final judgment of the so-called " Inventory Controversy " in Japan. As Takemura and Kanamori explain in their paper, Shimomura's "imported raw materials" involve not only crude raw materials but also semi-manufactured raw materials (*e.g.*, rolled steel, chemical products, *etc.*), while their's are restricted to crude raw materials. Shimomura too clarifies the source of his estimate in respect to the actual value of imported raw materials in 1955 and 1956 as follows :

Unit : million dollars

Fis. year	Crude raw materials	Fabricated raw materials	Total (A)	Timber and cork (B)	A—B
1955	1,278	289	1,567	69	1,499
1956	2,146	452	2,598	88	2,510

Shimomura thus adopted a wider definition, while the opponents in the controversy adhered to a narrower one. The difference in their definitions brought about a lengthy debate, which probably could not have been understood well by anybody other than the debaters themselves.

Then, what is the reason for the difference in the estimates of increase in inventories of imported raw materials in the fiscal year 1955 ? Shimomura would probably have changed his estimate of inventory increase in the imported raw materials in 1955 from $50 million to $100 million, mainly because he had first in mind only crude raw materials, but later he became aware that he should actually use a wider concept of raw materials. Whether or not his changed estimate is adequate will be beyond even Shimomura's confidence, and we will not take it seriously. However, the main skeleton of the " Inventory Controversy " has roughly been sketched here.

One problem remains : While the definitions of raw materials are different between Shimomura and Goto (and also Takemura=

Kanamori), the actual value of imports of raw materials in fiscal year 1955 are nevertheless the same ($1,500 million or $1,499 million). Even though the semi-manufactured raw materials are included in Shimomura's definition, and excluded from Takemura–Kanamori's definition of imports of raw materials, 1955 imports are the same. If we now assume that the portion of semi-manufactured raw materials is deducted from $1,500 million (f) in Takemura–Kanamori's figure, then it is quite clear that their final estimate of imports for inventory accumulation will be raised from $328–256 million to around $400 million, and the divergent views on the inventory accumulation of imported raw materials can be reconciled to some extent.   Thus, our pointing out of the difference in the raw material definitions and the above adjustment may throw some light in solving the technical confusions involved in the controversy.   Shimomura's estimate was not so exaggerated as was generally believed, but his definition was merely wider.   Goto and his collaborators adopted a narrower concept, but still there was some scope within which the divergence of their estimates can be reduced by the downward adjustment of the 1955 imports of raw materials, so as to include only the *crude* raw materials.

Other detailed discussions had been made in order to strengthen their points, and Shimomura even attempted to estimate the inventory increase in imported raw materials by two other methods.   However, it seems to me that the latter two were less reliable procedures, and we will not go into these discussions.

Anyhow, Shimomura placed great emphasis on the role of inventory fluctuations, while Goto emphasized the part of the rise in the investment for producer's durables.   The former accentuated the temporality of the balance of payments difficulty, whereas the latter its semi-structural nature.   The former believed that the oscillation of inventory investment had caused the increased import ratio in the 1956–57 boom, while the latter believed that the increased investment for producer's durables had had greater import-inducing effect.

As Fig. 1 " Inventory Investment and Imports " and Fig. 2 " Producer's Durables Investment and Imports " shows, both have

119

fairly close cyclical movements, and at first sight, it may be difficult to decide whether inventory investment or producer's durables investment had induced imports.   However, a further analysis is needed, and we will discuss this point in another chapter.[3]

Fig. 1.   Inventory Investment and Imports
— Seasonal fluctuations unadjusted —

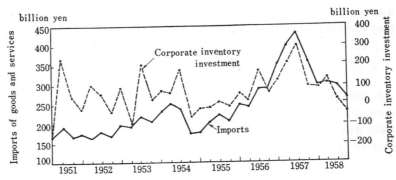

Notes :   1) Figures are in terms of quarterly rate.
2) Corporate inventory investment is estimated by the author.

Fig. 2.   Producer's Durables and Imports
— Seasonal fluctuations adjusted —

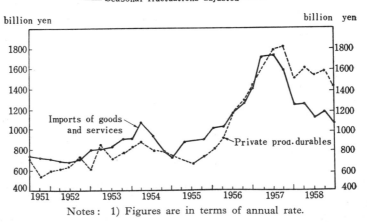

Notes :   1) Figures are in terms of annual rate.

3)   See Chapter 7.

120

Shimomura's view, however, depends upon the tendency that the imports-*GNP* ratio was almost constant (9–10%) in 1951–56, except for cyclical fluctuations, thus enabling him to use its constancy for future projection.   The trend was constant, but there were only cyclical fluctuations due to the inventory cycles.   But this observation is based on a very weak foundation, in so far as the imports-*GNP* ratio used is *in money terms*.   Actually for 1951–56 we see a fairly a large decline in the relative prices of imports, so the import ratio *in real terms* had a rising trend, even though it was constant in money terms.   In other words, let M denote the value of imports, P the *GNP* deflator and P_m the price index of imports, then $\dfrac{M}{P_m} \Big/ \dfrac{GNP}{P}$ will indicate a rising tendency if P_m/P is falling, even if M/GNP is constant.   Fig. 3 shows this relation up to 1959, and how the import ratio will be different, according to whether the money term or the real term be employed.   Therefore, we can say that Shimomura's

Fig. 3.   Imports-*GNP* Ratios in Money and Real Terms

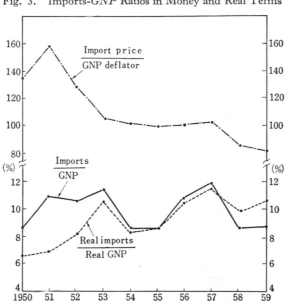

assertion of a 10% growth rate was based upon the assumption that the relative prices of imports would decline with such a speed as to keep the import ratio in money terms constant, or on the assumption that the import ratio in real terms would stop rising with stable relative prices of imports. Actually, as we can see in Fig. 3, the import ratio in real terms kept rising, and the money-term import ratio continued a secular stability only through the decline of relative prices of imports. The relative prices of imports declined twice very sharply after the Korean Incident and the 1957–58 recession. If we had not a sharp decline in import prices in the 1957–58 recession, we could not have attained the accelerated rate of growth in the coming period, accomplished by raising the balance of payments ceiling. In fact, the decline of import prices was drastic, and it made possible a huge investment boom in 1959–60 (the annual increase rate of private investment was 73% and 30% respectively in f.y. 1959 and 1960) without bringing about any deficit in the balance of payments until 1961. However, the decline of import prices in 1958 had never been anticipated by Shimomura. For 1956–59, we had a real growth rate of GNP of about 9–10%. If the decline of import prices were not to occur, then such a growth rate as anticipated by Shimomura would not have been realized.

It is not yet clear whether the real-term import ratio will continue to rise or slow down in future, but, to recognize that Shimomura's assertion of a high growth rate is based on a rather weak foundation as explained above, will be indispensable for the evaluation of his analysis.

3. The Capacity-Increasing Coefficient of Producer Durables

The second foundation of Shimomura's analysis was the assumption that the capacity-increasing coefficient of investment in private producer durables (producer's durable equipment plus business construction) is unity, i.e., denoting private producer's durables PD, the coefficient is defined as $(GNP_t - GNP_{t-1})/PD_{t-1}$ and it is assumed to be unity.

This assumption comes from his observation of the 1951–56 *GNP-PD* relation.   If we calculate the cumulative total of private producer durables for 1951–55, we obtain ¥3,661 billion, and if we compute the increase in *GNP* for 1951–56, we get ¥3,863 billion.   The ratio, ¥3,863 bil./¥3,661 bil., is supposed to give us the capital-increasing effect (=1.055).   This is almost unity, and Shimomura assumed this relation would not change even from 1957 onwards.   However, from 1957 on, investment in producer durables was always larger than the increment of *GNP* in the following year, and Shimomura advocates the adoption of a strong expansionist policy to combat the coming underutilization of plant and equipment, or to give full play to the potentialities of the Japanese economy which had been tremendously pushed up by the recent upsurge of the investment boom.

Against this very provocative opinion, which was then prominent among generally restrictive attitutes toward economic policy, there naturally emerged opposing arguments.   Professor Shigeto Tsuru of Hitotsubashi University, pointed out that in Shimomura's computation $\sum PD$ and ΔGNP were computed all in current prices, but if it were recomputed in constant prices, the capacity-increasing coefficient $\Delta GNP / \sum PD$ would be reduced to around 0.7.   Whether we use 1.0 or 0.7 as the capacity-increasing coefficient may make a great difference in our policy judgments, for the exaggeration in the under-utilization of plant and equipment would be mitigated if we use the latter ratio.

On the other hand, Saburo Okita, the director of the economic planning division of the Economic Planning Agency,   emphasized that, as we already passed the immediate-postwar stage of rehabilitation and arrived at the period when it became necessary to renew old equipment and introduce new innovational equipment, it is natural that the capital-output ratio would have increased (or the capacity-increasing coefficient would have decreased).

Toshihiko Yoshino, the associate director of the research division of the Bank of Japan, Yoshizo Yoshida, Professor of Osaka Metropolitan University, Tadao Uchida, Assistant Professor of Tokyo University, Tsunehiko Watanabe, Assistant Professor of Gakushuin University, and others also took part in this controversy, and it became one of the most excited debates among the postwar economic problems.

Shimomura's rejoinder was as follows : First, denoting total capital by K, tangible fixed assets by K_f, we obtain from Ministry of Finance, "Corporate Enterprise Annual Survey" (1954–57), $K_f/K=1/3$. Since gross profit P (incl. paid interest and discounts) as a ratio to total capital is almost 10% on an annual basis, $\dfrac{P}{K}\Big/\dfrac{K_f}{K}=30\%$. On the other hand, it will be necessary for a firm as a going concern to sustain an added value Y (wages and salaries, depreciation, repairs, rents, taxes and public charges and profit), which is about 4 times larger than P. In fact, the Corporate Enterprise Annual Survey suggests that this is the actual phenomenon. Then, we have the following relation, *i.e.*,

$$\frac{Y}{K_f} = \frac{P}{K} \cdot \underbrace{\frac{K}{K_f}} \cdot \frac{Y}{P}$$
$$1.2 \qquad 30\% \qquad 4$$

As Y/K_f is the average capacity-increasing coefficient for manufacturing industry, Shimomura guessed that his assertion that the capacity-increasing coefficient is about unity was roughly substantiated (at least it was greater than unity).

However, it seems to me that Shimomura's rejoinder is completely erroneous. First, on the one hand, book values of tangible fixed assets in the Corporate Enterprise Survey have still been under-valued owing to the postwar hyper-inflation, even though we had several revaluations in the post-war period. On the other hand, in the computation of the marginal capacity-increasing coefficient from the national income statistics, producer's durables are valued in current prices. Therefore, Y/K_f computed from the Corporate Enterprise Survey and $\varDelta GNP/PD$ computed from the national income statistics are incommensurable and the former cannot be a test for the latter. In the postwar period, the former should always be larger than the latter. Second, the tangible fixed assets in the Corporate Enterprise Survey are always net of depreciation allowances, while investment in producer durables as a denominator

124

of $\Delta GNP/PD$ in Shimomura's computation, is a gross concept. Thus, Shimomura compares with each other those which are not comparable, so his assertion of unity capacity-increasing coefficient is again on a shaky basis.

Shimomura further attempted to strengthen his proposition of unity capacity-increasing coefficient, by its international comparison. He found the coefficient in money terms, $GNP_{56}-GNP_{51}/\sum_{51}^{55} PD$ was 0.74 in the United States, 0.97 in the United Kingdom, 0.93 in West Germany, and 1.09 in Japan. Although the coefficient in the United States is a little lower than he expected, those in the United Kingdom and West Germany seem to him to substantiate his hypothesis. However, in case of Japan the private investment in producer durable equipment and private business construction are used as PD, while only the private investment in producer durable equipment (excl. of private construction) is used in case of the United States. Further, in case of West Germany, the total (private as well as public) investment in producer's durable equipment (excl. of private and public construction) is used. Concerning the computation of the U.K. coefficient, his computational procedure is not clear, but when I tentatively computed it in accordance with his definition in Japan's case from *National Income Statistics: Sources and Method*, H.M.S.O., 1956, it came out as 0.65 rather than 0.97. Therefore, his attempt to reinforce his proposition by the international comparison seems to make no sense again.

Shimomura's hypothesis on the unity capacity-increasing coefficient should thus be rejected. Of course, we see other defects in his computation. One of them can be found in his computation in money terms, as Tsuru pointed out. Another defect is his assumption that the level and change of GNP are the same as those of productive capacity for 1951–56, for which $\Delta GNP/PD$ was computed. However, during the same period the rate of capacity utilization had increased in manufacturing industry (from 73.2% in March of 1951 to 83% in September of 1956). Therefore, his assumption that GNP=capacity cannot be valid. According to my computation, the marginal private fixed capital-output ratio followed a rising

125

trend from 0.79 for 1946–51, through 1.50 for 1951–56, to 1.79 for 1956–59, and yet the rate of capacity utilization has not decreased (1955=100, 1957=107.2, 1958=94.1 and 1959=106.7). This means that there prevailed a rising trend of the marginal fixed capital-output ratio or a declining trend of the capacity-increasing coefficient. Therefore, Shimomura's assertion for the necessity of aggressive expansionist policy seems to depend upon a capacity-increasing coefficient which is constant and a bit too high. In fact, due to unprecedented technological innovation from 1956 onward, capital coefficients have actually increased, and the menace of overcapacity as Shimomura first imagined did not appear.

4. *International Comparison of Marginal Fixed Capital Coefficients*

It will be of interest at this stage to compute the differences in the marginal gross fixed capital-output ratios in various countries and explore their backgrounds. However, as far as this is an international comparison, the definitions must be on the same basis. A casual look at the U.N. summary of various countries' national income statistics suggests that it is impossible to make an international comparison of the marginal fixed capital-output ratios on Shimomura's definition of PD, *i.e.*, private producer durables. In many countries, private and public fixed investment is shown unseparated, and the definition of the scope of " private " or " public " may not be uniform according to the difference in the political system. Therefore, we attempt to compare the ratios of the real gross fixed investment I_f (incl. " private " and " public ") to the increment of real GDP (or GNP), *i.e.*, $\sum_{51}^{56} I_f/(GNP_{57}-GNP_{51})$ in constant prices (Table 2). Instead of breaking down this coefficient into " private " and " public ", we divide I_f into construction I_c and producer durable equipment I_e and comput the coefficient (Table 3). As the producer durable equipment is mainly " private ", and its productive effect is direct, Shimomura's intention in the use of PD will be almost satisfied when we use the latter ratio, $I_e/\Delta GNP$.

126

Table 2. Marginal Gross Fixed Capital-Output Ratios and Growth Rates in Postwar Various Countries

	Marginal gross fixed capital coef.	GDP annual growth rate		Marginal gross fixed capital coef.	GDP annual growth rate
Argentina	14.3	1.5%	Iceland	3.2	9.4%
*Australia	16.9	1.5	*Iraq	1.7	11.6
Austria	3.5	5.9	Ireland	9.7	1.5
Belgian Congo	7.1	4.3	Israel	2.7	8.5
Belgium	5.0	2.9	Italy	3.7	5.4
*Brazil	8.9	1.7	*Jamaica	1.1	9.4
*Burma	3.9	4.7	Japan	2.5	7.8
Canada	5.2	4.2	Luxemburg	6.9	3.0
Ceylon	3.2	3.4	*Mexico	2.4	5.9
Chile	3.9	2.7	*Morroco	7.9	2.7
*Taiwan	1.3	9.4	Netherlands	4.2	5.3
*Columbia	2.3	4.5	*New Zealand	7.6	2.8
Costa-Rica	2.9	6.8	Norway	7.7	3.8
Denmark	2.3	6.0	*Peru	5.0	3.8
*Dominican Rep.	2.0	8.9	*Philippines	1.1	6.8
*Ecuador	1.5	6.5	Portugal	3.5	4.1
*Finland	9.0	2.9	Puerto-Rico	4.5	4.1
France	3.6	4.6	Sweden	5.2	3.8
W. Germany	2.8	7.5	※Switzerland	4.0	2.7
*Ghana	5.4	2.1	*Union of South Africa	4.5	5.4
Greece	2.0	6.8	U.K.	5.6	2.5
※Guatemala	1.6	5.8	U.S.A.	5.7	2.9
Honduras	3.7	4.3	Venezuela	1.7	11.3

Source : Mainly from U. N., *Yearbook of National Accounts Statistics*, 1958.

Note : In principle, the gross fixed capital-output ratios were computed after dividing each cumulative total of fixed investment for 1951–56 in 1954 prices by the increment of *GDP* (or *GNP*) for 1951–57 in 1954 prices. * shows countries where we cannot get constant price series, so *GDP* and fixed investment were divided by a common deflator, the cost of living index. ※ shows countries where inventory investment cannot be separated from fixed investment. Growth rates were computed from 1951–57 real *GDP* comparisons.

127

As we can see in Tables 2 and 3, we find a great dispersion in the marginal gross fixed capital-output ratios of various countries, from the highest, 16.87 of Australia to the lowest, 1.06 of the Philippines. There is no constancy or stability of this ratio, as Shimomura had anticipated. Even if we pay attention to $I_e/\Delta GNP$ which use only producer's durable equipment in the numerator, we find a similar

Table 3. Composition of Postwar Marginal Gross Fixed Capital-Output Ratios in Various Countries

Marginal gross fixed capital-output ratios			Marginal gross fixed capital-output ratios			
	Residentail buildings	Other construction	Prod. durable equip.		Residential buildings	Other construction	Prod. durable equip.
Argentina	8.7		5.6	Italy	0.8	0.5	2.3
Austria	0.7	1.0	1.8	Japan	0.2	2.3	
Belgium	1.3	1.4	2.3	Luxemburg	1.4	2.7	3.3
*Burma	2.9		1.1	*Morocco	1.9	2.7	3.7
Canada	1.1	2.2	1.9	Netherlands	0.8	1.2	2.2
Ceylon	2.4		0.8	*New Zealand	1.8	1.3	4.6
*Taiwan	0.7		0.7	Norway	1.3	2.3	4.3
*Columbia	0.7		1.6	*Peru	2.4		2.6
Denmark	0.4	0.6	1.3	*Philippines	0.2	0.4	0.4
*Ecuador	0.2	0.5	0.8	Portugal	0.7	1.7	1.1
France	0.8	1.0	1.7	Puerto Rico	1.1	2.0	1.4
W. Germany	1.3		1.5	Sweden	1.3	2.0	2.0
*Ghana	3.5		1.9	Switzerland	4.1	6.3	6.2※
Greece	0.6	0.6	0.8	Union of South Africa	2.6		1.9
Ireland	1.9	3.6	4.2				
Israel	2.0		0.7	U. K.	1.2	1.5	2.9
				U. S. A.	1.5	2.1	2.1

Source: See footnotes of Table 2.

Note: ※ 6.2 involves inventory investment.

dispersion. If such is the case, the marginal gross fixed capital-output ratio cannot be used in economic projection. However, in Figs. 4 and 5, we find an inverse correlation between the marginal gross fixed capital-output ratios and the growth rates, not only in the total ratios $I_f/\Delta GNP$ but also in the truncated ratios, $I_c/\Delta GNP$ and $I_e/\Delta GNP$. Of course, the growth rate is not the sole factor explaining the differences in the marginal gross fixed capital-output ratios, but we should keep our eye upon such a remarkable inverse correlation between the two.

Then, what is the reason why such an inverse correlation exists? According to my speculation, it occurs mainly because the fixed investment used is in *gross* terms. The proportion of replacement investment in the total investment will be the larger, as the growth rate of an economy is smaller. In the extreme of simple reproduction, where a perfectly stationary condition prevails, fixed investment is wholly composed of replacement investment. However, in the stationary state, the increment of real GNP will be zero, so $I_f/\Delta GNP$ will be infinite. As the growth rate of an economy becomes larger, the proportion of replacement in total fixed investment becomes smaller. Therefore, $I_f/\Delta GNP$ too indicates a declining tendency. But this would not support the view that the *net* marginal fixed capital-output ratio will be constant regardless of the growth rate.

Such is our analysis in relation to Shimomura's capacity-increasing coefficient of private investment in producer durables, although the definition of investment is somewhat different and we have always used the reciprocal form, the capital-output ratio. This seems to be a digression from the main contour of the growth controversy. However, in view of the fact the capacity-increasing coefficient was one of the most important coccepts in the controversy, and the fact that we should ought to give our attention rather to its theoretical aspect, further digression may be interesting.

Although the inverse correlation of the capital-output raito and the rate of growth was found from international cross-section analysis, how about its intertemporal analysis? When the growth rate is higher, is the period also one of lower marginal gross capital-output ratio? Fig. 6 depicts this relation using the long-range series

Fig. 4. Marginal Gross Fixed Capital-Output Ratios and Growth Rates
for 1951–57 in Various Countries

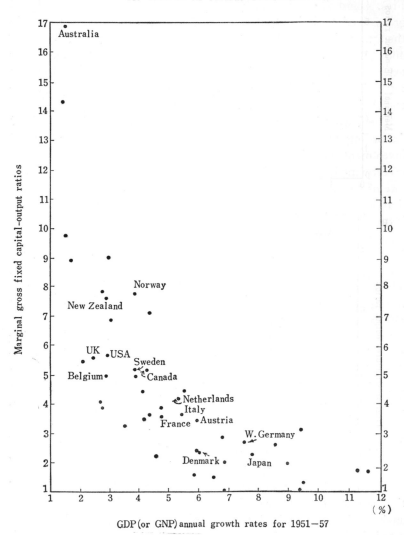

Fig. 5. Marginal Gross Fixed Capital Coefficient by Component and Growth Rates for 1951–57

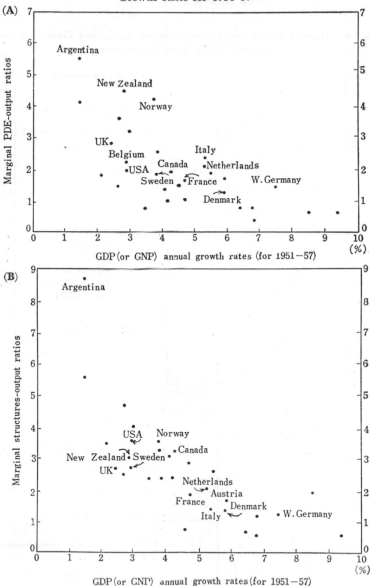

Note: PDE=producer's durable equipment.

Fig. 6.　Intertemporal Correlation of *MGFCO* Ratios and *NGP* Growth Rates

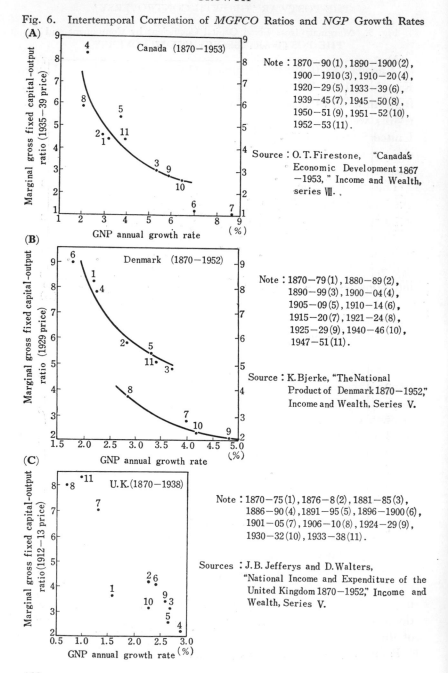

(A)

Canada (1870—1953)

Marginal gross fixed capital-output ratio (1935—39 price)

GNP annual growth rate　(%)

Note : 1870—90 (1), 1890—1900 (2),
1900—1910 (3), 1910—20 (4),
1920—29 (5), 1933—39 (6),
1939—45 (7), 1945—50 (8),
1950—51 (9), 1951—52 (10),
1952—53 (11).

Source : O. T. Firestone, "Canada's
Economic Development 1867
—1953," Income and Wealth,
series Ⅷ. .

(B)

Denmark (1870—1952)

Marginal gross fixed capital-output ratio (1929 price)

GNP annual growth rate (%)

Note : 1870—79 (1), 1880—89 (2),
1890—99 (3), 1900—04 (4),
1905—09 (5), 1910—14 (6),
1915—20 (7), 1921—24 (8),
1925—29 (9), 1940—46 (10),
1947—51 (11).

Source : K. Bjerke, "The National
Product of Denmark 1870—1952,"
Income and Wealth, Series V.

(C)

U.K. (1870—1938)

Marginal gross fixed capital-output ratio (1912—13 price)

GNP annual growth rate (%)

Note : 1870—75 (1), 1876—8 (2), 1881—85 (3),
1886—90 (4), 1891—95 (5), 1896—1900 (6),
1901—05 (7), 1906—10 (8), 1924—29 (9),
1930—32 (10), 1933—38 (11).

Sources : J. B. Jefferys and D. Walters,
"National Income and Expenditure of the
United Kingdom 1870—1952," Income and
Wealth, Series V.

132

of Canada (1870–1953), Denmark (1870–1952), and the United Kingdom (1870–1938). Again, we find a similar inverse correlation from time-series analysis. We can mention here that the same results were derived in relation to Sweden (1861–1930) and the United States (1879–1948), using a wider concept of investment including the changes in inventories, *i.e.*, the marginal gross capital-output ratio.

Thus, our analysis suggests a variability in the value of the marginal gross fixed capital-output ratio especially susceptible to the influences of the growth rate. In the short-run, it will be influenced by the changes in capacity utilization, and in the long-run, it will be influenced by the proportion of replacement in total investment, determined by the growth rate. Such should be cautiously be taken into consideration in any economic forecasting.

5. Three Concepts of the Capacity-Increasing Coefficient

So far, we have discussed the invalidity of Shimomura's assumption that the capacity-increasing coefficient of *gross* private investment in producer durables is unity. However, when various papers in the Growth Controversy were collected in a symposium *Nihonkeizai no Seichoryoku* (Growth Potential of the Japanese Economy), edited by Kinyujijo Kenkyukai (Institute of Monetary and Fiscal Situations) in 1959, Shimomura added a new comprehensive rejoinder, in which his concept underwent a complete conversion, *i.e.*, from the capacity-increasing coefficient of *gross* investment to that of *net* investment. As it means a change in his definitions, to net terms, in fact it may imply a switch to 0.7 in terms of *gross* private investment in producer durables. Therefore, his conversion to the *net* definition meant a complete concession to his opponents. Nevertheless, as he maintains the same outer appearance, *i.e.*, the " unity " capacity-increasing coefficient of investment in producer durables without mentioning his change to " net," there were few people who were aware of this change.

Before going into his procedure of conversion, it may be convenient to take up here Tsuru's discussion on the *gross* and *net* stock ratios.[4] He pointed out that there is a great difference between the capacity-increasing coefficient of gross *PD* computed from the national income statistics and the value added-tangible fixed assets ratio computed from the book-value summarized in the Corporate Enterprise Survey, apart from " average " and " marginal " differences.   I have already pointed out two other reasons for the divergence of the two concepts. However, Tsuru's is another point.

Assuming that a fixed asset is depreciated by the same amount year by year according to the straight line method during the years of its life, its book-value will decline along the book-value line indicated in Fig. 7.   However, the fixed asset will maintain the same efficiency for comparatively a long period, and only after a long elapse of time, it may fall, say, along the efficiency-value line (a).   But, let us assume here that the efficiency-value is constant over the whole period of life (the line (b)), and that as soon as this period is over, the value will suddenly decline to zero.

Actually, there are many fixed assets, and they will be arranged in a continuous distribution from the newest one to the oldest, which will soon be scrapped, along the book-value line in Fig. 7.   If simple reproduction prevails, *i.e.*, if replacement is made year after year in just the amount to replace the scrapped equipments, then we can say that the total book-value of fixed assets will be roughly 1/2 of their efficiency value.   Such is the conclusion derived under the stationary simple reproduction scheme, supposing that there is a uniform distribution of various assets over time and that there are no price changes.

From this point of view, Tsuru pointed out that in order to use the ratio of value added to tangible fixed assets, derived from book-values, as the capacity-increasing coefficient of *new* fixed investment, it must be multiplied by the adjustment coefficient 0.5.   However,

4)   Shigeto Tsuru, " Shihon no Sanshutsu-koka " (Productivity of Fixed Capital) (*Keizai Kenkyu*, January 1960).   The words, the gross stock ratio and the net stock ratio were quoted from *Productivity, Prices, and Incomes*, Joint Economic Committee Print, 91551, 1957, p. 93.   The original source is Machinery and Allied Products Institute.

Fig. 7. Book-Value and Efficiency-Value of a Fixed Asset

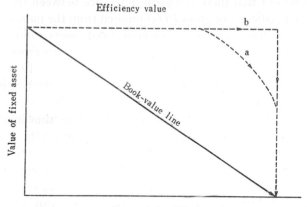

Efficiency value

Years of durability

this is the adjustment appropriate to the stationary state, and in a growing economy a bit larger coefficient must be used. Denoting the book-value of the fixed assets in existence as K, and the efficiency-value of them as K', then the ratio K_t/K'_t can be indicated by the following equation:[5]

$$\frac{K_t}{K'_t} = 1 - \left\{ \frac{1}{ng} - \frac{1}{(1+g)^n - 1} \right\}$$

where n is the years of durability and g is the annual growth rate. In the case $n=20$, $g=1\%$ gives $K_t/K_t'=0.543$; $g=5\%$ gives $K_t/K_t' =0.605$; and $g=10\%$ gives $K_t/K_t'=0.678$.

This algebraic relation can easily be understood intuitively in Fig. 7. Although in the case of simple reproduction, the various assets may be distributed uniformly over time along the line of de-

5) Tsuru, *op. cit.* As K' is the cumulative total of gross investments G growing from the past at a rate g, but excludes those which have been scrapped,

$$K'_t = G_t + \frac{G_t}{1+g} + \frac{G_t}{(1+g)^2} + \cdots\cdots\cdots + \frac{G_t}{(1+g)^{n-1}}$$

On the other hand, the book-value K is the cumulative total of fixed assets depreciated by the straight line method. Denoting the rate of depreciation as d $(=1/n)$,

$$K_t = G_t + \frac{G_t(1-d)}{1+g} + \frac{G_t(1-2d)}{(1+g)^2} + \cdots\cdots\cdots + \frac{G_t\{1-(n-1)d\}}{(1+g)^{n-1}}$$

By dividing K'_t into K_t we obtain the equation in the text.

creasing book-value, they will deviate upwards more and more, as the growth rate is higher. This is because the larger the growth rate, the larger the proportion of newer assets.

Tsuru named the capital-output ratio computed from book-values as the " net stock ratio ", and that computed from the efficiency-value as the " gross stock ratio ". He maintains as follows: We should use the gross stock ratio rather than the net stock ratio in our economic projections. If it is difficult to estimate gross stock directly, and easy to estimate net stock from the book-values, then it is possible to estimate the former indirectly through the latter. His convenient device was that using the value added-tangible fixed assets ratio (1.2) computed by Shimomura and applying $K/K'=0.6$ to it, so that a workable capacity-increasing coefficient of fixed investment of 0.7 is derived. This is equal to the value of the capacity-increasing coefficient of gross producer durables investment *in real terms* which Tsuru once computed from national income statistics. Therefore, he seems to believe that the latter ratio 0.7 can also be derived indirectly by multiplying the value added-fixed assets ratio based on book-values by K/K', and that this is a valid criticism of Shimomura's earlier procedure of checking with each other the two capacity-increasing coefficients based on the national income statistics and the Corporate Enterprise Survey respectively.

However, even Tsuru may not be correct. On the contrary, it seems to be that there appeared at least three kinds of capacity-increasing coefficients (or capital-output ratios) in the Controversy, apart from " marginal " or " net " difference.

1) Capacity-increasing coefficient of gross private investment in producer durables ($\Delta GNP/\sum PD$ based on the national income statistics)

2) Net stock ratio (This is a reciprocal form of (1), but based on book-values net of depreciation allowances).

3) Gross stock ratio (This is also a reciprocal form of (1), but in case of (1), the cumulative total of gross private investment in producer durables is used, without excluding equipment scrapped year after year. In this sense, (1) is *more gross* than (3) in which the efficiency value of fixed assets *exclusive of* rejected equipments is

used).

Therefore, according to my view, the following ranking

$$\frac{1}{(1)} > (3) > (2)$$

exists. Tsuru certainly raised an interesting point, but he is misled in believing that $(1) = \frac{1}{(3)}$.

The above has been a discussion of Tsuru's point, but we will go next to Shimomura's conversion to the " net " definition. First, in this conversion, Shimomura accepts Tsuru's proposition that the value added-fixed assets ratio based on book-values will be larger than the true capacity-increasing coefficient based on efficiency values. Second, although Shimomura computed the value added-fixed assets ratio in manufacturing and obtained 1.2, he revised it to 1.3–1.4, because in the former computation tangible fixed assets at the *end* of the year was used but he thought it correct rather to use the average of the values at the beginning and the end of the year. Third, in order to convert the value added-fixed assets ratio based on book values into efficiency-values, he assumed the adjustment coefficient to be 0.65 in 1955, 0.67 in 1956, 0.71 in 1957 and 0.76 in 1958. Of course, these adjustment coefficients were estimated on very arbitrary assumptions, so we will not discuss them here. Fourth, if the value added-fixed assets ratio, 1.3–1.4, based on book-values is multiplied by these adjustment coefficients, then the true capacity-increasing coefficient in terms of the efficiency value of equipments would be from 0.9 to 1.12, again becoming almost unity. Fifth, although Tsuru once estimated the capacity-increasing coefficient of *gross* investment in producer durables in *real* terms as 0.7, the fact that it is 0.7 in gross terms gives us the impression that the capacity-increasing coefficient of *net* investment in producer durables (excl. of replacement; this coefficient is the reciprocal of Tsuru's " gross stock ratio " and not of his " net stock ratio ") is rather larger than unity.

The above outlines the work of Shimomura's conversion, but it is clear that according to his revision (the capacity-increasing coefficient of "net" investment = unity) he would have to admit that the capacity-

137

increasing coefficient of gross private investment in producer durables would be rather 0.7. His analysis based on the net concept will be explained in the following section, but the variability of the capacity-increasing coefficient of gross investment in producer durables must now be admitted, by assuming changes in the proportion of replacement investment in total producer durables investment. However, Shimomura still adheres to the constancy of the capacity-increasing coefficient of net investment in producer durables.

6. *The Expansionist Policy of the Ikeda Cabinet and the Shimomura Plan*

After the Growth Controversy explained above, the Ikeda cabinet appeared on the scene (July 1960), and the program of Shimomura who is an economic consultant of Premier Ikeda entered the spotlight. In October 1960, the so-called Income-Doubling Plan was announced, whose content is the doubling of the real national income in ten years, with annual rate of growth of 7.2%. However, owing to the appearance of the Ikeda cabinet, the first three years' growth rate was raised to 9%. This was a compromise between the Income-Doubling Plan and the Shimomura Plan which will be discussed here.

Table 4 summarizes the formal aspects of his plan. The *GNP* growth rate ranges from 11 to 9%. First, investment in gross private producer's durables (col. 1) are given. From them, the replacement investment will be deducted according to an estimated proportion increasing from 11% to 20%, in order to arrive at the net private investment in producer's durables. As the capacity-increasing coefficient of net investment in producer durables is assumed to be unity, capacity next year is supposed to increase by the same value as net producer durables this year. The increments of capacity thus derived are compared with those of *GNP*, and $\Delta GNP/\Delta$Capacity is called here the " marginal demand-supply ratio ". The changes in this ratio were reflected in the changes in wholesale prices for 1952–59, and we see a close correlation between (5) and (6).

Table 4. Growth Rate and the Capacity-Increasing Coefficient in the Shimomura Plan

unit: 100 billion yen

Fisc. year	Private producer's durables (1)	Proportion of replacement investment (%) (2)	ΔCapacity (3)	ΔGNP (4)	Marginal demand-supply ratio (4÷3) (5)	Rate of change of wholesale prices (6)	GNP (7)	ΔGNP/GNP (%) (8)	Marginal gross fixed capital-output ratio. (incl. public invest.) (9)
1951	6.1	11	5.4	6.7	1.2	−1.4	54.4	12.3 (10.5)	1.9
1952	7.1	11	6.3	9.6	1.5	+2.4	61.2	15.7 (6.7)	1.6
1953	8.0	11	7.1	3.6	0.5	−2.9	70.8	5.1 (3.9)	4.1
1954	7.6	11	6.8	7.6	1.1	−0.5	74.4	10.2 (10.1)	2.2
1955	7.8	11	6.9	10.5	1.5	+6.2	82.0	12.8 (8.2)	2.1
1956	13.7	12	12.1	7.8	0.6	−0.4	92.5	8.4 (7.1)	3.5
1957	16.8	12	14.8	2.6	0.2	−5.6	100.3	2.6 (3.7)	10.6
1958	16.0	13	13.9	19.6	1.4	+2.3	102.9	19.0 (17.0)	1.8
1959	20.0	13	17.4	13.5	0.8		122.5	11.0	2.9
1960	23.5	15	20.0	15.0	0.8		136.0	11.0	2.9
1961	26.0	15	22.1	18.0	0.8		151.0	11.9	2.8
1962	26.8	16	22.5	20.0	0.9		169.0	11.8	2.8
1963	27.6	16	23.2	21.2	0.9		189.0	11.2	2.9
1964	28.5	17	23.7	22.5	0.9		210.2	10.7	3.0
1965	30.5	17	25.3	24.0	0.9		232.7	10.3	3.1
1966	33.0	18	27.1	24.5	0.9		256.7	9.5	3.3
1967	36.0	19	29.2	26.5	0.9		281.2	9.4	3.3
1968	39.0	20	31.2	28.1	0.9		307.7	9.1	3.4
1969	42.0	20	33.7	30.1	0.9		335.8	9.0	
1970	44.0	20					365.9		

Source: Osamu Shimomura, " Fundamentals in the Growth Policy " (in Japanese), *Riron Keizaigaku*, March 1961.

Note: *ΔGNP/GNP* in column (8) is shown in real terms in the brackets. Otherwise it is in money terms.

From this he speculates that the unity marginal demand-supply ratio represents a rather slight falling tendency of prices, and so assumes the future marginal demand-supply ratio to be 0.8–0.9 in order not to bring about inflation. In other words, he supposes that not all the increments of capacity but only about 80–90% of them will be supported by the increase in *GNP*. And yet, *GNP* can maintain a high growth rate, 11–9%, and attain an increase of 2.7 times in the ten years, 1960–70. On the other hand, exports are supposed to increase by 2.6 times, and the marginal propensity to import is assumed to be 9%. The rapid development of *GNP*, investment in producer durables and exports is thus to be accomplished without bringing about rises in wholesale prices or balance of payments difficulties.

In relation to the Growth Controversy, this program has the following features.

1) For 1951–55, the proportion of replacement investment (2) is assumed to be 11% and the capacity-increasing coefficient of net investment in producer durables to be 1, so the capacity-increasing coefficient of gross investment in producer durables is implicitly assumed to be 0.89. Moreover, the proportion of replacement investment in this plan will rise to 20% after ten years, so the implicit capacity-increasing coefficient of gross investment in producer durables is assumed to fall to 0.8.

2) Further, the marginal demand-supply ratio is assumed to be 0.8~0.9 for this period, so the implicit ΔGNP/gross *PD* will be $(0.89{\sim}0.80) \times (0.8{\sim}0.9) = (0.68{\sim}0.80)$. This suggests that in the new Shimomura plan the consequences of the Growth Controversy have been in large measure taken into consideration.

3) However, the cumulative totals of increase in capacity and increase in *GNP* for 1952–56 are ¥3.25 trillion and ¥3.8 trillion respectively, and the latter total is larger by 17% than the former.

4) As Tsuru pointed out, the capacity-increasing coefficient of gross investment in producer durables *in real terms* is computed as about 0.7 for 1951–57, while in this plan the implicit gross coefficient is supposed to be 0.89 (0.8 even after adjusting the marginal demand-supply ratio).

5) Although Shimomura seems to have maintained his position

that the capacity-increasing coefficient of *net* investment in producer durables is unity and constant, he admits its gradual decline in terms of gross investment. And in terms of the marginal gross fixed capital-output ratio (incl. of public investment), it must rise from 1.9 in 1951 through 2.9 in 1960 to 3.5 in 1970.

6) Shimomura assumed that the marginal demand-supply ratio $\Delta GNP/\Delta$Capacity would be 0.8 for 1960–62, and 0.9 for 1963–70, so the cumulative total of increases in productive capacity will become ¥27.54 trillion and that of increases in *GNP* ¥24.3 trillion, thus bringing about an excess capacity of ¥3.2 trillion. In his plan, the accumulation of such excess capacity is assumed to be normal.

7) Be that as it may, his point is the continuation of the extraordinary high rate of growth. However, his capacity-increasing coefficient of gross investment in producer durables implicitly assumed before 1960 is a little higher than our estimate. If it is assumed to be 0.7 and declining since then, a bit moderate plan than his may be called for.

Much more important in his plan than the above is his prophesy on the future agricultural population. According to his plan, the working population in primary industry (incl. mining) is supposed to diminish to one-third in ten years. (Premier Ikeda's amendment " to 40% " was due to the recalculation on the assumption of a 9% growth rate for the first three years and a 7.2% growth rate afterward).

His projection is as follows : When the real gross national product increases to 2.7 times the 1960 level, industrial production is assumed to increase to 3.8 times in the ten years. This figure is computed by assuming varying elastisities of industrial production (*O*) with respect to *GNP*, and this elasticity ($\Delta O/O \div \Delta GNP/GNP$) is supposed to decline from 1.63 to 1.22 in 1960–70. Shimomura computes the increase in the working population in three industries (manufacturing, construction industry, and service industry) on the assumption of the following employment elasticities in those industries with respect to industrial production.

The demand for labor in the three industries thus computed, however, surpasses the supply of labor considerably. The excess

141

demand cannot but be provided by the migration of labor from primary industry (incl. of mining). Thus, the working population in primary industry must diminish from 15,750 thousand in 1960 to 4,560 thousand (to less than one-third!). This is a main contour of the startling program which aroused hot debate in the economic as well as political field.

$$
\begin{bmatrix} \text{Industrial} \\ \text{growth rate} \end{bmatrix} \rightarrow
\begin{cases}
\begin{array}{l} \text{Employment elast. in} \\ \text{mfg.} \end{array} & 0.47\sim0.43\rightarrow & \begin{array}{l}\text{Estimate of working} \\ \text{population in mfg.}\end{array} \\
\begin{array}{l}\text{Employment elast. with} \\ \text{respect to mfg. prod.} \\ \text{in construction ind.}\end{array} & 0.48\sim0.43\rightarrow & \begin{array}{l}\text{Estimate of working} \\ \text{population in} \\ \text{construction industry}\end{array} \\
\begin{array}{l}\text{Employment elast. with} \\ \text{respect to mfg. prod.} \\ \text{in service ind.}\end{array} & 0.48\sim0.78\rightarrow & \begin{array}{l}\text{Estimate of working} \\ \text{population in service} \\ \text{industry}\end{array}
\end{cases}
$$

The following criticisms can be presented:

1) Even if the growth rate and the various employment elasticities assumed by Shimomura are correct, and the demand for labor in the secondary and tertiary industries will appear as his program predicts, there will arise a problem whether the farmers themselves will move to the urban district as the plan anticipates. In order to examine this question, it is necessary to refer to the variation in the agricultural working population classified by ages for 1950–55. As Table 5 shows, younger persons occupy a dominant proportion in the total decrease in the agricultural labor force in these five years. The young less then 24 years of age were about 90% of the total male decrease amounting to 704 thousand, and even more than 100% of the total female decrease amounting 518 thousand. But, instead of the migrating labor force, if we examine the age composition of the existing total agricultural working population, then 78.5% of the total labor force (14,911 thousand) belongs to the ages above 25, and 47% to those more than 40 years old. The fact that the exodus of the young from the villages occurs under the conditions of the aging of the agricultural labor force, presents us a serious problem. In prewar times, the second and third sons deserted the villages, but recently even the heir does so, thus it seems to be inevitable that the age composition of the agricultural population will become more and more top-heavy.

142

Table 5.   Age Composition of the Agricultural Working Population for 1950–55

unit: thousand

	Age	1950	1955	Changes
Male	More than 14	7,819	7,115	−704 (100.0)
	14—19	1,149	665	−484 (68.8)
	20—24	989	834	−155 (21.9)
	25—39	1,921	1,988	+ 67
	40—59	2,550	2,283	−167
	more than 60	1,208	1,245	+ 37
Female	More than 14	8,314	7,796	−518 (100.0)
	14—19	1,083	686	−397 (76.6)
	20—24	1,190	1,017	−178 (34.4)
	25—39	2,670	2,674	+ 4
	40—59	2,579	2,628	+ 50
	more than 60	790	789	− 1
Total	More than 14	16,133	14,911	−1,222 (100.0)
	14—19	2,232	1,351	−881 (72.1)
	20—24	2,179	1,851	−328 (26.8)
	25—39	4,591	4,662	+ 71
	40—59	5,128	5,011	−117
	more than 60	1,998	2,034	+ 36

Source: The Conference for Promoting Productivities in Agriculture, Forestry and Fisheries, *Nihonnogyo Kisotokei* (Basic Statistics for Japanese Agriculture), 1958, p. 158.

Such a tendency can clearly be recognized in the 1960 Census of Agriculture and Forestry. The decrease of persons less than 19 years old for 1955–60 accounted for 85% of the total decrease in the farm population of the same period.

Will things go successfully, if those who remain in the villages are only the aged and women when the numbers of farmers are reduced to one-third or 40% after ten years, considering that those who migrate are dominantly the young? Just when an " agricultural revolution ", the rapid advance in the agricultural productivity, is necessary and urgent in order to lessen the income gap between industry and agriculture, it will be a tragedy to see that those who should perform this work will merely be the aged and women. Of course, so as to reduce the agricultural labor force to 1/3 or 40%, some of the aged and women also must move to urban districts. However, it will cause trouble, for the peculiarity of the Japanese labor market is such that the large firms restrict their new employment to new graduates in principle. Therefore, it is too optimistic to think that the performance of the expansionist policy will automatically entail unprecedented migration without any friction, and reduce the income gap between industry and agriculture. It is clear that cautions and positive policies must be executed in order to expect such a radical migration.

2) Although we assumed Shimomura's employment elasticities, are they really correct? He assumed the employment elasticities as 4.7~4.3 in case of manufacturing, and as 4.8~7.8% in case of the service industry. He derived these elasticities, using the Labor Force Survey conducted by the Statistics Bureau of the Prime Minister's Office. But, the labor force consists of " employees " and " proprietors and family workers ". In the computation of these elasticities, however, he depended on the figures of " employees ", and actually attempted to estimate the trend of the " labor force " in a wider concept. But, in such a rapid economic expansion, there occurred and will occur a higher rate of increase in the number of " employees " than of the " labor force ", because the proportion of " proprietors and family workers " will decline. The employment elasticities were thus computed on figures biased toward a higher rate of increase, so that the estimated " labor force " was actually a projection in some kind of the past trend of " employees ". Such an estimate of future labor force (from the demand side) will naturally be overbiased.

The increase in " labor force " for 1953–58 was 1.275 times (8,620 thousand / 6,760 thousand), but that of " employees " for the same period was 1.396 times (6840 thousand / 4900 thousand), according to the Labor Force Survey. Therefore, it is clear that the increase rate of the number of " employees " is higher than that of labor force. Although the employment elasticity in manufacturing was computed as 0.47~0.43 in the Shimomura plan, our computation of it based on the 1951–59 figures of the index of manufacturing production and "labor force" gives us 0.18. Of course, this is merely a tentative computation based on the comparison of two years only, but seems to suggest that the estimate of the demand for labor in manufacturing was too high. The same check can be done in relation to the estimate of "labor force" in tertiary industry. The labor force in tertiary industry increased by 44.3% from 11,370 thousand in 1951 to 16,400 thousand in 1959. When this is compared with the increase rate of manufacturing production 193.5%, then the employment elasticity in the tertiary industry with respect to manufacturing production becomes 0.229 (44.3% / 193.5%). Nevertheless, in the Shimomura plan, this elasticity is assumed to be 0.48–0.78. Thus, our examination will be of some help in making clear the background of the remarkable argument for a radically diminishing agricultural population that Shimomura presented.

However, Shimomura will reply to such a criticism as follows: Since 1959, the employment elasticity with respect to manufacturing production seems to have shown a sudden rise, so the past " employees " - " production " relation can be projected without much error to the future " labor force " - " production " relation. This may be true, for according to the short report of the 1959 Census of Manufactures (covering establishments with 30 employees and over) the increase in the number of employees in 1958–59 was 15.2%. As the increase in manufacturing production was 25.9%, the employment elasticity was 0.59. This may be an overestimate, for it does not include establishments with 30 employees and over, but it may be a good evidence of a sudden change in the elasticity. However, whether this is a temporary phenomenon or not, is not clear. Although in relation to manufacturing employment such an apology may be given, no justification can be possible concerning the employment estimate in tertiary industry.

The conclusion is now evident. First, assume that Shimomura's estimate of the demand for labor in the secondary and tertiary industries were correct, then the resistance of the farmers to migration would make the labor force a bottleneck in the rapid growth program, and the growth rate cannot but slow down. Second, provided that he admits an overestimation of employment elasticities and corrects it downwards, then rapid growth will be at least possible on his plan. However, it is completely impossible that the agricultural labor force will be reduced to 1/3 or 40% in ten years. Thus, his plan involves a fatal defect.

3) In view of the sharp controversy concerning his reduction-of-agricultural labor force program, Premier Ikeda made an interesting statement during the election campaign. He stated that as the proportion of the side-work farmers (the non-agricultural incomes of whom are higher than their agricultural incomes) will increase in the future, we will arrive at the same situation automatically as if the agricultural labor force decreased to 40%. However, in the Labor Force Survey, the families working in other industries (in case of the side-work farmers) are dealt with as if they actually were working in other industries, and not in agriculture. When the same person works in agriculture and non-agriculture at the same time, he is assumed to be engaged in the industry in which his labor hours are longer. Such being the case, almost all of the side-work farmers are already treated as engaging in non-agriculture, so even when they lose the colour of agriculture completely, the supply of labor will not rise in order to satisfy the demand from the non-agricultural sector. In the Shimomura plan, the decrease of the agricultural labor force is supposed to arise perfectly due to the increasing demand for labor in other industries. However, the Ikeda statement employed the peculiar logic that the sidework farmers who will not satisfy the demand for labor in other industries will gradually disappear. These seems to be a great discrepancy between the Shimomura plan and the Ikeda statement.

Shimomura's new arguments are still being published in connection with the problem of the balance of payments deficits, the 1960–61 recession and so on, but the above summary and my criticism will give some idea to those foreigners who want to know the characteristics of his analysis. Even if his analysis has various defects and the techniques used are not so refined, he is one of a few economists who insisted the potentiality of 10% growth rate and who has had a strong influence upon the economic policy of the Ikeda

Cabinet. Moreover, the contents of his argument are extremely provocative and interesting. I believe that his argument will be of interest even to foreigners, as far as they are curious about the extraordinary high rate of economic growth in postwar Japan. This is why I have attempted to include one chapter dealing with the " Growth Controversy ".

PART II
CYCLES

CHAPTER 6

POSTWAR BUSINESS CYCLES

1. Have the Juglar Cycles Disappeared?

Although we can clearly recognize the regularity of three to four year cycles in the postwar period, nobody will accept the existence of the Juglar cycle the duration of which is about ten years. In the postwar years in which rehabilitation factors strongly prevailed, it may be difficult to find a ten year cycle. Moreover, we have not sufficiently long data to dig up such a swing, for only fifteen or sixteen years of time series are available to us. In such an economy as Japan's, where the rate of growth is exceedingly high, it is especially impossible to find such cycles from the *absolute* figures of the time series.

However, as the Juglar cycle seems to be a cycle of fixed investment and the absolute figures do not show any cycle of ten year duration, we have examined the private producer's durables / GNP ratio as depicted in Fig. 1.

It is surprising to see in the chart that the PD/GNP ratio indicates a rise until 1952 and then a decline until 1955. This suggests that this ratio shows about ten years duration from the immediate postwar depth. In this cycle, the upswing was 6–7 years in length and the downswing was three years (for 1952–55). From 1955, this ratio again follows an upswing until 1961 with a temporary standstill in 1958. It is not clear whether or not 1961 will be a peak, but in view of the fact that in the 1945–1955 cycle the upswing continued for 6–7 years, we should pay attention to 1961 when 6 years has already elapsed since 1955. The PD/GNP ratio shows a continuously rising trend and it may be that the postwar years so far are just the upswing of the long cycle. However, it seems to be interesting

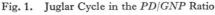

Fig. 1.   Juglar Cycle in the *PD/GNP* Ratio

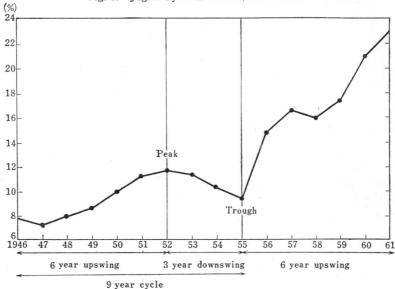

also to see that 1961 or 1962 should be the upper-turning point of the 10 year cycle, at least from the standpoint of a mechanical judgment based on the periodicity or the assumption of the regularity of the business cycle.   Furthermore, it seems to me that the rising trend of the *PD/GNP* ratio is likely to taper off at about the 1961 level, for such a high ratio cannot be found in other countries and it may not continue to rise forever in Japan.

2. *Periodicity of the Minor Cycle*

In each cycle, we find some specific causes which brought about it ; the Korean War, the Suez Incident, a tight money policy, *etc.*, yet we had fairly regular minor cycles of three to four years duration in the postwar period.   In Fig. 2, we have a business cycle barometer compiled by the Bank of Japan for 1951–59, by which we understand that in each minor cycle, the length of the downswing was always 16 months, while the length of the upswing became longer, from

Fig. 2.   Business Cycle Barometer of the Bank of Japan

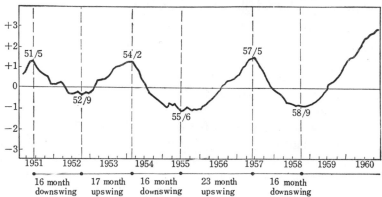

Source :   The Bank of Japan, *Wagakuni no Keikihendoshihyo* (Business Cycle Barometer in Japan), September 1959.

17 months in 1953 upswing to 23 months in the 1956 upswing. Probably, in the 1959–60 boom, the length of upswing has been a bit further prolonged.

If forty months are looked upon as the standard length of the minor cycle as are often done, then the upswing length of 17 months in the 1953 boom is too short, and the cycle from 1955 to 1958 fits almost correctly the standard length, for 23 months plus 16 months makes 39 months.   Probably, the length of the 1959–62 cycle will be a little longer than the standard.

Incidentally, the Bank of Japan's index of Business Cycle Barometer is a weighted average of 16 indices on the statistics of currency supply, bank clearings, volume of loans, commodity prices, shipments, transportation volume, employment, wages, consumption, foreign trade, *etc.*, and both the trend and the seasonal, irregular fluctuations are adjusted out of it.

3.   Some Characteristics of the Postwar Minor Cycles

We can mention a few characteristics in relation to the postwar cycles, although they may not be peculiar to the postwar Japanese economy.

First, the role of inventory fluctuations has been extremely important. Table 1 compares the inventory investment / GNP ratios in four countries, and shows that Japan's ratio is overwhelmingly high. The average ratio for 1951–58 was 6.5% for Japan, while the ratios for other countries were less than 2.4%. If so, it is clear that the inventory changes have had a much greater influence than in other countries.

Then, what are the reasons for the high inventory investment / GNP ratio in Japan? Before going into discussion of this ratio, it is necessary to consider the level of inventory ratio (in case of individual firms, the inventory-scales ratio). According to the research of the Statistics Bureau of the Bank of Japan, the ratio for manufacturing was 2.78 in the latter half of 1939, and 2.65 in the latter half of 1959, while it was 1.67 in the United States in the third quarter of 1957 according to the surveys of Federal Trade Commission and the Securities and Exchange Commission.

Table 1. International Comparison of Inventory Investment-GNP Ratio

	Japan	U.S.A.	U.K.	W. Germany
1951	12.0	2.8	4.5	4.4
1952	7.4	0.7	0.4	3.8
1953	8.1	0.1	0.8	1.5
1954	4.2	—0.4	0.3	1.1
1955	8.1	1.6	1.8	3.0
1956	7.0	1.4	1.5	1.3
1957	7.0	0.3	1.9	2.0
1958	—1.7	—1.1	0.2	1.9
Average	6.5	0.7	1.4	2.4

Sources: Japan . . . . E. P. A., *Kokumin Shotoku Hakusho* (National Income Report), 1961.

U.K. . . . . Central Statistical Office, *National Income and Expenditure*, 1959.

U.S.A. . . . *Economic Report of President*, Jan. 1959.

W. Germany . *Statistisches Jahrbuch für die Bundesrepublik Deutschland*, 1959.

Therefore, the first problem to be examined lies in the higher inventory-*GNP* ratio in Japan. We can enumerate five reasons :

1) As the growth rate in Japan is extremely high, this may give firms an optimistic view that even if they hold a large volume of inventories, stocks will soon be sold. In such circumstances, the firm's inventory-sales ratio will naturally go up.

2) Japan depends greatly for basic raw materials on foreign countries, and this will necessarily raise the inventory ratio for raw materials.

3) So far, we have had a foreign currency quota system, so that firms cannot help but raise their inventory ratios because they cannot import raw materials whenever they like. This hypothesis can be tested against the recent tendency of the inventory ratio to decline in anticipation of the coming liberalization of foreign trade.

4) In Japan, we have not so well-organized a net work of highways, and the roads are very bad and narrow, so it consumes much time for commodities to move from factory to factory, and the stocks in factories, warehouses, stations and in transit will become larger.

5) In such an economy as Japan where the number of small firms is so great, inventory holdings will necessarily be larger than under the hypothetical condition in which firms were consolidated.

The inventory ratio raised for these reasons will affect the inventory investment / *GNP* ratio in the following way. Denoting inventories by V, inventory investment will be ΔV. The inventory ratio in the economy as a whole is V/GNP. When V/GNP is assumed to be constant, then the marginal inventory ratio $\Delta V/\Delta GNP$ is also constant. Now, in the following identity,

$$\frac{\Delta V}{GNP} \equiv \frac{\Delta V}{\Delta GNP} \cdot \frac{\Delta GNP}{GNP},$$

the higher the *GNP* growth rate ($\Delta GNP/GNP$), the higher the inventory investment / *GNP* ratio ($\Delta V/GNP$), given the marginal inventory ratio ($\Delta V/\Delta GNP$). Thus, $\Delta V/GNP$ is doubly influenced by the high rate of growth. First, the marginal inventory ratio itself is a function of the growth rate. Second, in the above identity, $\Delta V/GNP$ depends upon the numerical value of $\Delta GNP/GNP$.

155

If we do not like to use the assumption that the average and the marginal inventory ratios are the same, then we may use the identity

$$\frac{\Delta V}{GNP} \equiv \frac{V}{GNP} \cdot \frac{\Delta V}{V}.$$

In this case, the growth rate of inventories $\Delta V/V$ may not be equal to $\Delta GNP/GNP$. However, in an economy where $\Delta GNP/GNP$ is extremely high, $\Delta V/V$ will also be high. Thus, it seems to be correct to assume that $\Delta V/GNP$ is high in an economy where the growth rate is high.

4. Downward Rigidity in Fixed Investment

When the fixed investment behavior in the postwar recessions is compared with that of the prewar period, we find that some fundamental changes have taken place. In Table 2, we see how in the recessions of the prewar period fixed investment was flexible downward, and how in those of the postwar period it is inflexible downward. For instance, in 1929–30, total gross investment in producer's durable equipment fell by 17.8% and in 1930–31, it fell by 31%, while in 1957–58 in the postwar period the decline of private producer's durables was only 2.5%.

Why has fixed investment increased rapidly in booms, but failed to decline easily in the recessions after the war? The first reason for the downward inflexibility of fixed investment may lie in the postwar rehabilitation effect. Second, the prevalence of technological innovation stimulated an immense investment demand, thus considerably increasing the backlog of unfilled orders for capital goods. Therefore, even the decline in new orders for capital goods in recessions had not a great influence upon deliveries of capital goods. Third, the existence of strong financial props to the big firms from the banks seems to have contributed to the downward rididity of fixed investment. Treasury investment and large scale loans have also contributed to it. Fourth, the cutthroat competition among firms in the oligopolistic industries pushed up the level of fixed in-

156

Table 2. Downward Rigidity in Fixed Investment

		Total gross fixed investment	Private gross producer's durables
Booms	1950–51 (F.Y.)	+49.1 %	+56.4 %
	1955–56 (″)	+45.8	+76.1
	1958–59 (″)	+26.6	+32·4
		Total gross fixed investment	Total gross producer's durable equipment
	1919–20 (C.Y.)	+ 19.9 %	+27.5 %
		Total gross fixed investment	Private gross producer's durables
Recessions	1951–52 (F.Y.)	+20.5 %	+16.8 %
	1953–54 (″)	− 4.0	− 5.1
	1957–58 (″)	+ 1.7	− 2.5
		Total gross fixed investment	Total gross producer's durable equipment
	1920–21 (C.Y.)	−19.0 %	−29.9
	1929–30 (″)	−23.6	−17.8
	1930–31 (″)	−23.0	−31.0

Sources : The figures for the prewar period come from the author's estimate by means of the commodity flow method (See *pp*. 178–202 in K. Ohkawa and others, *The Growth Rate of the Japanese Economy since 1878*, Tokyo, 1957, and the postwar figures were computed from the E.P.A., *Kokumin Shotoku Hakusho* (National Income Report).

Notes : 1) All the rates of increase are based upon current price data.
2) Private producer's durables includes business construction in addition to private producer's durable equipment.

vestment, for the most easiest procedure for expanding their market shares and of getting foreign currency quotas for raw material imports consisted in raising the level of fixed investment. Once the government economic plan was set up, each firm tried to invest far greater funds than the target rate of the economic plan. Such a brisk investment activity was also in background of the downward inflexibility of fixed investment in postwar recessions.

157

5. 'Increase Rate' Cycle

In such a speedily growing economy as Japan, the cycles tend to be embodied not in the *levels* of industrial production but in its 'increase rate', for the steeper the trend, the more obscure the recession in production, as far as the indices are expressed in *annual* series. Even in recessions, the level of industrial production will rise to some extent, and only the rate of increase of production will decline.

Fig. 3 shows that the index of manufacturing and mining production followed an unceasing increase for the entire span of the postwar years, but we see very clear cyclical fluctuations in the rates of increase of output and imports. In boom years; the Korean War in 1951, the so-called 'Jimmu Boom' in 1956–7, *etc.*, the increase rate became larger, and in recessions; 1949–50, 1952, 1954–55, and 1958, it became smaller. Compared with the increase rate of manufacturing and mining production, that of the machinery industry seems to have shown a wider oscillation. This is seemingly due to the acceleration principle which explains why the production of

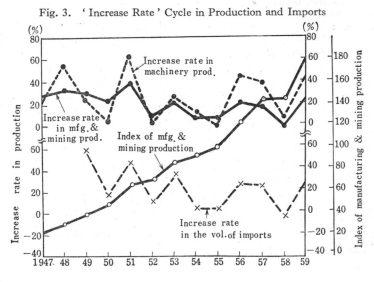

Fig. 3. 'Increase Rate' Cycle in Production and Imports

capital goods oscillates more severely than general production activity. Assuming a constant relation between fixed capital K_f and output, its marginal relation $\Delta K_f/\Delta O$ will also be constant. If we assume further that the production of capital goods is performed only by the machinery industry, then we can arrive at conclusion that even the absolute level of machinery production ΔK_f will fall when the *increment* of the general production level decreases, provided that we assume away here machinery production for replacement purposes. If this fact is taken into consideration, it is clear why machinery production is more oscillatory than total or consumer goods production.

However, in Fig. 3, two problems remain : 1). the rate of increase of machinery production is never negative, 2) in the 1957–58 recession the rate of increase of machinery production began to surpass that of manufacturing and mining production. The first point can

Table 3. ' Increase Rate ' Cycle of Machinery Production

	Mach. prod. (excl. electric, instrumental, and transp. machineries)	Machinery products			
		Standard induction motors	Spinnery frames (cotton and rayon staple)	Steel vessels (started)	Machine tools
1947	30.9 %	%	895.4 %	%	15.7 %
1948	58.5		180.4		45.2
1949	35.7		140.8	114.8	−17.0
1950	−10.7		21.8	−20.0	−39.5
1951	91.2	23.3	199.1	84.3	126.3
1952	−9.1	−15.9	−46.6	−11.8	26.8
1953	28.5	39.4	−32.4	−13.3	61.6
1954	6.9	16.0	40.5	−16.8	−3.2
1955	−5.2	−30.1	−47.9	130.5	0.1
1956	31.8	90.7	219.5	84.8	54.7
1957	26.9	43.5	−68.7	26.5	24.1
1958	−1.0	−45.8	−9.6	−26.8	−6.2
1959	24.2	67.6	32.4	4.5	46.5

Source : Ministry of International Trade and Industry.

be understood if we take into account of the existence of replacement production of machinery and the production of consumer durables which is unaffected by the working of the acceleration principle. The second point can be judged by the increasing proportion of consumer durables in total machinery production after 1956.

In order to make clear the first point, let us examine the ' increase rate ' cycle of machinery production excluding consumer durables, and of four machinery products in Table 3. In this table, it is surprising to see how frequently we come across the negative rates of increase in depression years. Especially in 1957, the increase rate of spinning frames became (−) 68.7%. In these alternations of plus and minus rates of change, we see the full working of the acceleration principle. This relation was extremely blurred in the behavior of total machinery production after 1956, when the share of consumer durables had considerably increased (the index of production

Table 4. Rates of Increase of Industrial Production and Imports

	Increase rate of mfg. and mining production (a)	Increase rate of the volume of imports (b)	Import elasticity with respect to production [b/a] (c)	Imports ———— Production (d)
1949	22.9 %	57.3 %	1.92 %	92.0 %
1950	22.5	17.1	0.76	87.8
1951	38.2	46.0	1.20	93.6
1952	7.2	10.2	1.42	96.3
1953	22.1	35.9	1.62	107.1
1954	8.4	3.6	0.43	102.4
1955	7.6	5.1	0.67	100.0
1956	22.4	27.0	1.21	103.8
1957	18.1	24.7	1.36	109.6
1958	0.2	−21.5	−107.50	85.8
1959	24.1	32.1	1.33	91.4

Sources : 1) Manufacturing and Mining production : Ministry of International Trade and Industry data.

2) The volume of imports : E. P. A., Research Section's index until 1951, and the Ministry of Finance, Customs Bureau index, later.

of consumer durables increased for 1956–60 by 3.89 times).

Another conspicuous relation in Fig. 3 is a similar movement in the rates of production and imports. This may be a representation of the tautological relation that when industrial production increases, imports, particularly those of raw materials, will also increase. However, a careful look at the graph will suggest the rates of change of imports are far more variable than those of industrial production. Table 4 computes the imports / industrial production ratios and the import elasticity of production. It is very evident that the elasticity declines in 1950 (the so-called Dodge deflation), 1954–55 (deflationary policy), and 1958 (a recession after the so-called 'Jimmu' boom) and rises in boom years. 1952 is the only exception, but if quarterly data were used, we should be able to find the above relationship.

6. Cycle in the Proportional Composition

Although the cycle is difficult to find in the curve of real output, we see it in the proportional composition of *GNP*. Recently, any projection based upon the input-output table depends upon the stability of the group of average coefficients. However, very often the average coefficients of various kinds will undergo a substantial change even during the short-run cycles. Not only the average but also the marginal coefficient may suffer from cyclical changes.

A simple example can be given in relation to the changes in the composition of aggregate demand. In this case, aggregate demand is equal to the sum of *GNP* plus imports. Fig. 4 shows how various coefficients follows cyclical changes. The import ratio increased steeply from 4.8% in 1946 to 11.3% in 1951, and from then on we see only a cyclical fluctuation. The inventory investment ratio fell in the depressions of 1949, 1954, and 1958, while the personal consumption ratio increased in each case.

It may be interesting to explore the empirical behavior of the composition of demand, not only in the macro-field, but also in the various input coefficients among various industries. For instance, if it

Fig. 4. Proportional Compositions of Aggregate Demand

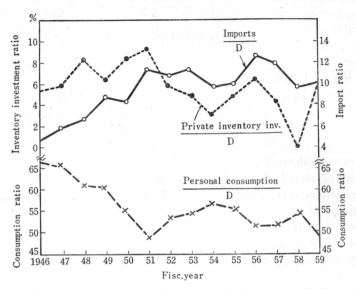

is correct to assume that machinery production (as capital goods) is far more variable than the production of construction materials, then the allocation ratio of rolled steel to construction activity may increase in depressions, while the same ratio of rolled steel to machinery industry will rise in the boom. We are not certain whether or not such a relation is universal, but it seems to be important to examin this proportion, not only for the study of the peculiarities of the economy, but also as one of the materials for short-run economic forecasting. Where we would like to establish some functional relation, it is useful first to compute the average coefficient and examine its fluctuations empirically. From such a study, some function, like the Modigliani type of saving function, for example, may be found to be appropriate.

Such is an observation of the postwar business cycle from only a few aspects. However, since we are much more interested in the aspects of the inventory cycle, in the next two chapters a study of their aspects will be taken up.

162

CHAPTER 7

PATTERNS OF INVENTORY CYCLES AND
CHANGES IN THE IMPORT RATIO

Postwar Japanese inventory cycles have many interesting aspects worthy of careful analysis. Particularly important is the fact that the inventory cycle of the small business always leads that of the big business. However, we are going to analyze this problem in the next chapter. In this chapter, the patterns of inventory cycles will first be discussed by industry and by type (*e.g.*, by finished commodities, goods in process, and raw materials), and second, the relation between inventory changes and changes in the import ratio will be taken up.

In any country, changes in inventory investment occupy a fairly large proportion of the changes of *GNP*, as far as the upswing or downswing in minor cycles of about forty months duration is concerned. In Japan too, this incremental ratio has been very large. For instance, in the upswing from July–September of 1954 to April–June of 1957, the ratio amounted to 44.5%. This example suggests the importance of the inventory cycle in the causation of short-run business cycles.

In the postwar Japan, the inventory cycle seems especially important, in view of the fact that the ratio of inventory investment to *GNP* is extremely high. For example, its ratio was, on the average, 6.5% for 1951–56 in Japan, whereas the corresponding ratios were 0.7% in the United States, 1.4% in the United Kingdom and 2.5% in West Germany, as I have explained in the previous chapter. I feel therefore that the role of inventory fluctuations in economic changes has been much more important in Japan than in other countries.

CYCLES

1. Some Patterns of Inventory Cycles

Inventory investment is the current value of physical changes in inventories, and in the official national income statistics it is mainly estimated from the book-value statistics of inventory assets of various enterprises, as the Corporate Enterprise Survey, *etc.* However, we have another source of data on physical inventories of various commodity items, issued from the Ministry of International Trade and Industry. The latter agency also computes indexes of the volume of inventories. By using these data, we analyze 1) the mode of behavior of inventories and inventory investment, 2) the behavior patterns of inventory investment, broken down into finished commodities, goods in process, and raw materials, and 3) those of inventory investment by industry, also cross-classified by type.

First, it may be useful to compare the changes of the level of inventories with the changes of inventory investment. Fig. 1 is based on the Ministry of International Trade and Industry indices of the physical volume of inventories (with 1955=100), and the levels and the increments (or decrements) are compared in terms of index numbers. The results are shown after being smoothed by four quarter moving average. The observations derived are as follows:

1) As the growth rate of industrial production is very large in Japan, the level of inventories too shows a steep upward trend, in both finished commodities and raw materials. At the same time, we can clearly see cyclical behavior in them.

2) The ups and downs of inventory investment lead the cycles of inventories. When the level of inventories reaches its peak, the increment in inventories will be zero, thus the latter being near the bottom rather than the peak. The derivative of $y=\sin x$ is $dy/dx=\cos x$, so that we can easily speculate on the course of the increments of a time series with cyclical behavior.

3) If some trend line is fitted to each of the inventory series, and the deviations from these trends are computed, we see that the deviations are negative in the upswing and positive in the downswing. From this, we may assume that the ratios of inventories to sales or

164

Fig. 1.   The Relation of Inventories and Inventory Investment in Manufacturing
—4 quarter moving averages—

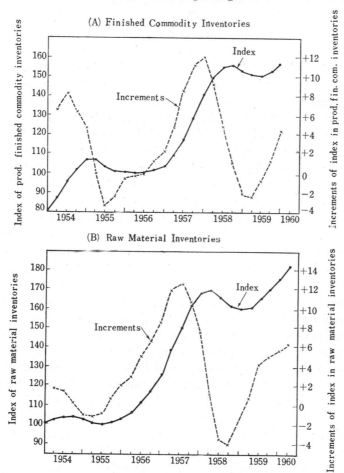

(A) Finished Commodity Inventories

(B) Raw Material Inventories

production will be inversely correlated to the business fluctuations,
or that they show so big a lag that we are tempted to believe that
they do move inversely.

4)   In comparison with the inventories of raw materials, those of
finished commodities lag behind by about two quarters.   Correspondingly, inventory investment in finished commodities too shows

a lag of about two quarters, as compared with that in raw materials.

Theoretically, inventory investment is often broken down into " intended " and " unintended " inventory investments. The reason why the finished commodity inventory investment lags behind that of raw materials is that in a recession in the former more unsold stocks (" unintended " one) are involved than in the latter.

In the inventory investment series for either finished commodities or raw materials, we see that the plus figures are overwhelmingly more numerous than the minus figures, and this is due to the steep rise in the inventory level itself, which is in turn made possible by the tremendously rapid rate of economic growth. Thus, one of the reasons why we see a higher inventory investment-*GNP* in Japan than in any other country can be sought in her rapid expansion.

The above are observations based on indices of the volume of inventories released by the Ministry of International Trade and Industry. However, we have another source of data based on book-values, among which particularly important is the Quarterly Report of the Corporate Enterprise Survey issued by the Ministry of Finance. Therefore, it may be interesting to check the results from the two data with each other. Fig. 2, A and B are the comparisons of the two results after being smoothed out by four quarter moving averages. Although the seasonally unadjusted series do not indicate a good coincidence between the two, it is to be noted that if they are adjusted by seasonal variations they indicate a fairly parallel movement.

We thus tested the two sources for mutual consistency, the next problem being to determine the difference, if any, in the behavior of investment in the different types of inventories,—finished commodities, goods in process and raw materials. Fig. 3 depicts the movement of investment in the three types of inventories, estimated from the Corporate Enterprise Survey, after they have been smoothed out by four quarter moving averages. From this, we find very clearly the existence of a lag in the peak and trough of the finished commodity inventory investment, as compared with the two other types. The goods-in-process inventory investment shows only a short lag behind raw material inventory investment, but much more noteworthy is the greater oscillation of the latter than the former in

Fig. 2. Comparison of the Corporate Enterprise Survey and the MITI's
Inventory Indexes in the Estimation of Inventory Investment
— 4 quarter moving averages —

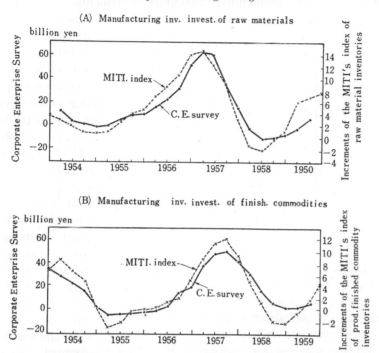

(A) Manufacturing inv. invest. of raw materials

(B) Manufacturing inv. invest. of finish. commodities

the 1956–57 boom.   In the trough of 1955, the lag between inventory
investment in finished commodities and in raw materials was one
quarter, in the peak of 1957 it was two quarters, and in the trough of
1958–59, we see a three quarter lag.   The reason of this gradually
prolonged lag is not clear.

Fig. 4 is a similar graph obtained from the Ministry of International
Trade and Industry indices of the volume of inventories, after they
are smoothed by four quarter moving averages.   In this case too,
we see an evident lag of finished commodity behind raw material
inventory investment.   However, unlike the case of Fig. 3, there
occurs a lag of two quarters, not three quarters, in the 1958 trough.
The greater oscillation of imported raw material inventory invest-

Fig. 3. Inventory Investment by Type in Manufacturing due to the Corporate Enterprise Survey

— 4 quarter moving averages —

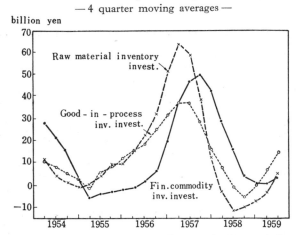

Sources: Computed from the Minstry of Finance, the Quarterly Reportos of the Corporate Enterprise Survey

ment than of total raw material inventory investment in the 1955–58 cycle, but their relatively parallel movements from 1959 on, are also interesting, in view of the probable psychological influence of the forth-coming liberalization of foreign trade upon inventory behavior. If import restrictions were taken away, manufacturers or merchants would be under reduced pressure to import foreign raw materials in a short period, so that the liberalization of trade may not only lessen the inventory ratio, but also mitigate the degree of oscillation of inventory investment, which might often be spurred by the strengthening of restrictions in balance of payments difficulties.

In the official national income statistics, inventory investment is not broken down into the detailed industries. Particularly, it is impossible to see its behaviors by subsectors of manufacturing industry. Therefore, we are going to estimate corporate inventory investment (for corporate enterprises with over ¥2 million paid-up capital)[1] by

1) This covers almost the whole of the corporate enterprises. According to the Annual Report of the Corporate Enterprise Survey in 1959, the proportion of inventories of corporate firms with under ¥2 million paid-up capital was only 16.5%.

Fig. 4.   Inventory Investment by Type (in terms of points on indexes) due to
the MITI's Indexes
— 4 quarter moving averages —

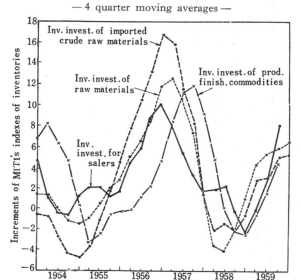

Sources :   Computed from the Ministry of International Trade and Industy,
various indexes of volume of inventories

subgroups of manufacturing as well as by size of firms, utilizing the
Ministry of Finance, Quarterly Report of the Corporate Enterprise
Survey.   Tables 1 and 2 represent these estimates.   From Table 1,
we see clearly that the peaks of inventory cycles are 1951, 1953, 1956–
7, and 1959 respectively, just corresponding to the actual movement
of business cycles.   The troughs, 1950, 1952, 1954, and 1958, also
represent those of the actual business fluctuations.

When examined by industry, the following points are made clear :
1)   For the boom years, 1951, 1956 and 1959, the industrial composition of inventory investment between the textile and the machinery
industry indicates a remarkable change.   On the one hand, in 1951,
the proportion of inventory investment in the textile industry in that
of manufacturing was 43.1%, falling to 29.7% in 1953, and to minus
4.1% in 1959.   On the other hand, the proportion in machinery industry was 29.4% in 1953, 43.9% in 1956, and 54.6% in 1959.

Table 1. Corporate Inventory Investment by Industry

Unit: billion yen

| Fiscal year | Manuf. ind. | Textile ind. | Machinery industry | | | | Metal industry | | | Chemical | Paper & allied prod. | Food | Construction ind. | Whole-sale & retail trades |
			Ma-chinery	Electric ma-chinery	Transp. equip.	Total	Prim. metals	Fabr. metal products	Total					
1950	-53.1												-20.3	
1951	325.4	140.4	-9.0	13.8			47.2	6.6	53.8	31.7		11.6	41.7	12.4
1952	24.7	-60.6	6.6	14.2			7 6	1.9	6.5	12.9		19.5	7.7	8.7
1953	190.6	56.6	10.6	28.5	16.9	56.0	47.8	4.2	52.0	3.5		21.3	30.2	143.1
1954	68.8	30.4	6.0	-.6	-13.0	-6.4	-5.5	2.0	-3.5	11.3	6.1	16.4	48.8	-51.0
1955	74.5	-45.5	-1.2	14.7	59.6	73.1	-11.3	-3.2	-14.5	13.3	1.3	16.4	11.6	61.4
1956	311.8	65.6	27.2	28.7	81.0	136.9	50.0	9.1	59.2	43.5	7.5	10.2	-1.7	166.6
1957	383.1	42.5	13.5	39.0	20.0	72.5	141.0	16.6	157.6	30.4	14.9	22.1	97.1	-5.9
1958	-28.4	8.4	4.8	-4.2	-45.1	-45.1	-19.8	-.2	-20.0	7.2	-5.8	6.5	-.3	40.2
1959	316.5	-12.9	19.4	89.0	64.5	172.9	78.5	16.9	95.4	51.0	13.6	-2.0	121.6	233.9

Note: Computed from the Quarterly Report of the Corporate Enterprise Survey each quarter, and then summed up by fiscal year. Adjusted for inventory valuation changes.

170

Unit: billion yen

Table 2. Corporate Inventory Investment by Industry by Type

Fisc. year	Manuf. ind.	Textile ind.	Machinery industry Machinery	Electric machinery	Transp. equip.	Total	Metal industry Prim. metals	Fabr. metal products	Total	Chemical	Paper & allied prod.	Food	Construction ind.
Inventory invest. in finished commod.													
1954	44.4	12.3	7.7	5.2	1.7	14.6	−6.7	1.9	−4.8	6.5	1.3	13.0	−.2
1955	−6.4	−21.8	−5.6	2.1	.3	−3.2	−6.6	−1.8	−8.4	4.1	.8	5.6	.5
1956	38.6	12.4	3.2	5.5	4.3	13.0	1.7	−.5	1.2	16.1	−2.3	7.5	−.8
1957	200.5	34.2	7.4	19.5	4.9	31.8	51.5	8.9	60.4	22.8	9.4	17.7	1.3
1958	6.7	−10.1	2.2	4.1	−.7	5.6	.3	0	.3	6.7	−4.5	.2	1.4
1959	84.3	−9.3	−1.6	29.5	6.7	34.6	16.6	9.4	26.0	23.4	6.2	.1	.6
Inventory invest. in goods-in-process													
1954	20.6	13.2	−3.0	4.2	8.5	−7.3	8.6	.5	9.1	.6	.7	.5	45.7
1955	41.1	−10.0	1.8	6.6	44.5	52.9	−5.6	−.9	−6.5	2.3	−.5	3.1	8.3
1956	110.4	19.2	12.3	12.4	45.0	69.7	13.4	3.2	16.6	5.5	.5	1.0	−7.2
1957	81.9	7.5	6.9	16.3	17.7	40.9	18.1	2.6	20.7	3.2	.9	1.9	94.5
1958	−12.2	.3	5.1	−3.0	−24.5	−22.4	−.9	1.5	.6	2.7	.1	.9	−8.2
1959	133.9	8.1	14.6	30.8	43.7	89.1	26.3	1.2	27.5	12.1	.5	−5.1	119.0
Inventory invest. in raw materials													
1954	4.0	5.1	1.2	1.7	−6.5	3.6	−7.5	.6	−8.1	4.0	4.3	2.6	3.2
1955	39.8	−13.7	2.7	6.2	14.7	23.6	1.0	.5	.5	6.9	1.1	7.9	2.9
1956	162.8	34.0	11.6	10.8	31.6	54.0	35.1	6.4	41.5	21.7	9.5	1.7	.5
1957	100.6	1.1	−.6	3.2	−2.7	−.1	71.5	5.0	76.5	4.5	4.5	2.7	1.3
1958	−23.0	18.8	−2.5	−5.4	−20.4	−28.3	−19.5	−1.9	−21.4	−2.0	−1.6	5.7	6.9
1959	98.7	−11.8	6.7	28.4	14.3	35.1	35.5	6.4	41.9	15.6	7.1	6.8	2.2

Note: See the note for Table 1. Adjusted for inventory valuation changes. The totals of the three types of inventory investment do not always coincide with the industrywise totals in Table 1, because of rounding.

171

Among the subgroups of the machinery industry, the inventory investment in electric machinery industry increased rapidly (¥28.5 billion in 1953, ¥39.0 billion in 1957 and ¥89.0 billion in 1959), reflecting the rapid expansion of production. Thus, the changing industrial structure will entail different behavior of inventory investments in different industries.

2) In textile industry, inventory investment decreased from ¥140.4 billion to minus ¥60.6 billion in 1951–52 just after the Korean war, amounting to a decline of ¥201.0 billion. This decline was 67% of the total decline in inventory investment for manufacturing as a whole, the latter decline being ¥300.7 billion. The textile industry, with such a dominant weight in total inventory adjustment, reduced its share in the later period. For 1958–59, for example, the increase in inventory investment in manufacturing was ¥344.9 billion (from minus ¥28.4 billion to ¥316.5 billion), and the share of machinery industry had become 63.2%, and that of the metal industry 33.5%.

3) Inventory investment in the construction industry consists mainly of the changes in goods-in-process (*i.e.*, the structures under construction), and there is some peculiarity in its cyclical movement. We see a rise in inventory investment rather in the recession years, such as 1954 and 1957, although this is not always a regular phenomenon. This reflects a tendency in depression to substitute construction for producer's durable equipment, as well as the lag of construction activity in response to the business cycle.

4) The behavior of inventory investment in corporate wholesale and retail trades is also very important. As compared with manufacturing as a whole, its ratio was 75.1%, 53.4% and 73.9% for the three boom years 1953, 1956 and 1959 respectively. In the recession of 1953–54, the decline of inventory investment was ¥194.1 billion in wholesale and retail trades, while it was ¥121.8 billion in manufacturing. Although wholesale and retail trades are aggregated in Table 1, the weight of the former is overwhelmingly larger, for in the case of retail trade only corporate stores are included. Moreover, the most influential in the inventory cycles of wholesale trade are the big foreign-trade corporations, which intend to increase im-

ports of raw materials, *etc.*, along with the expansion of domestic economy. Therefore, if the inventory investment series (seasonally unadjusted) in corporate wholesale trade is depicted, it actually indicates violent oscillations. Thus, even if the level of inventories in the wholesale sector is lower than that in manufacturing as a whole, the amplitude of the changes in inventory investment in the former is found to be extremely high.

5) As Table 1 indicates merely fiscal year figures, it is also necessary to check the quarter-to-quarter movement of inventory investment by industry. Figure 5 depicts this series by four quarter moving averages. In this chart, inventory investment in wholesale trade is most interesting in the sense that its peak and trough always lead those of other industries. For instance, in the 1956–57 boom, the peaks of inventory investment centered around April–June of 1957 in almost all industries, but its peak in wholesale trade was seen in October–December of 1956 (a two quarter lead). Moreover, the trough of inventory investment after the 1956–57 boom was reached in April–June of 1958 in the electric machinery and in the transportation equipment industries, in July–September of 1958 in the primary metal industry, and in January–March and April–June in 1959 respectively in the chemical and textile industries, but in the wholesale trade it had already been reached in October–December of 1957. Another point to be noted is the fact its upward trend is most conspicuous in the chart. Therefore, corporate inventory investment in wholesale trade (predominantly consisting of foreign-trade corporations) is one of the most important indicators in economic forecasting. It is also interesting that the trough in the textile industry shows the largest lag compared with other industries.

6) Based upon the data of Table 2, we can analyze the mode of behavior of inventory investment by type, *e.g.*, the finished commodities, goods-in-process, and raw materials. In Table 3, we explore the cyclical pattern of changes in the rank of the amounts of inventory investment in manufacturing in the three types of goods. In periods of depression, 1954 and 1958, the same ranking,—(F), (P), (R)—, holds true, *i.e.*, the relative amount of inventory investment in the finished commodities (F) is the largest and that of raw

Fig. 5. Corporate Inventory Investment by Industry

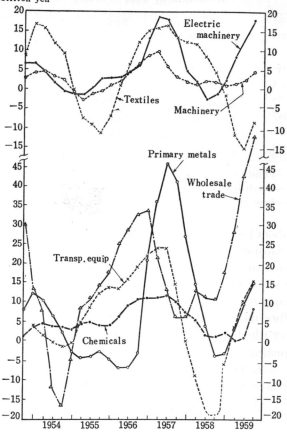

materials (R) is the smallest. Whereas, in 1955 and 1959, the periods of recovery, the ranking—(P), (R), (F)—is seen, and, in the boom of 1956, the ranking,—(R), (P), (F)—, opposite to the ranking in the depression was seen.

It is of interest that the ranking in the boom is quite opposite to that in the depression, but there was an exception in 1959, a year of rapid expansion, that even then the ranking,—(P), (R), (F)—can be seen, mainly because of a rise in the balance of payments ceiling

174

Table 3. Phases of the Cycle and Changes in the Rank of Values in Inventory Investment by Type of Goods

Fis. year	Rank			
	I	II	III	
1954	F	P	R	
1955	P	R	F	
1956	R	P	F	
1957	F	R	P	
1958	F	P	R	
1959	P	R	F	

Note: (F)—Finished Commodity inv. investment.
(P)—Goods-in-process inv. investment.
(R)—Raw material inv. investment.

brought about by a decline in the relative prices of imports and rapid export expansion, as well as due to the change in inventory behavior of entrepreneurs just being confronted with the liberalization of foreign trade. Moreover, in the recession of 1956 to 1958, we see the existence of the intermediate type of ranking, (F), (R), (P) in 1957, before moving to the ranking in 1958, (F), (P), (R). This is a case in which the inventory recession is prolonged.

7) Finished commodity inventory investment decreased from ¥44.4 billion to ¥38.6 billion, and goods-in-process inventory investment increased from ¥20.6 billion to ¥110.4 billion (about 5 times) in 1954–56, whereas the raw material inventory investment indicates about a 40 times increase for the same period, from ¥4.0 billion to ¥162.8 billion. Of course, it is conceivable that in 1954 the raw material inventory investment was particularly low in the depression of that year, but even in the 1955–56 comparison the goods-in-process inventory investment shows an increase of 2.67 times, and the raw material inventory investment of 4.08 times. Thus, the rapidity of the increase in raw material inventory investment as well as in that of wholesale trade in this period seems to support the view that in the 1956–57 boom there were highly speculative imports of raw materials.

8) We are going to examine the movements of the relative proportion of corporate inventory investment in each industry by type. Not only in total inventory investment but also in raw material inventory investment, there is a rising proportion in the machinery and metal industries. The peak of the raw material inventory investment in the metal industry was in 1957, despite the fact that the other industries in general showed peaks in 1956. This lag seems to have reflected the abrupt increase in imports of scrap iron and steel during the 1956–57 boom in the iron and steel industry. The movement of raw material inventory investments in the chemical, food, and construction industries is less oscillatory, and it seldom happens that they have a negative value.

On the other hand, in the case of goods-in-process inventory investment, the proportion of the machinery industry (particularly the transportation equipment industry) is large. In 1955, goods-in-process inventory investment in the machinery industry was ¥52.9 billion, rather larger than that in manufacturing industry as a whole, ¥41.1 billion, and in 1959 the former was ¥89.1 billion, still dominantly large, as compared with ¥133.9 billion in the latter. The goods-in-process inventory investment in the construction industry also matches that in machinery, *i.e.*, the former was ¥119.0 billion and the latter ¥89.1 billion in 1959.

In the case of finished-commodity inventory investment, in the 1956–57 boom, its peak was in 1957 in each industry, with a one year lag behind the other types of inventory investment.

Lastly, it would be useful to ascertain the movement of the relative proportion of the three types of inventories,—the finished commodity, the goods-in-process and the raw material inventories, in the process of business cycles. M. Abramovitz found that the cyclical change in the relative composition of goods-in-process have some similarity with that in the index of industrial production in the United States[2]. However, in such a highly growing economy as that of Japan, we cannot find clear waves of the business cycle in the level of industrial production itself. Rather, in the rates of increase of industrial production, a cyclical pattern is evident.

2) M. Abramovitz, *Inventories and Business Cycles*, 1950, p. 155.

Fig. 6 compares the latter with the fluctuations in the proportions of the three kinds of inventories. Although strict coincidence cannot be found, there is a roughly inverse movement between the relative composition of the finished-commodity inventories and the rates of increase of the industrial production, on the one hand, and a parallel movement between the goods-in-process and the raw material inventories and the rates of increase of industrial production, on the other. Therefore, we find a cyclical fluctuation in the relative composition of inventories.

However, even if the rate of increase of industrial production showed a clear upswing in 1959, there was rather a downward tendency in the relative proportion of raw material inventories. In 1957, it rose to about 43%, whereas in the 1959 boom it was still at the low level of about 38%, mainly reflecting a change in inventory behavior. The latter may be an important background to the still persistent surplus in the balance of payments in 1959, even when

Fig. 6. Cyclical Changes in Relative Compositions of Various Inventories

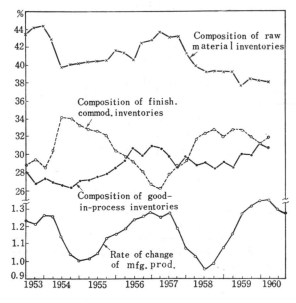

the annual increase rate of industrial production in that year amounted to 24%.

On the one hand, we notice a downward trend in the proportion of raw material inventories. The anticipation of the liberalization of foreign trade and the rationalization of inventory control in various firms in recent years seems to have stimulated this. The relative composition of goods-in-process inventories, on the other hand, follows an upward trend, just inversely to that of the raw material inventories. Thus, the inventory behavior mentioned above seems to have represented the tendencies of business enterprises to save the surplus inventory holdings piled up in the 1956–57 boom.

Table 4 shows the inventory-sales ratios in each quarter; in the 1956 boom the lowest of the ratio was 0.696, but in the 1959 boom it decreased further to 0.625. In terms of the fiscal year average, it was 0.733 in 1956, but 0.667 in 1959. We can also recognize here a change in the inventory behavior, which is supposed to have contributed to some extent in raising the balance-of-payments ceiling. Setting aside this trend, we see clearly a regularity of its behavior in that it declines in the boom and increased in the recession.

Table 4. Corporate Inventory-Sales Ratios in All Industries

Fiscal year	Apr.-Jun.	Jul.-Sept.	Oct.-Dec.	Jan.-Mar.	Fiscal year average
1952	1.018	0.870	0.936	0.844	0.917
1953	0.815	0.754	0.747	0.779	0.774
1954	0.893	0.795	0.784	0.770	0.811
1955	0.817	0.732	0.735	0.731	0.754
1956	0.731	0.696	0.720	0.781	0.733
1957	0.821	0.850	0.894	0.965	0.883
1958	0.865	0.806	0.754	0.747	0.793
1959	0.716	0.674	0.625	0.635	0.667

Source: The Ministry of Finance, the Quarterly Report of the Corporate Enterprise Survey.

2. *Inventory Changes and the Propensity to Import*

According to the Keynesian tradition, several economists attempted to compute linear import functions in Japan, but a casual look at the basic data makes me hesitate to follow this routine. Let me depict a simple graph which correlates the index of the volume of imports of raw materials with that of the volume of industrial production (Fig. 7).

Fig. 7. Imports of Raw Materials and Industrial Production

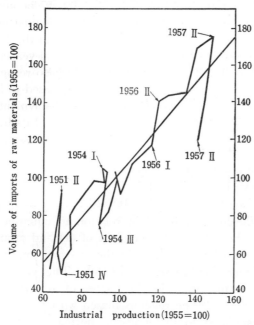

As can be seen from Fig. 8 we may fit a linear relation between imports of raw materials and industrial production. For the period 1950–1957 (1950=yearly and 1951–57=quarterly data), we get the following relation.

$$M_t = -16.45 + 1.2017 \ O_t \ ; \ R^2 = 0.8645 \quad \dots\dots\dots\dots\dots (1)$$

The correlation arrived at is very good, but the relation cannot be projected to the phases of boom or depression. The deviations from the straight line fitted by the least square method are not random. They reflect very exactly the process of business cycle, *i.e.*, in booms the deviations scatter above the line and in depressions the reverse prevails. For the years, 1951 (Korean war boom), 1953 and 1956–57, the deviations scatter upwards, and for the years, 1952, 1954 and 1957, they scatter downwards. Therefore, a glance at the chart suggests that some cyclical factor should be introduced in the import function together with the level of production. We find an asymmetry of changes in the propensity to import in booms and depressions. The imports of raw materials in a boom are greater than those in a depression even under the same level of industrial production.

Various equations can be fitted to the various phases of business fluctuations. The import function in the upswing (1954 III–1957 II):

$$M_t = -68.60 + 1.6689 \ O_t; \quad R^2 = 0.9635 \quad \dots\dots\dots\dots\dots\dots \quad (2)$$

Import function connecting booms (1951 II, 1952 IV, 1953, 1954 I, II, 1956, 1957 I, II);

$$M_t = -2.46 + 1.1787 \ O_t; \quad R^2 = 0.8223 \quad \dots\dots\dots\dots\dots \quad (3)$$

Import function connecting depressions (1951 III, IV, 1952 I, II, III, 1954 III, IV, 1951 I, 1957 III, IV):

$$M_t = -14.58 + 1.0375 \ O_t; \quad R^2 = 0.9220 \quad \dots\dots\dots\dots\dots \quad (4)$$

Regression coefficients computed in relation to equations (3) and (4) are close to the regression coefficient of (1) and around unity. However, the regression coefficient in the upswing import function (2) is much higher than these, *i.e.*, 1.6689. This constant cannot be used for the future projection in a sense of long-run as well as short-run predictions. The relation biased with the boom period cannot be extrapolated to the long-run normal relation. It also cannot be extrapolated to the coming period of depression, because in depressions we see a sudden cyclical decline in the propensity to import. Nevertheless, the E.P.A., White Paper of 1957 expressed an opinion that the rise in the propensity to import in 1956 has a semi-long-run structural tendency. This point of view was changed in the White Paper of 1958 in the face of the sharp decline in the propensity to import in the 1957–58 recession.

Thus, some cyclical factor should be injected into the import function. We have attempted to construct an equation taking account of this. Denoting corporate inventory investment by V_t and the rate of increase of industrial production compared with the same quarter of the preceding year by O_t/O_{t-4}, we get,

$$M_t = -98.34 + 1.03910 \ O_t + 0.01004 \ V_t + 0.77887 \ (O_t/O_{t-4}) ;$$
$$R^2 = 0.9485 \ \dots\dots\dots\dots\dots\dots\dots\dots\dots\dots\dots\dots\dots\dots \quad (5)$$

Readers may be aware of an improvement of the coefficient of determination R^2 from 0.8645 (in the simple linear one variable equation) to 0.9485. This means a considerable part of the systematic deviation from equation (1) can be explained by the additional variables V_t and O_t/O_{t-4}. The cyclical nature of variations of the propensity to import is now made clear.

Cyclicality of the import ratio depends in part upon fluctuations in the requirements of raw materials per unit of industrial production. It is the changes in imported raw materials *consumed* divided by industrial production. Another important factor is the changes in imported inventories. The importance of the latter can be illustrated by a simple numerical example. Assuming that the normal inventory ratio is 30% as compared with current production and the unit raw material requirement is constant (20%), the following example can be constructed (Table 5).

Total imports of raw materials consist of two parts; one part is proportional to industrial production (20%), and another part is induced by assumed entrepreneurial behavior—the maintenance of normal inventory ratio 30%, and expressed by the increments of inventories. The result obtained indicates more violent fluctuations in imports of raw materials than in industrial production. Thus a mere halt in the rise of production (142 to 142) entails a decline in imports of raw materials (33 to 28). A decline of production from 142 to 130 (8.45% decrease) causes a drastic decline in imports (28 to 22). This means a 21.43% decline. The production of 110 in the boom corresponds to raw materials imports of 25, while the production of 130 in recession corresponds to the low level of imports of 22. The import ratio is 23% versus 17%. This application of the

Table 5

Period	Production	Inventories of imported raw materials	Imported raw materials proportionate to production	Total imports of raw materials	Imports / Production
1	100	30	20 (100)	20 (100)	20 %
2	110	33 (+3)	22 (110)	25 (125)	23
3	125	38 (+5)	25 (125)	30 (150)	24
4	142	43 (+5)	28 (142)	33 (165)	23
5	142	43 (0)	28 (142)	28 (142)	20
6	130	39 (−4)	26 (130)	22 (110)	17

acceleration principle thus explains why imports and the import ratio decrease sharply in depression while production is constant or falls slightly. The above interpretation applies not only to imports of crude raw materials (cotton, iron ore, *etc.*), but also to imports of semi-finished raw materials, such as steel. Moreover, even finished products may be under the rule of this empirical law, in so far as they are imported as stocks of foreign trade merchants.

In the above analysis, we assumed a constancy in the ratio between imported raw materials consumed and industrial production. However, such an assumption is not realistic. It may change as time elapses. Therefore, it is necessary to introduce another device by which we can throw light upon the problem of inventories and imports.

Our device is very simple, but probably useful. Denoting imported crude raw materials consumed by M_c, the volume of imports of crude raw materials by M, total crude raw materials consumed by R_c, and industrial production by O, we get the following identity.

$$\frac{M}{O} = \frac{M}{M_c} \cdot \frac{M_c}{R_c} \cdot \frac{R_c}{O} \quad \ldots\ldots\ldots\ldots\ldots\ldots\ldots (6)$$

M/O is the import ratio or the propensity to import crude raw materials in physical terms in manufacturing industry. M/M_c is a barometer representing the variations in inventories of imported crude raw materials, since the difference between M and M_c is the inventory investment in relation to imported crude raw materials.

M_c/R_c is the proportion of imported crude raw material consumption to its total domestic consumption. R_c/O is the unit crude raw material requirements in industrial production. Therefore, we can imagine three important factors influencing the fluctuation of the import ratio M/O, *i.e.*,

Import ratio
- Inventory variation factor (M/M_c)
- Import dependence in raw material consumption (M_c/R_c)
- Unit raw material requirements (R_c/O)

Fig. 8 shows that the import ratio M/O is cyclically influenced by the variations of M/M_c and M_c/R_c, and also influenced by the marked downward drift of R_c/O. In this chart, the index of industrial production (incl. manufacturing, mining, gas and electricity), and the index of imported crude raw material consumption are as compiled by the Ministry of International Trade and Industry. However, the index of the volume of crude raw material imports corresponding to the coverage of the MITI's index of the imported crude raw material consumption has not been compiled by any official authority.

Fig. 8. Import Ratio, Unit Raw Material Requirements, Inventory Fluctuation Factor and Import Dependence in Raw Material Consumption

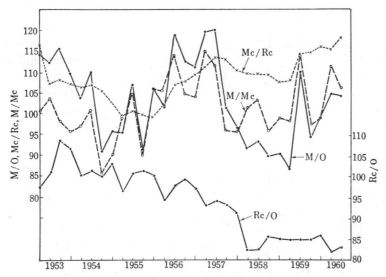

Therefore, I have compiled, by myself, a volume of imports index using the main 12 items of imports; wool, cotton, flax, iron ore, scrap iron, non-ferrous metal ores, phosphate ore, salt, coal, petroleum, hides, and crude rubber (88% of total imports of crude raw

Table 6. Index of the Volume of Imports of Crude Raw Materials
(Estimated by the author)

	Index of the value of imports of crude raw materials (A)	Index of the volume of imports of crude raw materials (B)	Index of the price of imports of crude raw materials (C) [A/B]
1953 I	96.4	91.8	105.0
II	98.7	96.8	102.0
III	98.9	100.0	98.9
IV	100.7	101.4	99.3
1954 I	98.5	100.1	98.4
II	104.2	103.3	100.9
III	80.5	80.9	99.5
IV	86.5	88.9	97.3
1955 I	93.2	93.4	88.8
II	102.9	103.3	99.1
III	92.3	90.3	101.7
IV	111.6	112.1	99.6
1956 I	119.4	117.5	101.6
II	146.2	142.9	102.3
III	147.9	140.5	105.3
IV	165.0	147.8	111.6
1957 I	196.9	167.1	117.8
II	219.0	177.0	123.7
III	175.3	145.6	120.4
IV	153.1	135.7	112.8
1958 I	135.9	131.5	103.3
II	124.2	130.6	95.1
III	113.6	127.6	89.0
IV	118.5	136.2	87.0
1959 I	119.6	140.2	85.3
II	155.1	190.8	81.3
III	146.3	170.7	85.7
IV	171.2	194.9	87.8
1960 I	198.0	223.2	88.7
II	194.8	227.5	85.6
III			
IV			

Note: As the price index is derived by dividing the value index by a quantity index of the Laspeyres type, it is itself of the Paasche type.

materials), with the 1955 structure of imports as weights (Table 6).

Interesting analyses can be introduced here: First, the unit raw material coefficient R_c/O follows the downward trend continuously from 1953. This may reflect the effect of the rapid introduction of technological innovations and the shifting of the industrial structure toward heavy industry, so that the declining R_c/O seems to have had the role of suppressing the potential tendency of an increasing import ratio. Particularly conspicuous were the decline of the unit raw material requirements in 1958.

Second, there is an extremely close correlation between M/O and M/M_c, and the cyclical and seasonal fluctuations in M/M_c are reproduced in the changes in M/O almost perfectly. However, M_c/R_c also shows a cyclical change, although its oscillation is not as severe as in M/M_c, for M/M_c reflects the seasonal fluctuation but in M_c/R_c only the cyclical fluctuation appears. Therefore, our problem is to ascertain which of the effects, M/M_c or M_c/R_c is greater.

Let us go into this analysis by observing Fig. 8 and computing year-to-year changes in the various ratios in Table 7. From fiscal 1955 to 1956, M/O increased by 13.8%, but M/M_c increased by 7.7%, i.e., the inventory variation factor M/M_c accounted for about 56% of the total variation of the import ratio M/O. Whereas, the other cyclical factor, M_c/R_c increased by 8.3%, so we can say that for this period the relative weight of M/M_c and M_c/R_c was almost the same. For fiscal 1958–59, on the other hand, M/O increased by 13.7%, but M/M_c by 6.3%, and M_c/R_c by 6.2%. The relative role

Table 7. Annual Changes in M/O, M/Mc, Mc/Rc, and Rc/O

Fis. year	$\dfrac{M}{O}$	$\dfrac{M}{Mc}$	$\dfrac{Mc}{Rc}$	$\dfrac{Rc}{O}$	Fis. year	$\dfrac{M}{O}$	$\dfrac{M}{Mc}$	$\dfrac{Mc}{Rc}$	$\dfrac{Rc}{O}$
1953	110.4	98.7	107.3	104.8	1956	115.9	109.4	109.1	97.0
1954	98.2	94.0	103.9	100.5	1958	89.9	99.1	108.5	84.5
Percent. Change(%)	−11.1	−4.8	−3.3	−3.6	Percent. Change(%)	−22.2	−9.4	−0.5	−12.9
1955	101.6	101.6	100.7	99.4	1958	89.9	99.1	108.5	84.5
1956	115.6	109.4	109.1	97.0	1959	102.2	105.3	115.2	84.3
Percent. Change(%)	+13.8	+7.7	+8.3	−2.4	Percent. Change(%)	+13.7	+6.3	+6.2	−0.2

of the two factors is about equal. From this point of view, we must observe the existence of the role of M_c/R_c, which was once pointed out by the late Mr. Yonosuke Goto (the author of the White Paper) in the so-called " Inventory Controversy "[3], as against the opinion of Mr. Osamu Shimomura who emphasized one-sidedly the role of the inventory changes. On the one hand, Mr. Shimomura's view was that the deficit in the balance of payments occurred then almost entirely because of the inventory increase in imported raw materials, so that it was unnecessary to enforce a tight money policy which would merely entail harm to the rate of economic growth of Japan. He forecasts the automatic decline of the import ratio due to the reaction from the excessive piling-up of imported raw materials. Mr. Goto, on the other hand, stuck to his view that the balance-of-payments difficulties occurred mainly due to the excessive investment in plant and equipment, so a tight money policy which will slow down the rate of growth was indispensable. However, in the recession of 1957–58, the import ratio actually declined sharply. Therefore, Mr. Goto could not but raise a new hypothesis to the effect that the import ratio could decline, even if there were no decline in inventory changes, when the proportion of imported raw materials in total domestic use of raw materials declined. Therefore, we can say that Mr. Shimomura's effect and Mr. Goto's are almost equal as far as the upswing of business cycle is concerned.

However, in the recession of 1956–58, M/O decreased by 22.2%, and M/M_c by 9.4%, while M_c/R_c decreased only by 0.5%. From this, we see that in the upswing M_c/R_c plays a role as great as M/M_c, but not in the downswing. This is due to the fact that there is not only cyclical change but also a secular upward trend in M_c/R_c.

In Fig. 8, we observe that part of the uptrend of M_c/R_c seems to be offset by the downtrend of R_c/O. This tendency, however, has stopped since 1958, for M_c/R_c has still been increasing but R_c/O has stopped decreasing since then.

The conclusion is as follows : The role of inventory fluctuation was persistently dominant in 1953–58, but the cyclical behavior of M_c/R_c was influential only in the upswing of 1955–56. On the other

3) See Chapter 5.

hand, the decline of unit raw material requirements (-12.9%) for 1956–58, played a great part in reducing the import ratio for the same period, amounting to about 58% of the decline of the import ratio. We should not, therefore, be carried away only by the inventory variation factor, neglecting the importance of the reduced unit raw material requirements.

The movement of M/M_c is extremely oscillatory, and its quarter to quarter changes show a close correspondence with those of M/O, while the fluctuation of M_c/R_c lacks seasonal changes, although it shows cyclical movements, and its cycle is very mild. Moreover, M_c/R_c has a rising trend, so it has a powerful effect only in the upswing of business cycles, but not in other phases. Therefore, from the view point of the observation of the overall period in question, the cyclical factor M/M_c have played a greater role than M_c/R_c, but if we restrict our analysis to the periods of upswing, e.g., 1955–56 or 1958–59, then both are equally influential, and the emphasis on inventory variation as if it were a sole factor, seems to go too far.

CHAPTER 8

INVENTORY CYCLES AND THE DUAL STRUCTURE

1. Hypothesis

One may regard the title of this chapter as a bit eccentric, because despite the general recognition of the influence of the dual structure on economic growth, its influence on short-run business cycles is not so well comprehended. We have not come across any empirical study of this problem for any other country.

Our problem is as follows: As we have discussed elsewhere[1], the dual structure which has evolved in Japan has a close connection with the concentration of capital into the big corporations. This connection may be due to the fact that the banks have intimate ties with the big corporations in the institutional arrangement of the *zaibatsu, etc.*, and certainly the long-term and short-term lending policies of the banks have a strong bias in favor of big firms. Our analysis here attempts to throw new light on the influences this basic fact may have on short-term business cycles.

In a series of postwar business cycles (tight money policy—recession—recovery—boom), the key point in the following discussion lies in the fact that the smaller businesses very often served as a cushion, *i.e.*, the disadvantages attendant on the process of the business cycles were shifted from the large to the smaller firms. As a model, we have a following picture in mind. When a policy of tight money was being pursued, loans to smaller firms were first curtailed, while for the time being, the big firms were not subject to restriction, sometimes continuing to receive loans even for inventory accumulation. If this is so, it is clear that the recession in the

1) See Chapter 1.

188

Fig. 1. Increments in Loans Outstanding: Big and Small Business

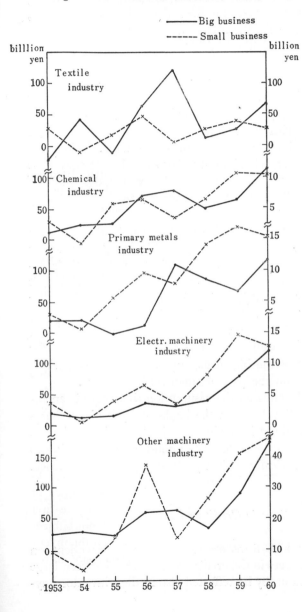

Sources:

The Small Business Finance Corporation, *Chusho Kigyo Kinyu Tokei Shiryo* (Statistics on Small Business Finance), *Chosa Jiho*, Vol. 1, No. 5; Vol. 2., No. 7.); and *Kinyu Tokei Hannenpo* (Semi-Annual Report of Financial Statistics), July 1961.

Note:

In order to trace data back to 1953, it was necessary to restrict financial institutions to all banks, and trust accounts of all banks in the case of big firms, and to all banks, trust accounts of all banks, and Credit Associations in the case of small firms.

credit cycle will begin with small business, and only with some lag will begin to show a downturn for the bigger firms. Therefore, according to our hypothesis, the upper turning point for small and medium firms will precede those for big firms.

Second, we can assume a situation in which, as a result of the tight money policy, imports decline, exports increase and the balance of payments shows a surplus. In such a situation, the money market becomes very easy; the banks, with surplus funds, will engage in lending competition, with the result that the hitherto suppressed loans to small and medium-scale firms will turn upward. The loans for bigger firms, however, will rise only after some lag, as they were not so severely curtailed. Therefore it is likely that the index of loans to smaller firms will lead that of the bigger firms in the recovery phase.

The third phase is the boom phase. As soon as the economy enters a "hot" boom like that of 1956, the big firms' demand for funds will increase sharply, and the banks will try to meet their demand as much as possible. Once such a situation commences, it places a drain on the funds which might be allocated toward smaller businesses, so loans to the latter begin to decrease. So the peak, lending to smaller businesses precedes the peak for big business. Thus, since the peak as well as the trough of the credit cycle for small firms leads that of the big firms, the credit cycle as a whole shows this precedence on the part of small business loans.

The above model depends on the assumption that there is an inseparably close connection between the banks and the big corporations, and that the supply of loanable funds is always insufficient to meet the rapidly growing demand. We intend in the following to test this inference numerically against postwar Japanese experience.

2. Lead of the Small Firms in Credit and Inventory Cycles

In an economy in which firms are extraordinarily dependent on bank borrowing, differences in the credit cycle patterns between large and small firms will naturally be reflected also in their inventory cycles. There seems to be an intimate relation between loans and inventory investment; in particular, movements in the supply of working capital directly regulate the movement of inventory investment in postwar Japan. Therefore, we shall take up here together, two aspects of the short-run cycles, viz., the credit and inventory cycles, in order to elucidate the influence of the dual structure on business cycle patterns.

In Figure 1, increments in loans outstanding from financial institutions are depicted by industry for large and small firms. By big firms, we mean those with paid-up capital of more than 10 million yen, and by small firms, those with less than that figure. Year-to-year increments in outstanding loans, both operating and equipment, are illustrated for five industries, viz., textiles, chemicals, primary metals, electrical machinery, and other machinery. We have disaggregated the series into industries to avoid the possibility that a lead on the part of small business loans for industry as a whole might reflect differences in the cycle between industries. But the lead of loans to small business is evident in each industry except electrical equipment, and even there, if four quarter moving averages of quarterly series were to be depicted, some lead could be found. In the 1954–55 depression, the small firm troughs are all found in 1954, while those of the big firms, except in electrical machinery, are all in 1955. In the 1956–57 boom, the small firm peaks come in 1956, and those of the big firms in 1957.

This duality in the credit cycles should naturally be reflected in different inventory cycles for big and small firms. By selecting four industries, viz., textiles, chemicals, machinery, and wholesale trade, from the Quarterly Report of the Finance Ministry's Corporate Enterprise Survey, we can depict the inventory cycles for large and small business in 1954–59. The dividing line here is 100 million yen paid-up capital. Although these figures are not adjusted by the changes in inventory valuation, they should suffice to show the lead and lag relation in the inventory cycle.

Figure 2 depicts the lead of the small business inventory cycles in the four industries named; a similar lag is also found in the paper and allied products, iron and steel, electric machinery, shipbuilding,

Fig. 2. Inventory Changes: Large and Small Business in Four Industries

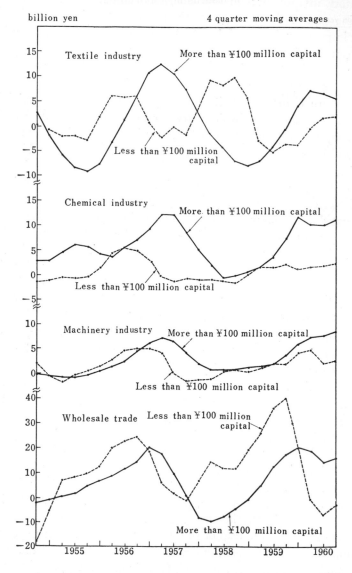

Fig. 3. Inventory Investment, 1952–1959, (4 quarter moving average) by Size
of Corporations in All Industries

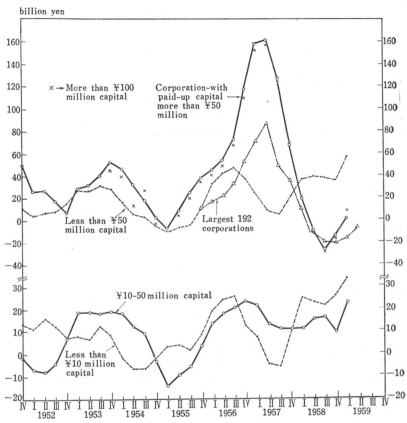

Source: Computed by the Ministry of Finance, Quarterly Report of Corporate
Enterprise Survey.

and other transportation equipment industries. Thus, the lead of
the smaller firms in both the credit and inventory cycles is almost
beyond doubt, and seems to be a pronounced trait of the Japanese
economy.

We have so far tested our hypothesis by using data divided only
into large and small firms. But there are series available dividing
the firms by size in more detail. Figure 3 depicts the inventory

193

cycles of different sizes of firms, although here the disaggregation by industry is abandoned. Here too we find that the large firms' cycles lag behind those of the smaller firms. In the 1956–57 boom, for instance, the inventory investment of the largest 192 corporations peaked in April-June of 1957, while firms with paid-up capital of less than 10 million yen had reached their peak in July–September of the preceding year. That is, the latter peak led by three quarters. In the following recession, the small business trough occurred in July–September, while that of the large firms occurred in October-December 1958, with a lag of five quarters.

3. Difference in the Cycles of Incorporated and Unincorporated Firms

We have shown above that the small firms always lead in the credit and inventory cycles. But does the hypothesis hold true for the lag-lead relationship between incorporated and unincorporated firms?

For estimates of inventory investment allocated between incorporated and unincorporated business, we can use data from the official national income statistics. There seems, however, to be serious doubt about the reliability of the official estimates of inventory investment, especially in relation to the unincorporated sector. Before proceeding with our analysis, therefore, it may be appropriate to discuss the basic data on inventory investment in the unincorporated sector.

In connection with inventory investment by unincorporated businesses, Mr. Nobuyoshi Namiki[2] has recently raised an interesting point. If the official inventory investment estimate for the unincorporated sector (inclusive of inventory valuation adjustment) is deducted year by year from the noncorporate, total inventories of the National Wealth Survey, 1955, we get a very strange result. The inventory balance for non-farm unincorporated enterprises

2) N. Namiki, *Zaiko Hendo ni kansuru Jakkan no Bunseki* (An Analysis of Inventory Changes), Economic Planning Agency, Economic Research Institute, Research Series No. 4.

would become negative from 1951 backward, and in the case of farmers' inventory balance, from September 1955 backward. Namiki believes that there was a very large undervaluation of farm inventories in the National Wealth Survey, and in the case of non-farm unincoporated firms, the inventory investment in the national income statistics has been greatly overestimated, in addition to the possible under-valuation (?) of inventories in the 1955 National Wealth Survey. In the case of farm inventories, if the inventories (¥206 billion) in December 1955 of the Wealth Survey were to be increased by about four times, then he finds that there would be no minus balances in the earlier period, and also that it would almost be compatible with estimates of inventories from the data of the Farm Household Economy Survey, (using the procedure: per unit inventories × total number of farm household).

In view of the statistics Mr. Namiki has cited, his judgment seems to be approximately correct. In this paper, we shall devote ourselves to a study of inventory investment in non-farm unincorporated firms. As the basic data in this field is from the Unincorporated Commerical and Manufacturing Enterprise Survey, by the Bureau of Statistics, Office of the Prime Minister, it is necessary to examine it in detail. Unfortunately, the size of the sample used in this survey is very small, about 500 units each in manufacturing and in commerce, respectively, inventory investment per unit of enterprise, which is the basis of the estimate in the official statistics, is derived in the manner suggested in Table 1.

Table 1 relates to manufacturing. As the basic data is essentially weak, we must strengthen the data to yield more reasonable figures. In *each quarter*, the inventories at the beginning and the end of the period per unit of enterprise are surveyed, and the difference is assumed to comprise inventory investment. This is, in turn, enlarged by some device to aggregate non-corporate inventory investment quarter by quarter in the national income statistics. The problem is that, as the sample is very small (around 500), the inventories at the end of one quarter from a given survey frequently differ from those at the beginning of the next quarter in the next survey. In a given firm, the two should be the same. Therefore, we have attempted to compute two other reference series (the second and the third column) in Table 1. The second column is computed as differences between inventories at the end minus those at the beginning of *each fiscal year*. Although the series in the first column does not show any marked cycle, the second series indicates clear ups and downs which correspond perfectly to the actual business cycle. However, since the figure at the beginning of the year is not equal to that at the end of the previous year, we have averaged the two and used the averages as inventory figures for each quarter. In this case, the sample may be presumed to be automatically doubled from about 500 to about 1,000 each in manufacturing and commerce respectively. Thus, the third column is the increment in each fiscal year of the averaged inventories. In this case also, we get a fairly reasonable cyclical fluctuation. The above three series is unadjusted with respect to inventory valuation changes, but the error due to this omission would be very much smaller in this sphere than that due to the incorrect treatment of the basic data.

Table 1. Inventory Changes per Unit of Enterprise in Unincorporated Manufacturing

Fiscal year	Inventory Changs, I (Total at the end *less* Total at the begin. *of each quarter*) Official estimates	Inventory Changes, II (Total at the end *less* Total at the begin. *of each fiscal year*)	Inventry Changes, III (Average of totals at the end of this quarter and at the begin. of next quarter *less* average of totals at the end of last quarter and at the begin. of this quarter)
1952	66,696 yen	— 9,558 yen	— yen
1953	30,254	22,027	9,190
1954	35,303	—26,556	5,440
1955	32,685	19,821	7,198
1956	35,717	59,777	45,649
1957	59,724	—58,938	—57,407
1958	41,207	76,960	41,078

Source : The Bureau of Statistics, *Kojin Shokogyo Keizai Chosa* (Unincorporated Commercial and Manufacturing Enterprise Survey).

From 1953 to 1958, the accumulated total of inventory changes is ¥234,894 according to the first column, but ¥93,191 according to the second column, and ¥51,148 according to the third column. The third series seems to be most reasonable and reliable, with the total of the third minimized to 22% of the total of the first. As the inventory investment is presumed to be overestimated in the non-farm non-corporate sector, this method of minimizing it would be a useful guide in improving the official national income statistics. When we look at the official statistics, we are surprised to see such high shares of noncorporate inventory investment in the total private investment. From fiscal year 1951 onward, this proportion moves as follows: 29.2% (1951), 41.1% (1952), 41.2% (1953), 57.4% (1954), 41.4% (1955), 13.8% (1956), 29.0% (1957), and 424.7% (1958). There may be something wrong in this. I feel confident that the weakness in the statistics can be overcome in some degree, if we carefully handle the basic data along lines suggested above.

Then, why is first column of Table 1 too high, and the second and third columns more reliable? What is the reason underlying this? The search for the reason is not simple, but there may be a tendency for firms to decrease the inventories on their books at the beginning of the period and increase them at the end, to hold down the amount of sales and profits subject to taxation. If this is the case, the inventory investment estimates in the first column are systematically over-stated. We should direct our attention, then, not to the *increase or decrease* of inventories in the sample at the particular period, but to the *level* of inventories at different periods. The level seems more dependable than the changes within the same sample, for it seems to reflect generally the changing inventory situation. From this point of view the average inventories in the third column would be more useful.

How about the quarter-to-quarter behavior of inventory invest-ment in the third column? The graphic representation in Figure 4, adjusted for inventory valuation changes and smoothed by the use of four quarter moving averages, clearly shows inventory cycles similar to those of small corporations with paid-up capital under 10 million yen in Figure 4 (A) and (B). It is interesting, moreover, that

Fig. 4 (A). Inventory Investment per Unit of Manufacturing Enterprise in the Non-Corporate Sector, 1953–1958

—Smoothed out by 4-quarter moving average—

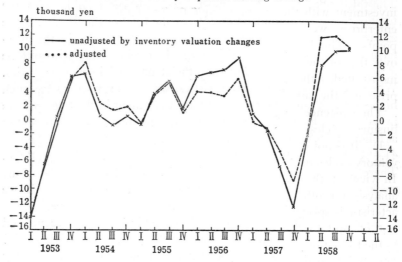

(B). Inventory Investment per Unit of Retail and Wholesale Enterprise in the Non-Corporate Sector, 1953–1958

—Evened out by 4-quarter moving average—

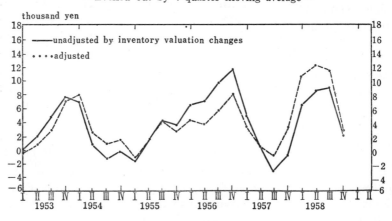

198

the pattern of fluctuations is similar in both manufacturing and commerce.

Comparing the movement of unincorporated non-farm inventory investment with the inventory investment of the smallest corporate enterprises, we find a similar timing of the upper and lower turning points. The lead of the unincorporated sector's inventory cycle over that of the corporate sector as a whole is hereby indirectly demonstrated, although the former data is given by individual enterprise and the latter (corporate enterprise) is in aggregate terms.

The existence of this lead-lag relation between the small and big business cycles suggests the following remarks:

1) It is not clear whether or not the duality of the credit and inventory cycles discussed above are peculiar to the Japanese economy. In view of the fact, however, that we have never seen such an analysis for other countries, there is a possibility that this characteristic is special to the Japanese economy. If so, the concentration of capital in the big firms seems to have played a role not only in the formation of the dual structure in a secular or structural sense, but also in creating a double sequence of credit cycles in the short-run or cyclical sense.

2) In such an economy, monetary policy would have a particularly differential effect between large and small business, and might even contribute toward widening the duality of the economic structure, as against the conventional view that it would have a uniform or " neutral " effect on the economy.

3) If there is a lead in the credit cycle of small business, we can use it in economic forecasting. By paying attention to the movement of loans to small business, we can predict the peak or trough in the big business credit cycle or in the aggregate cycle. We shall attempt a statistical analysis of this proposition in the following section.

4. The Duality of Credit Cycles and Economic Forecasting

If there has been an empirical rule that the inventory and credit cycles of small and middle-sized firms precede those of big firms by three or four quarters, we can make use of this relationship in economic forecasting. Let us take up here, for example, the quarter-to-quarter increments in outstanding loans for operating funds by all financial institutions to large and small enterprises, using a paid-up capital of 10 million yen as a dividing line. Figure 5, in four quarter moving averages, depicts very clearly the double sequence of the credit cycles in large and small business.

In the trough of the 1954–55 recession, we can see a lead by small business of about three quarters, and in the peak of the 1956–57 boom the lead is again about the same length. In the trough of the 1957–58 recession, the big business lag lengthened to about five quarters. This lengthened lag should be noted. Also to be noted is the fact that the big business curve intersects that of the small firms about nine months before the peak of the former (April–June 1957), and that this point of intersection (July–September 1956) was the peak of the small business cycle. In 1959, however, July–September became again the intersection point of the two cycles. Nevertheless, April–June 1960 was not a turning point in the big business cycle. The curve was still following an upward tendency. Moreover, the small firms' cycle does not peak at this point of intersection; it also continues to rise, although there was a conspicuous retardation of the rate of increase about this time.[3]

If the credit cycle picture for 1954–59 is taken as typical, then we may predict mechanically that, from the point of intersection (July–September 1959), a recession in the small firms' cycle should emerge. But actually, both the large and small business curves continued to rise after that date. Is this an indication that the duality of the credit cycles is not sufficient as a tool of economic forecasting? Perhaps it would not be sufficient. No tool, however, has been sufficient in itself. We believe that the comparison of these movements would be a useful addition to our tools of economic forecasting.

3) Rigorously speaking, the two trends in the big and small business cycles should be the same, in order that such a judgment on forecasting can be established. Therefore, our analysis will have also a limitation in this respect.

The different pattern of movement in the credit cycles after July–September 1959 from the pattern before that time may be explained by the extraordinary rise in fixed investment in 1959–60 (a 38% increase), motivated by a concern on the part of entrepreneurs to strengthen their competetive power in the face of the coming liberalization of foreign trade[4], and by the acceleration of the small business financing through policy measures. This boom in fixed investment

Fig. 5. Credit Cycles for Large and Small Business

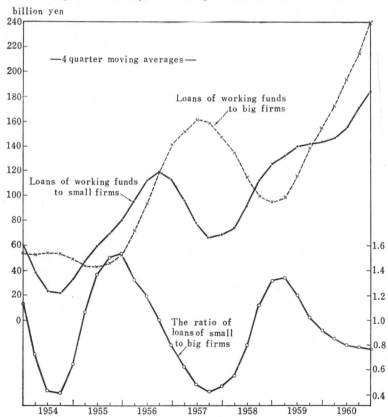

4) The Japanese government has declared its intention to raise the proportion of imports liberalized from 65% to 90% by September 1962.

probably pulled up inventory investment too, disturbing the tendency we have described above. We can note, however, the slowing of the upward tendency of the small firms' cycle toward the end of 1959. This may justify our view that the end of 1959 might have been the upper turning point of the small firms' credit cycle, had other things been equal.

Our analysis so far has contributed to some extent toward a prediction of the turning point of the inventory cycle. For instance, we have come across predictions that the inventory boom would end at the end of 1958, around April 1959, or around June 1959. But based upon the above analysis, we could have strongly contradicted these opinions, for the loans of working funds to the big firms reached their trough just around the end of 1958, as we can see in Fig. 5, so that could hardly have been the peak of the inventory cycle. April or June 1959 still could not be the upper turning point, because the upswing phase would have been too short in that case. Thus our analysis of the duality of credit and inventory cycles has been effective so far in judging the turning points, though the regularity of the cycles was disturbed somewhat after the middle of 1959. Probably because of the intense investment boom of 1959–60, the period of this inventory-credit cycle is being prolonged. Nevertheless, we note that the cycles thus analyzed show about a three year period. A similar period can be seen also in the ratio of loans to small and large business in Figure 5. It is probable that even if the peak-to-peak length of the big firms' credit cycle is prolonged to a little more than three years, we may soon see a cyclical decline in near future.

PART III

OTHER RELATED TOPICS

CHAPTER 9

THE STRUCTURE OF SAVING AND THE
CONSUMPTION FUNCTION IN THE
POSTWAR PERIOD

1. Introduction

The saving-consumption relation in the postwar recovery of Japan
is of special interest because the impact of her postwar dislocations
and her extremely rapid recovery were probably greater than in
most other countries. This paper is a part of my more comprehensive studies[1] on the prewar and postwar consumption functions
in Japan and outlines the peculiarities of the postwar saving-consumption pattern.

2. Saving-Ratio Discrepancies between Macro- and Microdata

Before considering the problems of the saving function, let us
analyze the post-war structure of saving in Japan. When computing
the personal saving ratio from the official national income statistics,
we get 16.0 per cent in the calendar year 1956. However, the saving
ratio computed from the family budget survey of all urban worker
families was only 11.8 per cent in the same year. The difference
between these figures is fairly great. The saving ratio of all farmers,
on the other hand, was only 4.1 per cent in 1956. Table 1 gives saving
ratios for these three categories for the period 1949–56 inclusive.

In this table saving ratios computed from the two budget surveys
are consistently lower than those from the national income statistics
in all the years covered. The propensity to save as computed from

---

1) M. Shinohara, *Shohi Kansu* (" The Consumption Function "), Tokyo, 1958.

Table 1. Comparisons of Postwar Saving Ratios from Individual Disposable Income

Calen-dar year	National income statis-tics (%)	All urban worker families (monthly data)*			All rural families (reduced to monthly figures)†‡		
		Disposa-ble income (¥)	Consump-tion ex-penditure (¥)	Saving ratio (%)	Dispos-able income (¥)	Consump-tion ex-penditure (¥)	Saving ratio (%)
1949	− 1.9‡				12,032	13,229	− 9.9
1950	13.8‡				15,815	14,429	8.8
1951	18.7	14,917	14,620	2.0	19,857	17,895	9.9
1952	17.5	18,991	18,161	4.4	22,782	21,048	7.6
1953	11.7	23,065	21,727	5.8	25,083	23,561	6.1
1954	11.1	24,922	23,067	7.4	26,014	25,133	3.4
1955	13.3	25,896	23,513	9.2	29,344	25,971	11.5
1956	16.0	27,464	24,231	11.8	27,836	26,699	4.1
1957	17.9	29,810	26,092	12.5			

Sources : Economic Planning Agency, *Showa Sanjuninendo no Kokuminshotoku* ("National Income in 1957 Fiscal Year"), Tokyo, 1958 ; Sorifu Tokei Kyoku (Statistics Bureau of Prime Minister's Office), *Kakeichosa Nempo*, 1957 ("Annual Report of Family Budget Survey, 1957), Tokyo, 1958 ; Economic Planning Agency, *Nihonkeizai Shihyo*, December 1957 ("Japanese Economic Indicators, December, 1957") Tokyo, 1958.

* Workers' data come from Statistics Bureau of Prime Minister's Office, *op. cit.*

† Farm-family data come from Ministry of Agriculture and Forestry, *Noka Keizai Chosa* ("Farm Household Economy Survey"), and cover all prefectures except Hokkaido.

‡ Fiscal year (from April 1 of the year to March 31 of the next year).

national income statistics is on the average twice as high as the propensity computed from survey data. Moreover, the propensity to save of the urban worker families follows an upward trend from 2 per cent (1951) to 12.5 per cent (1957), whereas the nation-wide saving ratios for total personal income and the saving ratios for farm income indicate cyclical movements.

The apparent contradiction among these ratios is not difficult to explain. In the United States, Friend and Kravis have found a similar relation and have provided an interesting interpretation.[2]   Let us apply the Friend-Kravis device to the Japanese income-saving statistics.

The personal income in the national income accounts is composed of employees' income, farm and non-farm independent proprietors' income, and property income.   Therefore, if we can estimate the saving from employees' income and farm proprieters' income, we are in a position to derive saving and the saving ratio from non-farm proprietors' income and property income as residuals.

Table 2 indicates the computational procedure.   It yields a strik-

Table 2.   Saving from Property and Non-farm Proprietors' Incomes

(In billion yen)

Calendar year (1)	Personal saving (National income statistics) (2)	Employees' income × Workers' saving ratio* (3)	Farm proprietors' income × Farmers' saving ratio† (4)	Col.(2) − Col.(3) − Col.(4) (5)	Col.(5) ÷ Col.(2) (Per cent)‡ (6)	Property and non-farm proprietors' income (7)	Col.(5) ÷ Col.(7) (Per cent)§ (8)
1951	664.4	32.7	87.3	544.4	81.9	1,046.0	52.0
1952	756.3	88.9	76.5	590.9	78.1	1,249.5	47.3
1953	564.8	136.6	61.0	367.2	65.0	1,332.3	27.6
1954	594.9	196.8	35.6	362.5	61.0	1,395.5	26.0
1955	772.0	257.4	137.8	376.8	48.8	1,563.2	24.1
1956	1,037.6	379.0	45.8	612.8	59.1	1,843.5	33.2

Source :   See Table 1.

   * The saving ratio to be applied to employees' income should be computed in this case as a ratio not to disposable but to pre-tax income.   The saving ratios thus computed are 1.8, 4.0, 5.1, 6.6, 8.2, 10.5 per cent, respectively, for the period 1951–56.

   † The saving ratios applied here are 9.0, 7.0, 5.6, 3.1, 10.6, and 3.7 per cent, respectively.   Farmers' saving ratios are on a fiscal-year basis but, neglecting probable small errors, are applied to the calendar-year figures.

   ‡ This column is a proportion of saving from property and non-farm proprietors' incomes in total personal saving.

   § This column is a saving ratio from pre-tex property and non-farm proprietors' incomes.

2)   Irwin Friend and Irving B. Kravis, " Entrepreneurial Income, Saving and Investment," *American Economic Review*, XLVII, No. 3 (June, 1957), 269–301.

ing and notable result. By applying the saving ratios computed from the workers' and farmers' family budget data to employees' income and farm proprietors' income, respectively, we get employees' saving and farm proprietors' saving (cols. [3] and [4]). By deducting these from total personal saving, we get property owners' and non-farm proprietors' saving (col. [5]). The ratio of this last figure to total personal saving (col. [4]) and the saving ratio from property income and non-farm proprietors' income (col. [8]) are surprisingly high. The share of property owners' and non-farm proprietors' saving in total personal saving was especially high in 1951 and 1952 (81.9 and 78.1 per cent, respectively) and was around 60 per cent in the succeeding four years. The surprising phenomenon found here was that this share amounts to 60 per cent in recent times. This seems to suggest that in personal saving as defined by the national income statistics workers' and farmers' saving are not very large when compared to saving from property and entrepreneurial income. This finding in Japan corresponds to the American finding by Friend and Kravis that entrepreneurial personal saving amount to 70 per cent of total personal saving, although there is some difference of definitions between the two.

The saving ratio from property and entrepreneurial income is also high, 52 and 47 per cent in 1951–52 and 25.9 per cent on the average between 1953 and 1955. In 1956 it again rises to 33.2 per cent.[3] Thus the saving ratio from property and non-farm proprietors' incomes was fantastically high compared with that of employees and farmers.

There are important reservations to the above analysis. (1) Strictly speaking, property income and saving are shared also by workers and farmers, but we are obliged to combine it with non-farm proprietors' income and saving. (2) Our conclusion depends upon the accuracy

3) In Japan there exists a close relation between small-scale firms and big firms through subcontracts, *etc.* Therefore, when there is an expansion of big firms, complementary small firms also undergo a parallel expansion. This is why investment through internal accumulation is fairly high even in case of small-scale industry, although 20–40 per cent of these firms' fixed investment is composed of used machines bought from big firms, according to the Census of Manufactures.

of the national income statistics as well as upon the accuracy of budget surveys. The writer is independently estimating personal consumption expenditure by the commodity-flow method. The result may be expected to be useful in checking the reliability of the official estimates, but it is not yet finished. However, since the estimate of personal saving is a residual—the difference between disposable income and consumption—it is inevitably subject to a wide margin of error.

Be that as it may, if we compare the total of personal and corporate saving (in the official national income statistics) with an independent estimate of national saving from financial statistics (published by the Bank of Japan), we can see the closeness of the levels and behavior of the two series except in 1951 (Fig. 1). However, the two series are not conceptually the same. (1) The Bank of Japan's estimate excludes changes of cash holdings. It is for this reason that, in 1951,

Fig. 1. Comparison of Saving Estimates from Financial and National Income Estimates

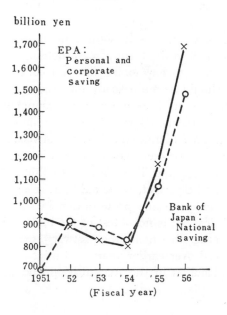

when, owing to the postwar inflation, much saving still took the form of cash balances, the Bank's estimate is so much lower than the official estimate of personal and corporate saving. (2) There are other, more intricate, differences between the two concepts. To make clear these conceptual differences, it may be convenient to use the following method. When personal and corporate sectors are combined, we have a relation

$$S = (M + D) - (F + d) + I,$$

where S=saving, M=changes in cash holdings, D=changes in deposits and security holdings, F=changes in liabilities (including paid-up capital), d=depreciation, and I=gross investment on physical assets. In this case, if we assume that $F+d=I$, as has been roughly shown in the postwar Japanese economy in which corporations' investment funds have been highly dependent upon financial institutions, then we get

$$S = M + D,$$

where S is saving estimated by the national income statistics and D is " national saving " estimated by the Bank of Japan. The difference between the two, M, is only significant in 1951, when quite a bit of saving was still in the form of cash holdings.

Thus, in order to harmonize the two concepts, these statistical adjustments should be numerically followed step by step. Since all these adjustments are here omitted, we cannot put too much faith in the fact that the two series are similar in Figure 1. However, we can expect *a priori* mutual offsetting between $F+d$ and I. Thus the behavior of the two series depicted in Figure 1 seems to give some hint that, although our inference as to the structure of personal saving may not be perfect, we should not reject it as complete nonsense. This creates some presumption in support of the national income statistics, but is not a test of the budget data used in Tables 1 and 2. On the other hand, the postwar Japanese budget data were vastly improved over earlier years and might be fairly dependable. (See the explanation in the statistical appendix.)

210

3. Farmers' Consumption-Saving Pattern

While the aggregate nation-wide saving-consumption function might be examined as a time series, it is more important to tackle saving functions by farmers, urban workers, and non-farm independent proprietors separately. These groups may have behaved very differently during the postwar period of widely disparate growth rates as between sectors of the economy. In particular, the prewar consumption standard appears to have been reached at different dates by the urban and rural populations (in 1951 in the rural sector and in 1957 in the urban sector). As will be argued later, this is very important in understanding differences in changing patterns of saving in the two sectors.

The Farm Household Economy Survey underwent a drastic revision in 1957, so we shall consider only the previous period, 1951–56. The saving ratio of farm families has already been shown in Table 1. By comparing it with the rate of change in farmers' real disposal income (see Table 3), we can fit the following saving equation

$$S_t/Y_t = .4015\,(Y_t/Y_{t-1}) - .3458\,;\ R^2 = .8917, \ldots\ldots\ldots \quad (1)$$

where S_t is real saving, Y_t current real disposable income, Y_{t-1} real disposable income in the preceding period, and R^2 the coefficient of determination. This means that the saving ratio will rise (or decline) according to whether real income rises more (or less) speedily than in preceding periods; alterations between good and bad harvests will bring about an oscillation of the saving ratio. However, provided Y_t/Y_{t-1} is constant, the saving ratio will also be constant in spite of the rise of real income. Figure 2 is a graphical representation of the Japanese farmers' postwar saving function as we have computed it.

This saving function differs from the Duesenberry type in one respect only—that, instead of Y_0 (preceding peak real income), Y_{t-1} is used. If the Duesenberry function is applied,[4] we get

4) J. Duesenberry, *Income, Saving, and the Theory of Consumer Behavior*, Cambridge, Mass.: Harvard University Press, 1949, Chap. 5.

Fig. 2. Saving Function for Farmers

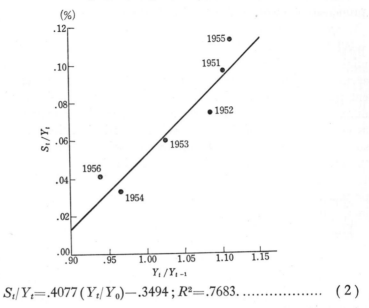

$$S_t/Y_t = .4077\,(Y_t/Y_0) - .3494\,;\, R^2 = .7683. \qquad\qquad (2)$$

The coefficient of determination in this case is less than in equation (1). Probably this reflects farmers' behavior, in which the desired consumption standard has more flexibility than would be required for dominance of Y_0 over Y_{t-1}. Incidentally, the farmers' prewar consumption standard seems to have been more flexible than the postwar one; that is, their saving behavior was symmetrical with respect to upward and downward income changes because the simple Keynesian saving function holds.[5]

Multiplying both sides of equation (1) by Y_t, and differentiating

---

5) The time series of income-saving data for farm families in the prewar period underwent two major revisions in 1924 and 1931. However, we can fit the following linear relations to them,

$$1921\text{--}23 \;.\;.\;.\quad S_t = -716.81 + 0.8173\ Y_t\,;\, R^2 = 0.8414,$$
$$1924\text{--}30 \;.\;.\;.\quad S_t = -603.57 + 0.6010\ Y_t\,;\, R^2 = 0.9756,$$
$$1931\text{--}36 \;.\;.\;.\quad S_t = -297.36 + 0.4592\ Y_t\,;\, R^2 = 0.8717,$$

when S_t and Y_t are in real terms and Y_t is pre-tax income. We see alterations of the saving function because of the revisions, but within each period linear relations exhibit good fits.

212

with respect to Y_t with Y_{t-1} constant, we get a short-run marginal propensity to save:

$$\partial S_t/\partial Y_t = .8030\,(Y_t/Y_{t-1}) - .3458 \quad\quad\quad (3)$$

By substituting each year's rate of increase of real income (Y_t/Y_{t-1}) in equation (3), we find each year's marginal propensity to save in Table 3. The derived marginal propensity to consume during this period is, on the average, .512. This is the *time-series* marginal propensity to consume.

However, we can compute the cross-section marginal propensity to consume of farmers from the Farm Household Economy Survey. By fitting a linear consumption function between income classes, we get the following three equations for 1951, 1953, and 1955:

$$(1951) \quad C = 62,361 + .6219\ Y;\ R^2 = .9826 \quad\quad\quad (4.1)$$
$$(1953) \quad C = 99,520 + .6869\ Y;\ R^2 = .9924 \quad\quad\quad (4.2)$$
$$(1955) \quad C = 115,463 + .6227\ Y;\ R^2 = .9861 \quad\quad\quad (4.3)$$

In the years of good harvest (1951 and 1955), the marginal cross-section propensity to consume is relatively lower, and in the year of bad harvest (1953) it is higher. For all three years it is between 62 and 68 per cent, greater than the time-series average of 51.2 per cent.[6] In agriculture, high income variability over time can be

Table 3. Marginal Propensity to Save of Farmers Derived from the Saving Equation (1)*

Fiscal year	Y_t/Y_{t-1}	$\partial S_t/\partial Y_t$	$\partial C_t/\partial Y_t$	
1951	1.105	.542	.458	
1952	1.085	.525	.475	
1953	1.022	.475	.525	Av. .512
1954	.965	.429	.571	
1955	1.114	.548	.452	
1956	.937	.407	.592	

* The saving function from which the above is derived is $S_t/Y_t = .4015\,(Y_t/Y_{t-1}) - .3458$.

6) The reader may be opposed to this comparison, for the cross-section function holds Y_{t-1} constant, and the time-series does not. However, we shall take up this argument in a later section.

213

expected. Therefore a time-series marginal propensity to save higher than the cross-section propensity might reflect the greater proportion of transitory income variation in total income measured by time series than in family income measured by cross-section, as suggested by Friedman.[7]

If this is so, does the same analysis apply to the consumption of urban workers' families as to that of farm families?

4. *Urban Workers' Consumption-Saving Pattern*

As a farmer's time-series saving function, an ordinary linear function does not fit well for 1951–56 ($S_t=-2,695+.195 Y_t$; $R^2=.111$). A modified Duesenberry function (or the Mack type) gives an excellent fit. On the other hand, a linear consumption function gives a good fit for urban worker families. The *time-series* consumption function using the Statistics Bureau's urban workers' Family Budget data for 1951–56 is computed as follows:

$$\text{(All cities)} \quad C_t=4,036+.726 Y_t; \quad R^2=.982 \quad\dots\dots\dots\dots \quad (5.1)$$
$$\text{(Tokyo)} \quad C_t=3,295+.785 Y_t; \quad R^2=.988 \quad\dots\dots\dots\dots \quad (5.2)$$

where C_t and Y_t are reduced to real terms by the urban and Tokyo consumers' price index. In both cases these typical Keynesian consumption functions imply that the average propensity to save will rise as real income increases. Then, how about the *cross-section* consumption function of all urban worker families? The results fitted to different income classes are as follows:

$$
\begin{aligned}
&\text{(1951)} \quad C=4,116+.690\ Y\\
&\text{(1952)} \quad C=4,858+.681\ Y\\
&\text{(1953)} \quad C=5,906+.683\ Y\\
&\text{(1954)} \quad C=5,653+.705\ Y \quad\dots\dots\dots\dots \quad (6)\\
&\text{(1955)} \quad C=5,737+.695\ Y\\
&\text{(1956)} \quad C=6,719+.650\ Y,
\end{aligned}
$$

7) M. Friedman, *A Theory of the Consumption Function*, Princeton, N.J.: Princeton University Press, 1957.

where the intercepts are in terms of current prices. If these are reduced to 1951 prices, then the intercepts will be 4,116 (1951), 4,627 (1952), 5,278 (1953), 4,746 (1954), 4,870 (1955), and 5,675 (1956). The intercept rose from 1951 to 1953, declined in 1954, and then rose again. This corresponds to the ups and downs of postwar Japanese business fluctuations. Furthermore, the cross-section marginal propensity to consume is relatively higher in recessions (*e.g.*, in 1954) and lower in booms (*e.g.*, in 1956). Anyway, it should be noted that the *time-series* marginal propensity to consume is larger than the *cross-section* marginal propensity to consume. This indicates that the transitory component in measured income is more volatile as between income classes than over time in the urban workers' family budgets. This result is exactly the opposite of that found in analyzing rural farm family budgets.

5. Some Observations

We have completed the computation of time-series and cross-section saving (consumption) functions not only in the urban sector but also in the rural sector. Now we have three problems to be considered. First, why are time-series saving functions of different types as computed between urban and rural sectors? Can they be explained in a consistent manner? Second, can the time-series marginal propensities to save computed directly from $S_t=-a+\beta Y_t$, and derived indirectly from $S_t/Y_t=a(Y_t/Y_0)-b$, be compared with one another? At first sight, the addition of another variable Y_o in the latter function seems to have some influence on the determination of the marginal propensity to save. Therefore, it may differ from that computed from a single variable equation. This seems to invalidate the mutual comparison. Third, can the cross-section marginal propensity to save computed from a linear single-variable function be compared with the time-series marginal propensity to save derived from a type $S_t=f(Y_t, Y_0)$? In this case, too, there is reason for doubt and on similar grounds. Let us go into the first problem.

The first problem is why different changing patterns of consumption and saving have prevailed as between rural farmers and urban workers. To answer this question is very important, for it will throw light upon the economic background of the peculiar saving-consumption patterns in the postwar Japanese economy.

As Table 4 indicates, the year when the real per capita consumption level overtook the prewar standard[8] was 1951 at the latest in the rural sector, whereas it was 1954 or 1955 in the urban sector. Of course, the real per capita consumption or income level is not always a good indicator for showing how far the prewar living standard is from the present one or by how much it is surpassed, since we should take account of asset items as well as income levels and since asset value may have decreased in the postwar period. Therefore the year the prewar standard was surpassed may be much later than 1955 (perhaps 1957), particularly in the urban sector. In my view, the difference between the saving patterns of two sectors is related to the

Table 4. Real Per Capital Consumption-Level Indexes (1934–36 = 100)

Fiscal year	Urban	Rural	Total
1951	70.0	109.4	85.8
1952	83.3	122.3	98.9
1953	95.9	127.9	108.7
1954	100.9	128.5	111.9
1955	108.4	131.2	117.5
1956	110.1	133.6	119.5
1957*	118.4	134.8	125.0

Source : Economic Planning Agency, *Keizai Yoran 1958* (Economic Handbook 1958) Tokyo, 1959.

* Calendar year.

8) In Japan the 1934–36 level of living is very often regarded as the prewar normal in the postwar period, for the Sino-Japanese incident occurred in 1936, and the increase of level of living was retarded or even suppressed thereafter. From 1934 to 1941 the per capita real consumption expenditures were ¥164, ¥155, ¥158, ¥165, ¥161, ¥153, ¥137, and ¥131 in 1934–36 yen, so we can roughly take the 1934–36 average level as the normal prewar standard of living.

year in which each sector surpassed its prewar consumption standard.

To explain this, it is convenient to refer to the so-called Modigliani saving function:

$$S_t/Y_t = a\left(\frac{Y_t - Y_0}{Y_t}\right) + b \quad\dots\dots\dots\dots\dots\dots(7)$$

If we assume that Y_0, the preceding peak income, is constant in the above function, we can derive the following from equation (7):

$$S_t = -[aY_0] + (a+b)\,Y_t \quad\dots\dots\dots\dots\dots (7')$$

Consequently, if the preceding peak income as a standard of consumption-saving behavior is constant at the prewar level, the the saving function will take a simple Keynesian form $(S_t = -a + \beta Y_t)$, for Y_0 is involved in a as a constant. In this case $a = aY_0$ and $\beta = (a+b)$. Thus the linear saving function with one variable $(S_t = -a + \beta Y_t)$ is a special case of the Modigliani function, where Y_0 is assumed as constant and Y_0 is less than Y_0 each year.

My interpretation is as follows: As the prewar living standard seems not to have been surpassed before 1956 in the urban sector, that is, $Y_0 > Y_{51}\dots\dots Y_{56}$, equation (7'), the linear Keynesian saving function, fits very well for the urban worker families. On the other hand, in the case of farm families, the prewar consumption standard had already been surpassed before 1951,[9] and Y_0 changed to a postwar standard. When the farm real income grows steadily, $Y_0 = Y_{-1}$, and the real income of the preceding year will become the previous peak income, changing its value every year. Therefore a function $S_t = -a + \beta Y_t$ does not fit $(R^2 = .111)$, for theoretically it assumes a constancy of Y_0. Although there are slight formal differences between the Duesenberry and Modigliani saving functions, the two are

---

9) Before 1950 we cannot get a clear picture of the real per capita consumption level of farmers. Moreover, there was a complete revision in the Farm Household Economy Survey between 1948 and 1949, and it is difficult to get comparable series. However, we know that before 1948 farmers' family budgets showed surpluses, while their real incomes were relatively constant. Thanks to the black market in rice, they enjoyed a higher *relative* income position (compared with urban workers) than they had ever experienced before. This might be why they maintained a budget surplus, even if their absolute income was lower than the prewar standard.

essentially the same. The reason for fitting a modified Duesenberry function as farmers' saving function can thus be stated simply.

During the period 1951–56 the two saving functions in the urban and rural districts were completely *heterogeneous*. The problem is what will happen when both will become homogeneous in the near future. The saving ratio of urban workers has risen to a high of 11.8 per cent in 1956. This might be close to the prewar normal saving ratio of workers. In 1957 it rose to 12.5 per cent. Probably this percentage will be the maximum. To guess that the urban saving ratio will follow the equation $S_t/Y_t = a(Y_t/Y_{t-1}) - b$ henceforward is not unreasonable. Of course, it remains a question whether Y_0 or Y_{t-1} will be more influential. However, it is almost certain that the urban workers' saving function will depart from the Keynesian linear type and become homogeneous with the farmers' saving function in the very near future. I suspect this movement will begin in 1958. (After the original draft had been written, I saw the 1958 urban saving ratio. This is 12.6 per cent, almost the same as the 1957 ratio, in spite of the increase of real disposable income per household of 7.3 per cent. From this, we may also assume that the prewar living standard was reached in 1957 in the mind of urban workers.)

The second problem is whether or not we can compare the marginal propensity to save (or consume) computed from the equation $S_t = -a + \beta Y_t$ with the marginal propensity derived from $S_t/Y_t = a(Y_t/Y_0) - b$. However, as explained above, the validity of $S_t = -a + \beta Y_t$ is limited to the period when Y_0 is constant and higher than Y_t each year. In the United States the linear Keynesian consumption function exhibits a fine fit for 1929–39, when the 1929 peak per capita disposable personal income in 1958 prices ($1,148) had not been surpassed (1933=$812, 1939=$1,119, and 1940=$1,188).[10] This relation, however, could not be projected correctly before 1929 or to the postwar period. The same holds true for the postwar Japanese consumption functions. It is important to keep in mind that the key point lies in the fact that, if Y_0 were constant, the Modigliani function would reduce to a simple linear function, and it fits only in

10) *Economic Report of the President*, Washington, D. C., 1959, p. 155.

218

the depression or postwar period, when Y_t is lower than Y_0 and when Y_0 is constant. Thus, explicitly or implicitly, Y_0 operates in both functions.

The third problem surrounds the comparability between the *cross-section* marginal propensity to save computed from a linear single-variable function and the *time-series* marginal propensity derived from a type $S_t=f(Y_t, Y_0)$. In this case, too, Y_0 does not appear in the former equation, but it does in the latter. However, we may imagine that some desired living standard is given socially every year. Both the relative and permanent income hypotheses actually assume this relation. As discussed in the second argument, Y_0 is implicitly assumed in the cross-section function, too, and I believe the two marginal propensities can be compared with each other.

Let me summarize the results computed concerning the two sectors (Table 5). First, it seems clear that the farmers' time-series marginal propensity to consume is less than the urban workers' time-series marginal propensity to consume. This could be due to the higher transitory component in the measured farmers' income, which is in turn subject to changes of harvest and to some entrepreneurial factors.

Second, one might expect farm income to vary much more than urban workers' income in cross-section as well as in time series. However, the cross-section data show about the same marginal propensity to consume among farmers as urban workers. Let me explain this. In the time series the income variations are discontinuously distributed over time, but in the cross section the income variations due to good and bad harvests are fairly *common* phenomena to any income class of farmers, particularly in a small country like Japan. Therefore, we have a particular reason why the farmers'

Table 5. Marginal Propensity to Consume

	Time series	Cross-section
Farmers	.45—.59	.62—.68
Urban workers	.72—.78	.65—.70

219

cross-section marginal propensity to consume is not always less than the urban workers'.

6. Conclusions

Some characteristics of the saving-consumption relations in post-war Japan have been made clear. They may be summarized as follows:

1. The saving functions are quite *heterogeneous* as between urban workers and rural farmers from 1951 to 1956. I have argued that this is due to the difference in the year when the prewar level of living was exceeded. Therefore the heterogeneity of saving functions should disappear in the immediate future. (The appearance of the 1958 result has supported this view.)

2. Therefore, it is bad procedure simply to extrapolate the saving function (*e.g.*, for the years 1951–56) to the future in long-range economic projection. There may be a transformation, particularly in the workers' saving function (*i.e.*, from the type $S_t = -a + \beta Y_t$ to the type $S_t/Y_t = a[Y_t/Y_{t-1}] - b$), when the prewar consumption standard is surpassed. The Duesenberry, the Modigliani, or the Friedman function enables us to deal with the above synthetically, whether we use Y_0 or Y_{t-1} as our strategic variable.

3. As shown in the United States by Friend and Kravis, the saving ratio from individual proprietors' and property owners' incomes is extremely high. Their saving amounts to about 60 per cent of total personal saving. This may be due either to their high internal investment or to the high transitory to permanent income ratio, as suggested by Friedman's hypothesis.

4. Using time-series data, a function of the type $(S_t/Y_t = a(Y_t/Y_{t-1}) - b$ fits better than the type $S_t/Y_t = a(Y_t/Y_0) - b$ as an estimate of the farmers' time-series saving function. Whether Y_0 or Y_{t-1} is more dominant in the saving equation may indicate the rigidity or flexibility of the past consumption standard.

5. The time-series marginal propensity to save for farmers is higher than that for urban workers, as may be expected from the perma-

nent income hypothesis. However, the same does not hold for the cross-section. In the time series, farmers' income will change in an erratic way, but, in the cross-section, the effects of harvests on income variability are expected to be fairly *common* to any current income class. This is why different results follow from time series and cross-section analyses. In the urban workers' data, the time-series marginal propensity to save is lower than the cross-section marginal propensity to save, whereas the reverse result is evidenced in the data for rural farmers.

APPENDIX

Two major family-budget surveys have been made in postwar Japan : the " Family Income Expenditure Survey " of urban workers and the " Farm Household Economy Survey " of farmers. Let us explain in brief the contents of and the methods used in these two surveys.

a) *Family Income and Expenditure Survey (F.I.E.S.)*

The origin of F.I.E.S. was the Consumer Price Survey (C.P.S.) started in July, 1946, by the Statistics Bureau of the Prime Minister's Office. It aimed at obtaining consumer price data as well as family expenditures in all urban areas. C.P.S. was a survey of urban family expenditures only; the parallel Family Income Survey (F.I.S.) was introduced two years later, in July, 1948. However, the sample basis of F.I.S. was different from that of C.P.S.

Beginning with September, 1950, C.P.S. and F.I.S. were combined in one survey, F.I.E.S., while price data have been left to be obtained from a different survey, the Retail Price Survey, commenced in June, 1950. In F.I.E.S., income and expenditures are surveyed for worker families only, while for other families only the expenditure side is covered.

The subjects of the survey are about four thousand households selected from all urban areas by stratified multistage random sampling. Each of the six largest cities constitutes a stratum. All cities other than the six largest were grouped in twenty-two strata, each stratum representing approximately the same size of population and geographical area; thus both size and regional differences in consumer prices, incomes, and expenditures were taken into account. One city from each stratum was then selected, for a total of twenty-eight cities. These are shown in Table A.

Table A

Population of 400,000 and over	Population of 100,000—400,000	Population of 50,000—100,000
Tokyo	Sapporo	Obihiro
Osaka	Sendai	Aomori
Yokohama	Chiba	Takasaki
Nagoya	Kofu	Matsumoto
Kyoto	Toyama	Matsusaka
Kobe	Hamamatsu*	Nara
	Tokushima	Otsu
	Hiroshima	Tottori
	Fukuoka	Hofu
	Nagasaki	Imabari
	Kagoshima	Miyakonojo

From each of the twenty-eight cities a definite number of unit areas were selected, and from each unit area four to five households with two members and over were selected (excluding agricultural, fishery, and other special households). The number of households to be surveyed in each city is proportional to the size of the stratum: 650 households from Tokyo, 350 from Osaka, 200 from each of the four other largest cities, and 100 from each of the remaining twenty-two cities.

The period for making entries of items is six months, and one-sixth of the families rotate each month.

Since 1953 expenditures have been classified, according to their *use*; for example, food and drink expenses for the treatment of visitors are classified in the miscellaneous group as social expenses. Prior to January, 1953, however, expenses were classified according to the kind of *commodities* purchased irrespective of their use. For the sake of comparability between the present data and the series before the revision, expenditures in one-third of the monthly sample are retabulated according to the classification of commodities.

The inflow and outflow in the family budget are surveyed according to the system shown in Table B. The cross-section figures on disposable income and consumer expenditures, classified by income classes, are summarized in Table C. Incidentally, the figures on the lowest-income families here present a striking confirmation of the idea that people in that bracket are there only temporarily: consumption exceeds disposable income tenfold!

Table B

Inflow	Outflow

1. Income before tax
  a) Wages and salaries
  b) Income from business and home work
  c) Other incomes, including social benefits
 	
2. Receipts other than income
  d) Deposits cashed
  e) Insurance proceeds
  f) Debts and credit purchases
  g) Others
 	
3. Cash holdings at the beginning of the month
	4. Consumer expenditures
	  a) Food
	  b) Housing
	  c) Fuel and light
	  d) Clothing
	  e) Miscellaneous
	
	5. Income tax and other public charges
	
	6. Disbursements other than expenditures
	  f) Deposits
	  g) Insurance premium payments
	  h) Debts and credit purchases repaid
	  i) Others
	
	7. Cash holdings at the end of the month

Note: (1+2+3)=(4+5+6+7).

b) *Farm Household Economy Survey*

Before the war the number of families surveyed with respect to farm household budgets was extremely small; 200 in 1924, 342 in 1931, and 1,400 in 1942. However, in 1949 the scale and method of the survey were significantly improved; the number of farm households to be surveyed was raised to 5,500, and the stratified random sampling method was introduced. To data on incomes and expenditures was added information on physical and liquid assets.

223

Table C. Monthly Disposable Income
Families by Pre-
(In

Pre-Tax Incomes	1951 Y_d	1951 C	1952 Y_d	1952 C	1953 Y_d	1953 C
Under ￥ 3,999	947	9,498	813	11,770	1,004	13,382
￥ 4,000-￥ 5,999	4,861	7,980⎫	6,039	9,213	6,020	10,354
￥ 6,000-￥ 7,999	6,684	8,431⎭				
￥ 8,000-￥ 9,999	8,509	9,609⎫	9,789	11,339	9,710	12,095
￥10,000-￥11,999	10,262	10,942⎭				
￥12,000-￥13,999	12,012	12,264⎫	13,317	13,582	13,279	14,203
￥14,000-￥15,999	13,795	13,692⎭				
￥16,000-￥17,999	15,460	14,995⎫	16,831	16,234	16,680	16,740
￥18,000-￥19,999	17,130	16,071⎭				
￥20,000-￥21,999	18,653	17,341⎫	20,081	18,749	20,076	19,491
￥22,000-￥23,999	20,367	18,351⎭				
￥24,000-￥25,999	21,947	19,445⎫	23,459	21,174	23,389	21,848
￥26,000-￥27,999	23,477	19,885⎭				
￥28,000-￥29,999	25,187	25,351⎫	26,696	23,247	26,551	24,724
￥30,000-￥31,999	33,143	25,991⎭				
￥32,000-￥35,999			29,921	24,846	29,690	26,734
￥36,000-￥39,999			33,002	27,332	32,731	28,918
￥40,000-￥43,999			44,035	34,158	35,844	31,181
￥44,000-￥47,999					39,019	33,357
￥48,000-￥51,999					41,526	34,305
￥52,000-￥55,999					45,077	37,145
￥56,000-￥59,999					47,260	35,812
￥60,000-￥63,999					59,586	43,785
￥64,000-￥67,999						
￥68,000-￥71,999						
￥72,000-￥75,999						
￥76,000-￥79,999						
Over ￥80,000						
Av.(Jan.-Nov.)	13,737	13,787	17,565	17,045	21,400	20,502
Av.(Jan.-Dec.)	14,917	14,620	18,991	18,161	23,065	21,727

Sources : Sorifu Tokei Kyoku (Statistics Bureau of Prime Minister's Office),
Sengo Junen no Kakei (Family Income and Expenditure in Postwar
Ten Years) Tokyo, 1956 ; *Kakeichosa Nempo*, 1956 (Annual Report
of Family Budget Survey, 1956).

Notes : 1) Y_d=Disposable income ; C=Consumer expenditure.
2) Figures classified by income classes are monthly averages for the

and Consumption of Urban Worker
tax Income Classes
yen)

| | 1954 | | 1955 | | 1956 | 1955 Numbers of Families |
Y_d	C	Y_d	C	Y_d	C	
718	14,543	772	15,324	713	15,904	530
6,061	11,270	6,034	10,399	6,006	10,882	781
9,780	12,266	9,760	12,290	9,806	12,258	1,752
13,356	14,367	13,500	14,373	13,561	14,512	3,199
16,852	16,890	16,898	16,773	17,082	16,889	4,069
20,164	19,675	20,236	19,340	20,443	19,466	4,147
23,443	21,985	23,713	21,995	23,814	21,945	3,343
26,884	24,833	26,881	24,712	27,122	24,644	2,651
29,829	26,989	30,179	26,915	30,619	26,911	1,953
32,852	28,627	33,207	28,776	33,520	29,086	1,489
35,652	31,367	36,332	31,931	36,747	31,308	1,110
38,958	33,539	38,979	32,722	39,505	33,334	750
41,425	34,263	41,747	36,134	42,721	35,814	688
44,676	37,084	45,049	38,071	45,619	37,776	435
47,568	40,312	48,352	38,769	48,832	39,622	294
49,624	40,010	50,745	41,133	50,291	41,446	259
52,861	42,292	54,643	43,850	54,237	41,438	179
54,515	43,012	56,025	45,017	57,832	43,401	154
57,953	46,481	58,083	46,210	59,678	43,763	121
62,939	51,210	62,421	47,178	63,444	45,740	81
77,507	54,606	80,923	54,326	91,792	54,498	330
22,361	22,090	23,996	22,328	25,254	22,950	28,315
24,922	23,067	25,896	23,513	27,464	24,231	

period from January to November.
3) Numbers of families surveyed are accumulated ones from January to November, so they must be divided by 11 in order to get average numbers per month.
4) These relate only to the urban *worker* families in all cities. This is why the total number is less than 4,000 per month.

Further revisions were made in 1952 and then (in detail) in 1957. The exposition here relates to the survey before the 1957 revision.

The period surveyed ranges from April 1 through March 31; for the period 1952–56 coverage was 5,800 families.

The selection of towns and villages for the survey was done as follows:

1. All Japan was divided into eleven major " agricultural districts " by meteorological and geographical conditions, by the type of farm management, and so on.
2. All cities, towns, and villages in each " agricultural district " were classified by the percentage of cultivated land and then by the percentage of irrigated land.
3. The next step was to set up unit areas comprising about 10,000 farm households (8,000 in case of Hokkaido), taking into account the border lines of various prefectures.
4. Homogeneity of each of the units was a major criterion of boundary determination; hence all the unit areas are classified as follows:

Table D.

Inflow	Outflow

1. Farming receipts
  a) Rice
  b) Wheat, Barley, *etc.*
    .
    .
    .
    etc.
2. Receipts from non-farming business
3. Wages and salaries
4. Rental and interest income
5. Gifts, subsidies, *etc.*, received
6. Sales of assets, debts, withdrawal from deposits. *etc.*
	7. Family expenditure
	8. Farming expenditure
	9. Non-farm business expenditures
	10. Taxes and public charges
	11. Purchases of assets, deposits, debt payments
	12. Changes in cash-holdings

Notes: $(1+2+3+4+5+6)=(7+8+9+10+11+12)$.
Disposable income $=(1+2+3+4+5)-(8+9+10)$.
Farm economic surplus $=$ Disposable income $-(7)$.

A) Purely farm area
  a) Grain farming   d) Fruit-growing
  b) Vegetable farming   e) Tea-growing
  c) Sericulture   f) Others
B) Urban area on the periphery of large cities
C) Mountainous area
D) Fishing area

5. Each unit area within a city, town or village was further divided into five strata by the size of cultivated land per farm household, and each stratum was regarded as a sampling universe.
6. The number of surveyed cities, towns, and villages was 580;

Table E. Annual Disposable Income and Consumption of Farm Households
Classified by Income Classes
(In yen)

Pre-tax income	1951		1953		1955	
	Y_d	C	Y_d	C	Y_d	C
Farmers with deficit					-131,583	265,270
Under ¥100,000	84,112	95,664	62,475	143,255	64,423	154,927
¥100,000–¥150,000	127,453	133,242	117,239	170,951	118,398	171,891
¥150,000–¥200,000	175,362	171,305	167,076	203,172	163,719	206,710
¥200,000–¥250,000	224,321	206,938	207,898	242,458	208,196	242,590
¥250,000–¥300,000	273,197	240,091	251,407	281,591	251,923	276,550
¥300,000–¥350,000	322,424	271,475	314,897	327,467	316,787	328,461
¥350,000–¥400,000	372,680	310,180				
¥400,000–¥450,000	424,693	337,591	401,383	387,175	414,794	384,780
¥450,000–¥500,000	476,075	364,311				
¥500,000–¥700,000	623,434	423,030	583,865	486,870	516,838	463,120
Over ¥700,000					764,030	565,589
Average	242,302	215,949	265,115	284,089	322,091	312,757

Sources : Norinsho (Ministry of Agriculture and Forestry), *Noka no Sozeikoka-shofutan ni kansuru Chosa* (Survey of the Taxes and Public Charges on the Farm Households), 1951, 1953, and 1955.

Notes : 1) Y_d=Disposable income ; C=Consumption.
        2) These relate to the figures of fiscal years for the whole country, including Hokkaido. In this respect, it differs from the time series in the text, which exclude Hokkaido.

that of surveyed farm households was 5,800. Therefore, from each city, town, or village surveyed, ten farm households were selected. Of these, there was one household for each of five strata (classified above by the scale of cultivated land) ; the other five were picked up by systematic random sampling from the entire unit area.

The items surveyed are very comprehensive and detailed, but this discussion is restricted to the system of inflow and outflow (Table D).

Table E gives the national farm family disposable income-consumption data classified by income classes for the fiscal years 1951, 1953, and 1955 (Hokkaido is included).

CHAPTER 10

SAVING AND CONSUMPTION PATTERNS IN JAPAN : A POSTMORTEM AND FURTHER ANALYSES

1. Introduction

This chapter will attempt to supplement the analyses in the preceding chapter on the structure of saving and consumption in Japan. First, it may be interesting to test the foregoing analysis of the saving behavior of urban worker and farm households using more recent data, for this will enable us to judge the validity of our hypothesis, and indicate any necessary revisions.   Secondly, it will be desirable to extend our analysis with more detailed family budget studies for the period before and after the Second World War.

A. POSTWAR STUDIES

2. A Postmortem

The first problem is to find to what extent our saving function fitted for 1951–56 for farm households also fits an extended period, 1951–59. As indicated on p. 211 in the preceding chapter, the saving equation computed, for 1951–56, was,

$$S_t/Y_t = .4015\,(Y_t/Y_{t-1}) - .3458\,;\quad R^2 = .8917 \ \ldots\ldots\ldots \quad (1)$$

where S_t is real saving, Y_t current real disposable income, and Y_{t-1} real disposable income in the preceding period. However, if the longer period 1951–59 is staken, including the three years 1957–59, recomputed saving function becomes as follows :

$$S_t/Y_t = .4031\,(Y_t/Y_{t-1}) - .3448\,;\ R^2 = .8767 \ \ldots\ldots\ldots \ (2)$$

The parameters in the two functions are almost the same. The two saving equations are shown in Fig. 1. Although there is a very slight difference between the two, it shows that our saving function (a modified Duesenberry type) is of almost the same form, and supports the validity of our hypothesis.

For the time-series consumption function of urban worker families linear curves were fitted for 1951–56 (p. 214), with extremely high coefficients of determination, (.982 for all cities, and .988 for Tokyo). However, as pointed out by Bean and Haavelmo,[1] consumption expenditures comprise a major portion of disposable income (80–90%), so that even an extremely high correlation between consumption and income may sometimes be spurious. Particularly, the non-

Fig. 1. The Saving Function of Farm Households (1951–59)

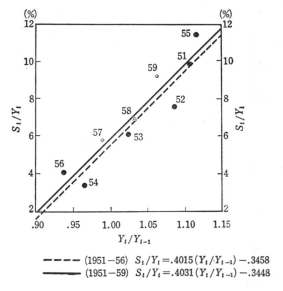

$$----\ (1951-56)\ \ S_t/Y_t = .4015(Y_t/Y_{t-1}) - .3458$$
$$————\ (1951-59)\ \ S_t/Y_t = .4031(Y_t/Y_{t-1}) - .3448$$

1) Louis H. Bean, " Relation of Disposable Income and the Business Cycle to Expenditures ", *Review of Economic Statistics*, Nov. 1946; Trygve Haavelmo, " Methods of Measuring the Marginal Propensity to Consume ", *Journal of the American Statistical Association*, Vol. 42, 1947.

linearity of the function which may be apparent in the form of the saving function tends to be obscured in the consumption function. Therefore, in Fig. 2, the saving-income and the saving ratio-income relations are depicted.

Conspicuous kinks can be seen around 1953 and 1956 in the saving-income relation, as well as in the saving ratio-income relation. The kink around 1953, which could not been clearly seen, in the form of the consumption function, is now very evident. For 1951–53, the slope is moderate, but, for 1953–56, it becomes steeper. The problem to be explained here is the occurrence of the kinks in 1953 and 1956. In Chapter 9, we have argued that the linear Keynesian consumption function with a positive intercept holds true with respect to urban worker families, and concluded that this would not

Fig. 2.   The Saving-Income Relation for Urban Worker Households, 1951–59

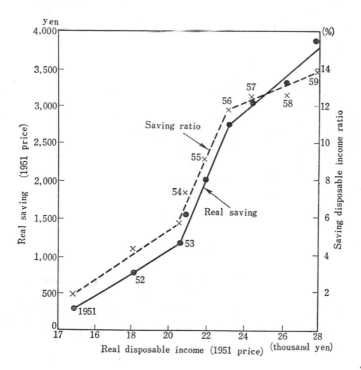

be so after the current real incomes have exceeded the prewar peak level. The unchanged saving ratio for 1957–58 (12.5%, 12.6%) might have supported our view. However, in 1959, the saving ratio of the urban worker families rose again to 13.9%, continuing to increase to 15% in 1960. Of course, whether this tendency will continue or not is a question, but some of our conjectures, presented in the preceding chapter, may have to be amended. These are reasons why a postmortem is also necessary with respect to the saving-consumption relation of the urban worker families.

One reason for the kink around 1953 may be that the rate of increase in real disposable income of the urban worker families declined in 1952–54 (21.3% in 1952, 14.0% in 1953, and 1.5% in 1954), but rose in 1955–56 (4.8% in 1955, and 5.5% in 1956). This may partly explain the kink, if we assume that real saving is a functon of real disposable income, and changes in the latter. We derive the following saving function, which satisfies this condition,

$$S_t = -6,381 + 0.3854\ Y_t + 0.0231\ \Delta Y_t, \quad R^2 = 0.8974\ \ldots. \quad (3)$$

for 1952–56.

Another reason can be stated as follows: Before 1954, the rate of increase of the consumer price index was higher than in the following period. This probably explains why the rise in savings was larger after 1954 than before, for in an inflationary situation the savers might incur a loss due to the decline of real outstanding liquid assets. Table 1 indicates that the increase in time deposits was relatively slow for 1951–54 at a time when the consumer price index was increasing at a relatively higher rate (over 5% per annum), while, after 1955 when prices were stabilized, time deposits rapidly increased from ¥290 billion (1955) to ¥691 billion (1959). Of course, this increase was partly due to the rise in national income during this period, amounting to 47.5%, but the rise in time deposits for the same period was 2.38 times. It is very clear that the stabilization of consumer prices since 1953–54 has contributed tremendously not only to the increase in time deposits, but also to the increase in other types of liquid asset holdings. In Table 1, the real rate of interest is computed, according to Irving Fisher's definition.[2] During this

2) Irving Fisher, *The Theory of Interest*, New York, 1930, Chapter 2.

232

Table 1. Price Stability and Increase in Time Deposits

	Interest rates on time deposits	Changes in C.P.I	Real rates of interest	Increase in time deposits of all banks
1951	5.43 %	16.5 %	—9.50 %	197 billion yen
52	6.00	4.9	+1.50	297
53	6.00	6.6	—0.56	247
54	6.00	6.4	—0.38	233
55	6.00	—1.1	+7.18	290
56	6.00	0.4	+5.58	445
57	6.00	3.1	+2.81	494
58	6.00	—0.5	+6.53	632
59	6.00	1.1	+4.85	691

Note :   Real rate of interest = (1 + money rate of interest) / (1 + rate of increase of C.P.I.) − 1.

Source :   The Bank of Japan, *Hompo Keizai Tokei* (Economic Statistics of Japan), 1960.

period, the rate of interest on time deposits was almost constant, so the changes in the real interest rate were accounted for by the changes in the consumer price index.   Strictly speaking, changes in prices, as deflators of the money rate of interest, should be anticipated changes but this table would be a useful approximation for over-all judgment.

Another kink in the saving curve around 1956, indicated on Fig. 2, might be explained as follows.   In the previous chapter, we have stated that the saving ratio of urban worker families would stop rising after 1957, for in 1957–58 it was 12.5% and 12.6% and we have concluded that this might have been the turning point.   It seems to us that as the upward trend in the saving ratio comes to a halt, the linear Keynesian saving function with negative intercept, so far valid, would not show a good fit in the future.   Instead, a saving function, like Duesenberry's, seems to be more appropriate, with rural and urban saving patterns tending to become increasingly homogeneous.   However, actually in 1959, the saving ratio increased to 13.9%, rising to 15% in 1960.   This shows that the upper limit of the urban worker saving ratio is not around 12.3%, but rather around 15%. This leads us to the following consideration: the prewar saving ratio should not be the sole criterion in setting up the postwar normal ratio. As an indicator of the postwar normal ratio, the liquid assets-national income ratios before and after the war must be taken into consideration. Although adequate data on urban worker's families are not available, the ratio between the cash in circulation plus all deposits and national income is quoted for reference.

As Table 2 indicates, the ratio of " cash plus deposits " to national income fell drastically after the war (1.76 in 1935 and 0.62 in 1951). However, after that, the ratio has made a substantial recovery towards the prewar level, and in 1960 it was 1.58. We do not intend to make the unlikely assertion that this ratio should normally be constant. On the contrary, as the historical experience of advanced countries shows, this ratio (or the Marshallian k) always tends to rise. What we would like to emphasize here is that for the four years, 1951–55,

Table 2.　Cash-Deposits *vs.* National Income Ratio, 1935, 1951–60

(Unit＝billion yen)

	National income (a)	Cash in circulation (b)	Deposits of all financial institutions (c)	$[b+c]$ (d)	$\left[\dfrac{d}{a}\right]$ (e)
1935	14.4	2.0	23.3	25.3	1.76
1951	4,535.3	510.2	2,307.7	2,817.9	.62
1955	6,528.0	695.0	6,277.0	6,972.0	1.07
1956	7,352.2	812.1	7,907.6	8,719.7	1.19
1957	8,201.2	868.8	9,416.7	10,285.5	1.25
1958	8,340.9	930.8	11,267.6	12,198.4	1.46
1959	9,630.8	1,083.1	13,300.1	14,383.2	1.49
1960	11,229.0	1,296.8	16,396.3	17,693.1	1.58

Notes :　These figures are crude, in the sense that (b), (c) and (d) are the amounts outstanding at the end of the year, and also do not exclude the amounts held by the governments.

Source :　National income ; The Economic Planning Agency, *Kokuminshotoku Hakusho* (National Income Report) 1959, Cash and Deposits ; The Bank of Japan, *Hompo Keizai Tokei* (Economic Statistics of Japan), 1960.

the ratio increased by 72.6%, but for the remaining four years, 1955–59, it only increased by 39.3%. Clearly, the rate of increase of this ratio declined, and it will continue to decline, as it approaches a ratio people will consider normal, or a normal rate of increase. The decline in the rate of increase in the ratio may suggest that it is approaching normality.

Thus, the extremely rapid increase rate in cash and deposits, relative to national income, in the post-war period will partly explain the rising trend in the saving ratio, especially for the urban worker households. After the liquid assets-income ratio declined sharply due to the postwar hyperinflation, there would have been a natural desire to pull up the ratio to a normal level. Such being the case, the restoration of per capita real income to prewar levels cannot solely account for the stopping or slowing down of the rising trend in the urban worker's saving ratio. Even if real income has reached the prewar level, the saving ratio might still continue to rise, provided that the assets-income ratio is lower than the prewar ratio or lower than the ratio that people now take to be normal under the changed conditions of the postwar economy.

Our analysis in the preceding chapter assumed that the upward trend in the urban worker's saving ratio will stop when people believe that the prewar level of real income is reached. However, we did not take into account the assets side nor the adoption of a new postwar consumption standard due to the rapid transformation of the consumption pattern with the introduction of western consumer durables, *etc.* But, even if these are considered, it is not plausible to suppose that the saving ratio of urban worker families will just continue to rise to 17%, 18%, and so on. It is my guess that about the 15–16% line will be the ceiling.

As explanations of the changes in the postwar saving ratios of urban worker families, we have already considered two hypotheses, the relative income hypothesis and the liquid assets hypothesis. However, the postwar Japanese data enable us to make an analysis based on the permanent income hypothesis. Table 3 computes the transitory income proportions as % of disposable income for urban worker families in 1951–60.

Table 3. Transitory Component in Incomes of Urban Worker Families, for
1951–60

	Disposable income (a)	Incomes of transitory nature			
		Temporary income & subsidiary jobs (b)	Business & home work (c)	Total (d)	$\left[\dfrac{d}{a}\right]$
1951	14,917	1,409	250	1,659	11.1 %
52	18,991	2,046	317	2,363	12.4
53	23,065	3,220	516	3,736	16.2
54	24,922	3,281	514	3,795	15.2
55	25,896	3,156	610	3,766	14.5
56	27,464	3,864	635	4,449	16.4
57	29,810	4,488	669	5,157	17.3
58	31,824	4,692	664	5,356	16.8
59	34,122	5,361	737	6,098	17.9
60	37,708	6,605	912	7,517	19.9

Source : The Statistics Bureau, Prime Minister's Office, *Kakeichosa Nempo* ("Annual Report of Family Budget Survey "), 1951–60.

Notes : 1) (b) is composed of various allowances for overtime work, bonuses, *etc.* and of worker's income from subsidiary jobs.

2) (c) is composed of renumerations for writing, tutorage, *etc.* and of various business income, like those from sales of tobacco, cake, grocery, *etc.*

We can make the following remarks on the basis of this table : 1) Corresponding to the steep rise in the saving ratio for 1951–60, the proportion of transitory income too shows a rise from 11.1% (1951) to 19.9% (1960).   2) From 1955 onwards, the cyclical changes in the proportion of transitory component are almost in parallel with those in the saving ratio.   If this aspect is taken seriously into account, the recent continual rise in the urban worker's saving ratio can be interpreted as reflecting an increase of transitory income (bonuses, *etc.*) due to the acceleration of economic growth.   However, the proportion of transitory income cannot be expected to rise beyond 20%, when we see the relative stability of this ratio for 1956–59 (16.4%, 17.3%, 16.8%, 17.9%).

Thus, we have argued the movement of the urban worker's saving

Fig. 3. Saving Ratio and Transitory Income Proportion for Urban Worker Families

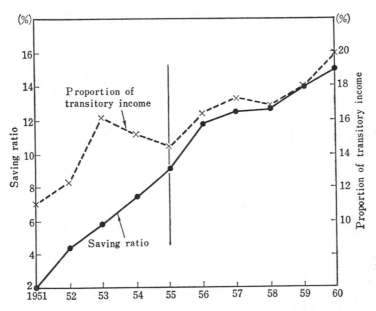

ratio in terms of the three hypotheses, *i.e.*, the relative income hypothesis, the liquid assets hypothesis and the permanent income hypothesis. It is of course difficult to combine these three into one composite model given the present state of statistical information, but when more useful and longer time series are available in the near future, we may be able to ascertain to some extent the relative merit of each hypothesis.

3. *A New Survey of Savings by Occupations in 1959*

The Statistics Bureau of the Prime Minister's Office has recently announced a new survey, *Chochiku Doko Chosa* (A Survey on Saving Behavior) 1959, from which information on the savings of non-farm individual proprietors, as well as of administrators of corporations, *etc.*, and professional classes has become available for the first time.

Table 4. Saving Ratios by Occupation, 1959

(Unit : yen)

Occupations	No. of households	Annual incomes before taxes (a)	Liquid savings (b)	Investment in household assets (c)	Investment for business use (d)	[b+c+d] (e)	$\left[\dfrac{e}{a}\right]$ (f)
Total	2,370	474,876	48,726	26,698	—	75,424	15.9 %
Worker households	1,628	453,582	45,035	25,465	—	70,500	15.5
Regular laborers	551	353,087	25,429	13,303	—	38,732	11.0
Day laborers	56	202,958	−988	8,089	—	7,101	3.5
Non-official staff	704	539,144	65,909	38,287	—	104,196	19.3
Official staff	317	482,516	40,886	21,195	—	62,081	12.9
Other households	742	521,596	56,825	29,406	—	86,231	16.5
Proprietors & artisans	551	497,657	48,203	21,895	36,534	106,632	21.4
Administrators	44	937,677	182,914	49,136	—	232,050	24.7
Professional services & others	58	739,928	82,384	120,762	—	203,166	27.5
Without-occupations	89	321,810	31,207	6,601	—	37,808	11.7

Sources : The Statistics Bureau, Prime Minister's Office, *Chochiku Doko Chosa* (A Survey on Saving Behaviors), 1959.

Notes : 1) Liquid savings (b) do not include net decrease in installment and credit purchases.

2) Investment for business use (d) excludes changes in inventories.

3) Investments (c) and (d) do not exclude second-hand physical asset.

As discussed in the preceding chapter, there is a big discrepancy between the personal saving ratio from the official national income statistics and the corresponding ratios from the two sample surveys of urban worker families and farm households. For 1959, the respective personal saving ratios were 19.0% from the former and 13.9% and 9.2% from the latter. By a tentative computation, we have arrived at a guess that the saving ratios from property incomes and of individual proprietors may have been considerably higher than any of the above. However, this is an estimation made on the assumption that the national income statistics and sampling surveys are correct and that urban workers and farmers do not receive a significant amount of property income. Fortunately, the above mentioned new survey provides us with useful information, although the data may not be too convincing until results of future surveys are compared.

Table 4 indicates that the saving ratio of non-farm proprietors is 21.4%, even excluding changes in inventories and even when compared with the before-tax income. If it were compared with disposable income, and inventory investment were taken into consideration, it may rise to about 30%. On the other hand, the saving ratio of the corporate administrators, *etc.* is 24.7%, and that of those engaged in professional occupations is 27.5%. Of course, these figures contain the deficiencies noted in the footnotes of Table 4, and so the saving ratio of worker households (15.5%) in Table 4 does not coincide with that computed from the family budget survey of urban worker families (13.9%). Biases to this extent may exist in every saving ratio computed in Table 4, but these ratios will give an approximate picture, indicating how high the saving ratios from personal property and entrepreneurial incomes are, even if a close numerical agreement with the results from the official national income statistics cannot be expected.

4. Changes in Cross-Section Differences of Saving Ratios in Post-war Period

So far, our analysis were focused on the time-series saving function and the structure of personal saving, but the intertemporal changes in cross-section differences of saving ratios, would also be of interest. Let us take up the survey of the budgets for urban worker families made by the Statistics Bureau of the Prime Minister's Office. In Table 5, we have checked changes in the saving ratios over time, corresponding to various real income classes (in terms of 1951 price). This comparison of saving ratios is made only among the similar real income levels, but even this rough check will help to make clear the variations in the saving ratios corresponding to the

Fig. 4. Cross-section Saving-income Relation for Urban Worker Households in 1951–59

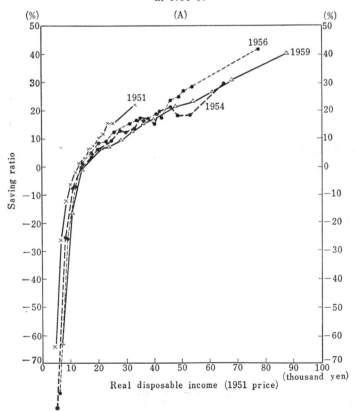

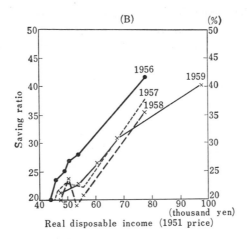

Real disposable income (1951 price)

various real income levels. From Table 5 and Fig. 4, we see that the curve of saving ratios between income classes clearly shift downward for 1951–53. For instance, the saving ratio under income class of about the ¥15,000 shows a steep decline (3.5% in 1952, and −0.4% in 1953). The saving ratio of the income class of under about ¥32,000 also decreased from 20.7% (1952) to 13.0% (1953). For 1951–52, the saving ratio-real income relation did not show any marked change, but for 1952–53 there was a drastic change. From 1954 to 1959, there were some variations, but not as large as that for 1952–53. However, in 1956 when a sharp boom occurred, the curve of the saving ratio shifted upward. From 1956 on, the year-to-year movements of the saving ratios in the upper income classes are depicted in Fig. 4 (B). In the recession of 1956–58, the savings curve tended to move downward. In 1959 when a strong boom again developed, it tended to shift upward, but not as much as in 1956. Thus the saving ratio of the urban worker families in the upper income classes has shown a downward drift with constant real income. However, at the same time, there has been a shift of households in each class toward a higher income class. The latter effect may offset to some extent a tendency in the overall saving ratio for urban workers to decline in 1956–59.

Table 5. Cross-section Saving-Income Relations of All Urban Worker Families

1951		1952		1953		1954	
Real disposable income	Saving ratio	Real disposable income	Saving ratio	Real disposable income	Saving ratio	Real disposable income	Saving ratio
15,460	.030	16,030	.035	14,906	−.004	14,149	−.002
21,947	.114	22,342	.108	20,902	.066	19,683	.062
25,187	.152	25,425	.148	26,533	.100	25,045	.095
33,143	.218	31,430	.207	32,032	.130	32,710	.139
—	—	41,938	.289	42,234	.242	41,666	.194
—	—	—	—	53,249	.265	52,845	.186
—	—	—	—	—	—	65,077	.296

1956		1957		1958		1959	
Real disposable income	Saving ratio	Real disposable income	Saving ratio	Real disposable income	Saving ratio	Real disposable income	Saving ratio
14,427	.011	14,146	.002	14,221	−.005	13,768	−.008
20,113	.078	19,871	.060	20,110	.058	21,105	.066
25,861	.121	25,690	.112	25,903	.098	24,714	.069
33,366	.156	33,845	.166	31,657	.123	31,955	.131
41,243	.189	42,108	.187	42,762	.182	40,359	.163
53,584	.279	51,632	.269	53,232	.192	54,170	.228
—	—	—	—	—	—	67,913	.309
77,527	.417	77,543	.377	77,290	.356	—	—
—	—	—	—	—	—	97,402	.402

Source: The Statistics Bureau, Prime Minister's Office, *Kakeichosa Nempo* ("Annual Report of Family Budget Survey"), 1951–1959.

Notes: 1) Real disposable incomes are the averaged incomes in various income classes, deflated by the Consumer Price Index of all cities (1951= 100).

2) Only those classes which are comparable over the years 1951–1959 were used.

3) The saving ratio is derived by dividing saving by disposable income in each size.

As we have explained in the appendix of the last chapter, the Family Income and Expenditure Survey makes clear the following inflow and outflow relations with respect to the urban worker families :

[Inflow]	[Outflow]
1. Income before tax	4. Consumer expenditures
2. Receipts other than income	5. Income tax and other public charges
a) Deposits withdrawn	
b) Insurance proceeds	6. Disbursements other than expenditures
c) Debts incurred and credit purchases	a) Deposits
d) Others	b) Insurance premium payments
3. Cash holdings at the beginning of the month	c) Debts and credit purchases repaid
	d) Others
	7. Cash holdings at the end of the month

From this table, savings can be computed by two methods :

  1. (1)—(4)—(5)   (Current account method)

  2. (6)—(2)+(7)—(3)   (Balance sheet method)

Therefore, we can depict a graph in which three curves are involved as follows :

(1) Deposits, insurance premium payments, debts and credit purchases repaid, and other property or security purchases.

(2) Deposits withdrawn, insurance proceeds, debts incurred and credit purchases, and property and securities sold.

(3) Changes in cash holdings.

Let us take up the four years 1951, 1953, 1956, and 1959, as representative of the period 1951–59, drawing a chart in which the above three items are indicated. If we can assume for a moment that positive savings (1) and negative savings (2) are made by different persons, we can infer from the graphs as follows : The group with positive savings (1) increases their positive saving as disposable income rises. However, even in the same income group there are household with deficits as well as with surplus. Not only in the very low income classes but also in the upper income classes, we will find household with considerable deficits. Particularly to be noted, is a very large amount of deficit in the lowest income class. This indicates that those whose incomes have temporarily dropped to zero cannot but depend on liquid assets, the selling of physical assets and borrowing.

Fig. 5.   Cross-section Relations of Positive and Negative Saving Flows for Urban Worker Households in 1931–59

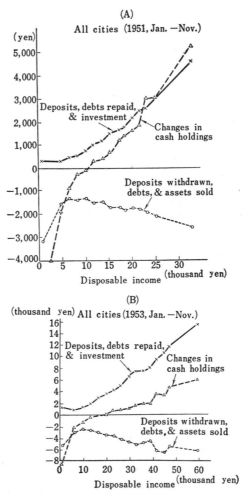

(A)

All cities (1951, Jan. –Nov.)

(B)

All cities (1953, Jan. –Nov.)

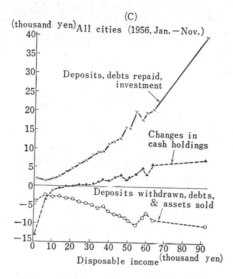

(C)
(thousand yen) All cities (1956, Jan. –Nov.)

Deposits, debts repaid, investment

Changes in cash holdings

Deposits withdrawn, debts, & assets sold

Disposable income (thousand yen)

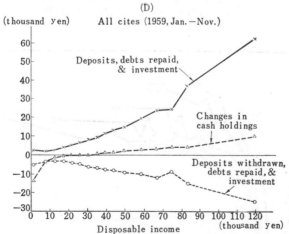

(D)
(thousand yen)   All cites (1959, Jan. –Nov.)

Deposits, debts repaid, & investment

Changes in cash holdings

Deposits withdrawn, debts repaid, & investment

Disposable income   (thousand yen)

This tendency will temporarily diminish, but will again rise continually as income increases. However, the plus and minus sides of savings are not always due to different persons. One person may withdraw his deposit and repay his debt. In this case, his actions have a bearing on both sides. Thus, the Family Income and Expenditure

245

Survey does not separate the deficit households from the surplus households, so rigorously speaking it is impossible to make here an analysis similar to James Tobin's.[3] But if we have in mind the liquid assets behind the curves in the graph, we can introduce here the so-called liquid asset hypothesis as an explanation. Further, the fairly large amount of deposits withdrawn, debts, and assets sold, can be explained by the existence of negative " transitory incomes " due to the temporary decline of incomes. Here, the so-called " permanent income " hypothesis may come up. The upper income classes do not always have a large amount of saving. Those whose incomes declined relative to preceding incomes may attempt negative savings, even if they belong to the upper income classes. In this sense, we can speculate on the existence of income variability underlying Fig. 5. Our data has a defect in the sense that we cannot test these speculations rigorously.

Fig. 6. The Cross-section Relation of Changes in Cash Holdings as % of Income for Urban Worker Households in 1951–59

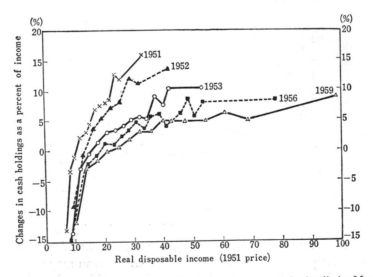

3) James Tobin, " Relative Income, Absolute Income, and Saving ", in *Money, Trade and Economic Growth*, in honor of John Henry Williams, New York 1931.

The comparison of (A) and (B) of Fig. 5 suggests that the curve of changes in cash holdings was drastically flattened between 1951 and 1953. In 1951, the cash holdings curve crosses that of positive savings around the income class of ¥25,000, but in 1953 the former curve shows a conspicuous shift downward. In Fig. 6, we see that the downward shift of the cash holdings curve is most pronounced for the two years, 1951–53. Compared with it, the shift in the following six years is not as great. The gap for only the two years 1951–53, is even larger than the gap for the next six years, 1953–59. The reason for this sudden shift around 1952–53 needs to be examined. Our hypothesis is that the large increase in cash holdings in 1951 (Fig. 6) is due to the persistent fear of postwar hyper-inflation, but after the end of the Korean incident, people become confident of the ending of inflation, and increased their savings in the form

Fig. 7. Cross-Section Relation of Positive Saving Flows as % of Incomes for Urban Worker Households in 1951 59

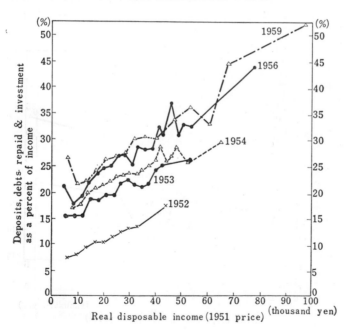

247

of deposits, insurance, *etc.* The savings in terms of cash holdings were reduced, and, instead, deposits and their withdrawal, debts credit purchases and their repayments, were bilaterally widened respectively. Fig. 7 and 8 indicate these tendencies.

In Fig. 4, and Table 5, we have seen that the saving ratio curve shows a sharp drop for 1952–53. However, in Fig. 7, the curve of " deposits, debts repaid, and investment " as a % of disposable income shows the most distinct upward shift for the same year. In terms of the *net* saving ratio, (positive minus negative saving), there occured a decline, but in terms of the positive saving ratio, these developed an upward shift. This apparent discrepancy can be reconciled by Fig. 8, in which the " deposits withdrawn, debts and assets sold " as a % of disposable income also increases steeply for 1951–53. Thus, it is clear that the rises in the positive saving ratio

Fig. 8. Cross-section Relation of Negative Saving Flows as % of Income for Urban Worker Households in 1951–59

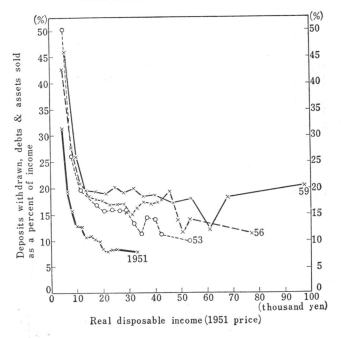

and the negative saving ratio offset each other. The " deposits, debts repaid and investment " ratio increased on the one hand, and the " deposits withdrawn, debts and assets sold " ratio too, on the other, thus decreasing, as a net balance, the saving ratio, which also takes into account the increase of cash-holdings. These are caused by the fact that in a hyper-inflation cash-transactions prevail (sometimes barter-transactions also), but, as the inflation ends, people tend to expand credit transactions. If the foregoing analysis is valid, the kink in the saving curve in 1953 for the urban worker households

Table 6. Saving Structure for Urban Worker Families, 1951–1959
All cities (Jan.–Dec. Av.)   (Unit: yen)

	Disposable income	Deposits withdrawn, & assets sold	Deposits, debts repaid, & investment	Changes in cash holdings
1951	14,917 (100)	1,753 (11.75)	1,453 (9.74)	627 (4.20)
1952	18,991 (100)	2,055 (10.82)	2,251 (11.85)	644 (3.39)
1953	23,065 (100)	3,809 (16.51)	4,587 (19.89)	560 (2.43)
1954	24,922 (100)	4,189 (16.81)	5,548 (22.26)	493 (1.98)
1955	25,896 (100)	4,166 (16.09)	6,128 (23.66)	420 (1.62)
1956	27,464 (100)	4,559 (16.60)	7,265 (26.45)	526 (1.92)
1957	29,810 (100)	5,010 (16.81)	8,220 (27.57)	508 (1.70)
1958	31,824 (100)	5,448 (17.12)	8,968 (28.18)	505 (1.59)
1959	34,122 (100)	6,269 (18.37)	10,314 (30.23)	702 (2.06)

Tokyo (Jan.-Dec. Av.)

1951	16,851 (100)	1,708 (10.14)	1,435 (8.52)	859 (5.10)
1952	21,017 (100)	2,106 (10.02)	2,372 (11.29)	802 (3.82)
1953	25,264 (100)	3,650 (14.45)	4,482 (17.74)	421 (1.67)
1954	29,107 (100)	4,232 (14.54)	6,015 (20.67)	459 (1.58)
1955	30,404 (100)	4,683 (15.40)	6,838 (22.49)	302 (.99)
1956	31,613 (100)	4,757 (15.05)	7,817 (24.73)	460 (1.46)
1957	35,506 (100)	5,915 (16.66)	9,626 (27.11)	593 (1.67)
1958	37,694 (100)	6,564 (17.41)	10,271 (27.25)	348 (.92)
1959	39,777 (100)	6,816 (17.14)	11,065 (27.82)	815 (2.05)

Source: The Statistics Bureau, Prime Minister's Office, *Annual Report on the Family Income and Expenditure Survey.*

(in Fig. 2) may have been an intensified result of the end of the hyper-inflation (1946–51), with a long lag of two years. If this line of argument is plausible, it would be somewhat artificial to attribute the kink in 1953 in the saving function to the difference in the rate of increase in consumer prices with 1953 as a borderline. It may be a consequence of the end of the inflation with a two year lag. However, we do not have conclusive evidence to indicate which hypothesis is more plausible.

The same kind of analysis can also be made in relation to the time series averages from the Family Income and Expenditure Survey for the urban worker households. In Table 6, we see that the " deposits withdrawn, debts, and assets sold " as a ratio of disposable income shows a sudden increase in 1953, and continues to rise up to 1959, but the " deposits, debts repaid, and investment " ratio shows a much more rapid increase. While, the increase in the cash holdings ratio indicates a declining tendency, although there are ups and downs in the ratio due to the business cycle. This table is quite consistent with the analysis so far made, concerning the intertemporal shifts in the cross-section relations.

B. PREWAR STUDIES

5. *Time Series Consumption and Saving in the Prewar Period*

The estimates of consumption expenditures in the " prewar " official national income statistics are very weak. We will soon return to the discussion of its reliability, but let us, first, present a chart correlating personal consumption expenditures and personal disposable income, deflated by the aggregate consumer price index (1934–35＝100) and divided by the total population. The apparent peculiar relation may partly be attributed to the lowering of consumption propensity due to the development of the war economy since the Manchurian Incident (1931). However, the tendency for the consumption ratio to fall may be seen, surprisingly enough, even before 1935 when the influence of the war on the economy was not so great, *i.e.*, .946 in 1930, .888 in 1932, .831 in 1935, .790 in 1938 and .725 in 1940.   It seems to me that this extraordinary drift of consumption-saving relation is probably partly due to the deficiencies in the official national income statistics.   An examination of the data points up the following.   The procedure for estimating consumption is :   per household family expenditures × the number of households, using the *Nokakeizai Chosa* (Ministry of Agriculture and Forestry, *Farm Household Economy Survey*) and the *Kakei Chosa Hokoku* (Statistics Bureau of Cabinet, *Report on Family Budget Survey*).   There is probably a substantial downward bias in per capita household family expenditures from these sampling surveys, particularly since the size of the samples was much smaller than in the postwar sampling surveys as explained in the Appendix of the last chapter.   Of course, some adjustments are introduced with respect to size of households in both surveys, and to size of household incomes in the case of farm household expenditures.   However, the estimates of urban consumption

Fig. 9.   The Consumption-Income Relation in 1930–40, based on the Official National Income Statistics

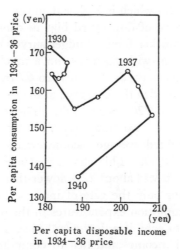

Per capita disposable income in 1934–36 price

251

expenditures, are very dubious, for it is clearly evident that the average per household consumption expenditures for urban workers are too low in the *Report on Family Budget Survey*.

The above survey before the war is limited mainly to income classes ranging from 50 yen to 100 yen per month, and households who live in rented houses. Because of these restrictions in coverage the survey results are necessarily underestimated. When average family expenditures are rising, those from the sample surveys are bound to be understated, for the data are limited to groups earning less than 100 yen. Some modifications were made in the survey during the war to include income groups earning more than 100 yen, but the serious defect discussed above could not be completely overcome.

Table 7 indicates that the number of households surveyed above the ¥100 level was 24.6% in 1931–32 and rose to 71.3% in 1939–40. Four income classes below ¥70–79 comprised 40% in 1931–32 and only 6% in 1939–40. This probably means that owing to the general rise in income the relative number of surveyed households in the lower income classes was reduced. Nevertheless, the survey was not extended to income classes much above ¥100. The average income of the class above ¥100 was ¥111.98 in 1931–32, but it was ¥126.31 in 1939-40, which is higher than the farmer by only ¥14.53.

Another evidence of downward bias in consumption expenditure from the urban worker family budget survey can be best presented by comparing them with figures from a much larger (once-for-all) family budget survey conducted in 1926–27 by the Cabinet Statistics Bureau which extended the coverage of the survey to include income classes up to around ¥200 per month. The total average income for manual and salaried workers was ¥113.62 in the latter survey, whereas the weighted average income for the income classes below ¥100–119 was ¥88.99. This shows that average of the survey for classes below ¥100 was about 22% lower than that for classes below ¥200. Thus, not only the rate of increase but also the very level of personal consumption expenditures in the official national income statistics seems to exhibit a downward bias. Therefore, we shall not use the national income statistics to compute macro consumption

Table 7. Number of Households by Income Classes in the Cabinet Statistics Bureau's, *Report on Family Budget Survey*

	Income Classes								
	-¥49	¥50-59	¥60-69	¥70-79	¥80-89	¥90-99	¥100-	Total	Average income over ¥100
1931-32	15 (.99)	78 (5.13)	251 (16.52)	254 (16.72)	289 (19.03)	258 (16.99)	374 (24.62)	1,519 (100.00)	111.98 yen
1934-35	5 (.30)	76 (4.55)	222 (13.29)	285 (17.06)	294 (17.59)	278 (16.64)	511 (30.58)	1,671 (100.00)	115.65
1937-38	5 (.31)	25 (1.56)	109 (6.81)	195 (12.18)	283 (17.68)	286 (17.86)	698 (43.60)	1,601 (100.00)	117.76
1939-40	—	1 (.06)	21 (1.32)	73 (4.59)	139 (8.73)	223 (14.01)	1,135 (71.29)	1,592 (100.00)	126.51

Source: The Statistics Bureau, Prime Minister's Office, *Sengo Junen no Kakei* (Family Income and Expenditure in Postwar Ten Years), 1956.

Notes: 1) Numbers in brackets are percentages.
2) These include both salaried and manual workers.

function here.

Although the sample survey of the urban worker family budget has the above drawback as a basis for estimating nation-wide consumption expenditures, this is not a defect inherent in the data itself. Therefore, it may be useful to analyze the family budget survey for workers as a time series, even though the construction of the consumption (or saving) function will not be attempted. The income statistics in Table 8 are biased as explained above, so their magnitudes in real terms may not represent the actual changes in real income per household. However, it will provide a clue for understanding the relation between the changes in the propensity to consume and the movements of real income during this period.

The real disposable income of workers fell during this period, but the average propensity to consume was also declining, particularly after 1935 with the intensification of the war economy. This is an extraordinary phenomenon and can only be understood, by taking into account the psychological effect on consumption behavior of the transition to the war economy.

Thus, as is argued above, the time-series from the family budget data for urban workers are very weak in reliability. Even less reliable is the time-series data on the farm household saving-income relation. The sample was very small, as explained in the Appendex of the previous chapter. Therefore, we can only present the table of the farm household data here. Saving functions computed from this data (in Table 9) were already mentioned in the footnote on p. 212. As the survey design underwent two revisions, one in 1924 and another in 1931, the saving function for this period is not very meaningful. This is why we have fitted three equations to the three periods, although this has reduced the size of the sample considerably.

6. Cross-Section Analysis of the Prewar Consumption Functions

The Family Budget Survey conducted for September 1926 to August 1927, by the Cabinet Statistics Bureau, was on a larger scale than any survey of this kind in the prewar period, although the sample

Table 8. Income and Consumption in Urban Workers Family Budget, 1926–1940, Statistics Bureaus' Survey —All cities—

(Unit: yen)

	Before-tax income	Income taxes & other public charges	Disposable income	Consumption expenditures	Propensity to consume	Cost-of-living index	Real disposable income
1926, Sept.-27, Aug.	113.62	.43	113.19	101.80	.899	99.0	114.33
1931, Sept.-32, Aug.	86.47	.15	86.32	76.18	.833	75.2	114.79
1932, Sept.-33, Aug.	88.66	.16	88.50	77.24	.873	76.9	115.08
1933, Sept.-34, Aug.	90.35	.16	90.19	78.75	.873	79.5	113.45
1934, Sept.-35, Aug.	90.26	.17	90.09	79.87	.887	82.5	109.20
1935, Sept.-36, Aug.	90.59	.18	90.41	79.93	.884	84.8	106.62
1936, Sept.-37, Aug.	93.60	.18	93.42	82.05	.878	90.3	103.46
1937, Sept.-38, Aug.	98.09	.18	97.91	83.75	.855	99.4	98.50
1938, Sept.-39, Aug.	104.70	.22	104.48	86.88	.832	111.0	94.13
1939, Sept.-40, Aug.	115.42	.31	115.11	97.00	.843	138.0	83.41

Source: See footnote in Table 7.

Notes: 1) This is for manual and salaried workers.
2) The cost-of-living index (1926=100) here is a combined one: the Ueda index for 1926-33, the Asahi index for 1933–36 and the Morita index for the later period. The latter takes account of changes in black market prices. The yearly index is adjusted for the period, September to August.

Table 9. Farm Household Saving-Income Relation, 1921–1936

(Unit: yen)

Fiscal year	Farm household income	Farm household saving	Real farm household income	Real farm household income	Propensity to save
1921	1,067.63	86.07	972.13	82.13	8.06 %
22	962.55	6.60	887.96	6.08	.69
23	1,198.74	191.26	1,105.85	185.33	15.96
					·········· revision
24	1,393.79	223.98	1,334.54	214.95	16.07
25	1,563.33	308.44	1,446.86	286.12	19.73
26	1,373.92	189.29	1,318.54	181.66	13.78
27	1,219.24	101.81	1,186.01	99.04	8.35
28	1,197.37	107.14	1,194.85	106.93	8.98
29	1,150.35	75.90	1,184.71	78.17	6.60
30	722.64	−77.83	823.85	−89.75	−10.77
					·········· revision
31	541.79	−7.30	691.94	−9.33	−1.35
32	624.13	65.39	786.59	82.98	10.48
33	726.08	119.39	900.84	148.74	16.44
34	732.28	94.54	879.09	113.49	12.91
35	876.46	132.79	1,008.58	152.80	15.15
36	933.33	150.33	1,050.89	169.10	16.11

Source: The Ministry of Agriculture and Forestry, *Farm Household Economy Survey*.

Notes: 1) In this table the incomes are before taxes.

2) There were changes in the survey methods in 1924 and 1931.

3) As there is no adequate deflator for farm household incomes, the urban cost-of-living index is used as a rough substitute.

was still smaller than those of the postwar period. The number of households surveyed was 7,220, of which 1,575 were households of salary earners, 3,210 of wage earners and 670 of farm households. In the Family Budget Survey from 1931, the objective was mainly households, with incomes of ¥50–100 per month, but in the 1926–27 survey groups with incomes up to ¥200 and above were included. In the Family Budget Survey for 1931–1940, the number of salary and wage earner households was 1,519–1,670, while it amounted in the 1926–27 survey to 4,785. Moreover, three times as many farm households were surveyed than in the Farm Household Economy Survey for the prewar period.

In Fig. 10, the propensities to consume for farm households, wage earners and salary earners are shown in relation to the monthly disposable incomes by income classes, and the data are given in Table 10. The curve of the consumption ratio is the steepest for the farm households, the flattest for the salary earners, and the wage earners fall in between. Thus, the consumption functions are computed as follows:

Salary earners $\quad C = 12.30 + .812\ Y;\ R^2 = .999$ .... (4.1)

Wage earners $\quad C = 18.49 + .711\ Y;\ R^2 = .993$ .... (4.2)

Farm households $\quad C = 37.87 + .599\ Y;\ R^2 = .940$ .... (4.3)

In the logarithmic expression,

Salary earners $\quad \log C = .19815 + .8879\ \log Y;\ R^2 = .999$ (5.1)

Wage earners $\quad \log C = .29688 + .8284\ \log Y;\ R^2 = .998$ (5.2)

Farm households $\quad \log C = .67642 + .6606\ \log Y;\ R^2 = .980$ (5.3)

The order of magnitude of the marginal propensity to consume or the income elasticity of consumption is salary earners, wage earners, and farmers, respectively. The relatively lower propensity to consume of farm households in the prewar Japan is also found for both postwar Japan[4] and the United States.[5] This may be due to the lower proportion of the variance of permanent income than that in measured income (Friedman's P_r) in the case of farm households which are more entrepreneurial in character and are subject to the vagaries of harvests.

In this sample survey, the average propensity to consume of farm households as a whole was 1.0024, with .974 for the owner farmers and 1.027 for the tenants. It is to be expected that the owner farmers whose incomes are relatively higher (and who are engaged in agriculture by themselves) would have the lower propensity to consume. There is no doubt that the cross-section marginal propensity to consume for the owner farmers would be considerably

4) See p. 219 of the last chapter.
5) Milton Friedman, *A Theory of the Consumption Function*, Princeton, 1957, p. 62.

Table 10. Cross-section Consumption-Income Relation, Family Budget Survey,
Cabinet Statistics Bureau 1926–27

(Unit: yen)

Income classes	Salary earners		Wage earners		Farmers	
	Disposable income	Consumption expenditures	Disposable income	Consumption expenditures	Disposable income	Consumption expenditures
¥ – 59	53.00	53.79	52.60	52.34	46.42	59.11
¥ 60– 79	71.01	69.03	71.01	67.33	69.27	74.87
¥ 80– 99	89.80	85.37	89.62	81.82	88.29	91.86
¥100–119	109.24	102.38	108.75	97.40	108.22	106.07
¥120–139	129.18	119.18	128.16	111.53	129.14	124.48
¥140–159	147.86	131.45	148.28	127.65	146.20	136.78
¥160–179	168.57	151.12	167.86	141.03	165.26	138.01
¥180–199	186.41	163.52	187.56	153.27	187.12	136.51
¥200–	226.42	194.22	229.29	175.23	218.92	167.29

Note: All figures in monthly averages.

Fig. 10. Cross-section Consumption-Income Relation, Farm and Worker Households, 1926–27

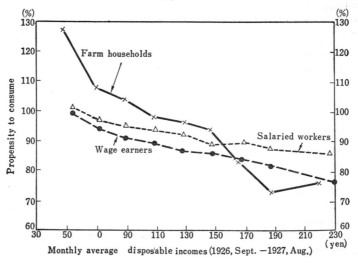

258

lower if it could be separated out. In Table 10, we note a kink in the farm household income-consumption relation around the disposable income level of ¥146.20. The marginal propensity to consume for the upper-income classes above the ¥146.20 level may even be about 0.25, and it is in these upper income classes that the owner farmers are likely to be numerous. The following figures may be suggestive:

	Owner farmers	Tenants
Disposable income (yen)	110. 29	78. 48
Consumption expenditures (yen)	107. 42	80. 58
Propensity to consume (%)	97. 4	102. 7

As to cross-section consumption functions computed from the Family Budget Survey for 1931–40, we already have a study by Professor Isamu Yamada of Hitotsubashi University. Since his computation was based on incomes before deduction of taxes, strictly speaking his figures do not represent disposable income-consumption relations. However, since income taxes and other public charges

Table 11. Yamada's Cross-Section Consumption Functions for Workers, 1931–1940

—All cities—

	Salary earners	Wage earners
1931, Sept.-1932, Aug.	$C = 11.41 + .77\ Y$	$C = 9.82 + .76\ Y$
1932, Sept.-1933, Aug.	$C = 7.48 + .81\ Y$	$C = 12.33 + .72\ Y$
1933, Sept.-1934, Aug.	$C = 11.56 + .77\ Y$	$C = 12.97 + .72\ Y$
1934, Sept.-1935, Aug.	$C = 5.70 + .83\ Y$	$C = 9.95 + .77\ Y$
1935, Sept.-1936, Aug.	$C = 8.00 + .81\ Y$	$C = 12.94 + .73\ Y$
1936, Sept.-1937, Aug.	$C = 14.98 + .73\ Y$	$C = 9.87 + .77\ Y$
1937, Sept.-1938, Aug.	$C = 15.77 + .71\ Y$	$C = 15.97 + .68\ Y$
1938, Sept.-1939, Aug.	$C = 9.41 + .76\ Y$	$C = 10.23 + .73\ Y$
1939, Sept.-1940, Aug.	$C = 20.75 + .67\ Y$	$C = 10.29 + .75\ Y$

Source: Isamu Yamada, *Keiryo Keizaigaku no Kihonmondai* (Fundamentals of Econometrics), Chapter 1, " Measurement of the Consumption Function ", p. 17. This is based upon the Cabinet Statistics Bureau, " *Report on the Family Budget Survey*."

were not significant in these lower income classes, they may be worth citing here.

A notable fact is that excluding two years, 1936–37 and 1939–40, the marginal propensity to consume for salary earners is significantly larger than that for wage earners.   This corresponds with the results for 1926–27.

As Mr. Yamada's study centers around the before-tax income-disbursement relation, we have attempted to compute consumption functions as the disposable income-consumption relation for salary and wage earners as a whole.   The marginal propensities to consume computed in Table 12 seem to move up and down inversely with the changes in the intercepts.   The cross-section marginal propensity to consume generally rises in a depression, and falls in the upswing. It fell from 1931 to 1933 (.772—.727), but rose in 1934 when whole-sale prices and the bank clearings declined (.785).   After that, it continued to fall until 1938 (.785—.668).   In 1939, it again rose. However, this is the only exception to our generalization.   The average propensity to consume as well as the income elasticity of consumption behaves similarly.

For reference, the consumption function for Tokyo was also computed for three years.   The intercepts, the marginal and average propensity to consume are always higher for Tokyo than all cities, taken together.

The intercepts in Table 12 are in current prices; when these are divided by the cost of living index given in Table 7, we get the inter-cepts in real terms.   By inserting these real term intercepts in the consumption functions computed in Table 12, and by applying the formula $(a/(1-\beta)$ where $C=a+\beta Y)$ to estimate real incomes at the break-even point $(C=Y)$, we have the following results :

	1926	1931	1932	1933	1934	1935	1936	1937
Real term intercepts	11.51	12.81	13.93	16.94	11.02	13.73	9.82	15.48
Real incomes at the break-even point	56.98	56.18	56.40	62.05	51.26	57.21	45.46	51.09

It is to be noted that during these ten years, there was no upward drift in real income at the break-even point (or at the zero-saving point).   In the period when there was a rapid expansion of in-

Table 12.   Cross-section Consumption Functions, Salary and Wage Earners
Combined, All Cities and Tokyo, 1931–1940

—All cities—

	Consumption functions	R^2	Propensities to cosume in the sampling averages	Income elasticities in the sampling averages
1931, Sept.-1932, Aug.	$C= 9.63+.772\,Y$	.996	.883	.874
1932, Sept.-1933, Aug.	$C=10.71+.753\,Y$	.998	.873	.863
1933, Sept.-1934, Aug.	$C=13.47+.727\,Y$	.997	.873	.833
1934, Sept.-1935, Aug.	$C= 9.09+.785\,Y$	.999	.887	.885
1935, Sept.-1936, Aug.	$C=11.64+.760\,Y$	.990	.884	.860
1936, Sept.-1937, Aug.	$C= 8.87+.784\,Y$	.998	.878	.893
1937, Sept.-1938, Aug.	$C=15.39+.697\,Y$	.996	.855	.815
* 1938, Sept.-1939, Aug.	$C=16.99+.668\,Y$	.997	.832	.803
* 1939, Sept.-1940, Aug.	$C=11.23+.748\,Y$	.998	.843	.887

—Tokyo—

1926, Sept.-1927, Aug.	$C=12.54+.813\,Y$	.997	.913	.890
* 1934, Sept.-1935, Aug.	$C=17.12+.740\,Y$	.971	.918	.806
* 1935, Sept.-1936, Aug.	$C=13.52+.763\,Y$	.996	.904	.844

Source :   The Statistics Bureau, Prime Minister's Office, *Sengo Junen no Kakei*
(Family Income and Expenditure in Postwar Ten years), 1956.

Notes :   1)   Income elasticities of consumption were derived by dividing the
marginal propensities to consume with the average propensities to
consume for the average samples.

2)   For years (*), the functions were computed, after excluding the
lowest income class.

dustrial capacity due to increases in military and export demand, the
upward pressure of consumption was weak.   Moreover, it is striking
that even in the lower-income classes there prevailed high saving
ratios, and consumption ratios tended to decline even with real incomes constant.   For example, if we put ¥200 into the disposable
income of the cross-section consumption function (the intercept=
in real terms) in Table 12, the consumption ratio would be 85.6%
in 1926, and 77.4% in 1937.   If we put ¥100 into the same function,

then the consumption ratio would be 91.3% in 1926, and 85.2% in 1937.

7. *Deposits, Borrowing, and Repayments and the Saving Structure*

The term, saving structure, may not be adequate, but here we will attempt to analyze the cross-section behavior of the positive saving, (deposits, insurance and annuity premiums, repayments and others) and negative saving (deposits withdrawn, insurance proceeds, debts and others), and make clear the structure of saving in terms of the behavior of these component gross concepts.

First, let us take up the deposits withdrawn, and insurance and annuity proceeds as a % of disposable income from Table 13, and compare it among wage earners, salary earners and farm households. This ratio is generally higher for salary earners than for wage earners, and particularly in IX the former is twice as high as the latter. This seems to be a vital point in understanding the relatively high propensity to consume of salary earners. In the case of farm

Table 13. Cross-Section Saving Structure in 1926
—in terms of deposits, debts, repayments, *etc.*—
A. Salary earners

Income classes	Deposits withdrawn insurance & annuity proceeds	Increase in debts, credit purchases, etc.	Increase in deposits & insurance annuity premiums	Debt repayments	Increase in eash holdings
	yen %	yen %	yen %	yen %	yen %
I	2.10 (3.96)	17.01 (32.09)	2.45 (4.62)	16.46 (31.06)	−.59 (−1.11)
II	7.10 (10.00)	14.55 (20.49)	8.59 (12.10)	14.66 (20.64)	.38 (.54)
III	8.46 (9.42)	18.81 (20.95)	12.18 (13.56)	19.10 (21.27)	.42 (.47)
IV	10.97 (10.04)	21.46 (19.64)	17.16 (15.71)	21.88 (20.03)	.25 (.23)
V	14.55 (11.26)	24.41 (18.90)	23.52 (18.21)	25.00 (19.35)	.44 (.34)
VI	15.61 (10.56)	26.79 (18.12)	30.27 (20.47)	28.40 (19.21)	.14 (.09)
VII	19.47 (11.55)	31.44 (18.65)	35.68 (21.17)	41.49 (24.61)	1.19 (.71)
VIII	24.13 (12.94)	30.54 (16.38)	43.60 (23.39)	33.64 (18.05)	.32 (.17)
IX	31.73 (14.01)	36.11 (15.95)	57.89 (25.57)	40.65 (17.95)	1.50 (.66)

B. Wage earners

	yen	%	yen	%	yen	%	yen	%	yen	%
I	3.51	(6.67)	14.69	(27.93)	4.57	(8.69)	13.74	(26.12)	.23	(.44)
II	5.87	(8.27)	20.21	(28.46)	8.92	(12.56)	20.24	(28.50)	.60	(.85)
III	7.93	(8.85)	24.67	(27.53)	14.26	(15.91)	25.34	(28.27)	.80	(.89)
IV	10.38	(9.54)	24.05	(22.11)	19.46	(17.89)	25.07	(23.05)	1.25	(1.15)
V	10.97	(8.56)	26.31	(20.53)	24.55	(19.16)	28.01	(21.86)	1.35	(1.05)
VI	12.91	(8.71)	30.31	(20.43)	29.90	(20.16)	32.67	(22.03)	1.37	(.92)
VII	17.60	(10.48)	29.94	(17.84)	41.30	(24.60)	31.77	(18.93)	1.30	(.77)
VIII	16.91	(9.02)	31.93	(17.02)	46.43	(24.75)	43.80	(23.35)	1.90	(1.01)
IX	16.81	(7.33)	41.97	(18.30)	63.62	(27.75)	45.15	(19.69)	4.07	(1.78)

(As percent of disposable income, in brackets)

C. Farm households

	yen	%	yen	%	yen	%	yen	%	yen	%
I	13.30	(28.65)	21.96	(47.31)	8.85	(19.07)	14.57	(31.39)	−.85	(−1.83)
II	13.69	(19.76)	21.91	(31.63)	13.60	(19.63)	17.10	(24.69)	−.70	(−1.01)
III	16.62	(18.82)	24.66	(27.93)	17.57	(19.90)	20.57	(23.30)	−.43	(− .49)
IV	15.61	(14.42)	24.49	(22.63)	21.46	(19.83)	21.22	(19.61)	−.43	(− .40)
V	19.94	(15.44)	30.88	(23.91)	25.02	(19.37)	28.92	(22.39)	1.53	(1.19)
VI	12.34	(8.42)	30.86	(21.11)	22.96	(15.70)	31.05	(21.24)	1.78	(1.22)
VII	15.53	(9.40)	27.45	(16.61)	31.11	(18.82)	33.13	(20.05)	5.99	(3.62)
VIII	15.96	(8.53)	28.15	(15.04)	56.08	(29.97)	27.07	(14.47)	11.57	(5.94)
IX	41.31	(18.87)	36.73	(16.78)	65.32	(29.84)	54.34	(24.82)	10.01	(4.57)

Source: The Cabinet Statistics Bureau, *Kakei Chosa Hokoku* (Report on the Family Budget Survey), summarized in Iwasaburo Takano *ed.*, *Hompo Shakai Tokei Ron* (Social Statistics of Japan), 1933, pp. 238–278.

Notes: 1) Income classes, I, II, . . .IX ranges from less than 60 yen to more than 200 yen. See Table 10.

2) The percentages in brackets are derived by dividing the figures in this table by the disposable incomes in Table 10.

households, this ratio is considerably higher in the lowest five and the top income classes.

263

Percent of the Deposits withdrawn & Insurance and Annuity Proceeds
to Disposable Income, 1926

Income classes	I	II	III	IV	V	VI	VII	VIII	IX
Salary earners	3.96	10.00	9.42	10.04	11.26	10.56	11.55	12.94	14.01
Wage earners	6.67	8.27	8.85	9.54	8.56	8.71	10.48	9.02	7.33
Farm households	28.65	19.76	18.82	14.42	15.44	8.42	9.40	8.53	18.87

This is why the average propensity to consume of farm households is 1.0024 in 1926 as a whole. At the same time, the ratio for farm households declines very steeply from the very high ratio (28.65%) in the I class to the low ratio (8.53%) in the VIII class, except for the highest income class IX. This probably accounts for the comparatively lower marginal propensity to consume of farm households than of the other two. 1926 was a poor harvest year. So, we must take into account a factor, bad harvest, in order to explain the enormous amount of deposits withdrawn particularly in the lower income class. Next we will consider the ratio of debts, credit purchases, *etc.* to disposable incomes.

Percent of Debts, Credit Purchases, *etc.* to Disposable Income

Income classes	I	II	III	IV	V	VI	VII	VIII	IX
Salary earners	32.09	20.49	20.45	19.64	18.90	18.12	18.65	16.38	15.95
Wage earners	27.93	28.46	27.53	22.11	20.53	20.43	17.84	17.02	18.30
Farm households	47.31	31.63	27.93	22.63	23.91	21.11	16.61	15.04	16.78

The ratio for salary earners is a bit lower than that for wage earners in the above table. However, the ratio of the *sum* of debts, credit purchases, *etc.*, and deposits withdrawn, insurance and annuity proceeds to disposable income is higher for wage earners in the lower income classes, and higher for salary earners in the higher income classes. This may suggest one of the reasons for the cross-section marginal propensity to consume of salary earners to be higher than that of wage earners. Compared with those of salary and wage earners, the ratio of debts, credit purchases, *etc.* of farm households is higher in the lower income classes, and about the same level in the higher income classes. This is also one of the reasons why the cross-section marginal propensity to consume of farm households is relatively low.

SAVING AND CONSUMPTION PATTERNS

Percent of Deposits and Insurance & Annuity Premiums to Disposable Income

Income classes	I	II	III	IV	V	VI	VII	VIII	IX
Salary earners	4.62	12.10	13.56	15.71	18.21	20.47	21.17	23.39	25.57
Wage earners	8.67	12.56	15.91	17.89	19.16	20.16	24.60	24.75	27.75
Farm households	19.07	19.63	19.90	19.83	19.37	15.70	18.82	29.97	29.84

Then, how about the percent of deposits and insurance and annuity premiums to disposable income?

The ratio is computed in the above table. It is generally higher for wage earners than for salary earners. In this aspect too, we find a factor which raises the average and marginal propensity to consume for salary earners. On the other hand, the ratio for farm households is higher than for the other two, except for classes VI and VII, and especially in the lower income classes. Another noteworthy is that in the case of farm households the ratio of deposits and insurance and annuity premiums was almost constant (around 19%) for the range of incomes, I to V. Leaving aside the deficit households, there seems to be a tendency for this ratio to be almost independent of the level of income in the farm surplus households. This probably indicates that even in the poor families there was a propensity to deposit a fairly constant proportion of income before they began to consume. It was noticed that in the prewar period postal savings showed a remarkable increase even in the rural districts. Our analysis may have some relevance to this.

We will omit the table indicating the ratio of repayments to disposable income, but it can be noted that the ratio of repayments for wage earners was higher than for salary earners. However, there is not too much difference between farm households and the urban worker households in the high ratio of repayments.

Finally, there is the ratio of the increase in cash holdings to disposable income. Although this ratio is very small, compared with others, the ratio for wage earners was higher than that for salary earners, and the farm households had a higher ratio than wage earner households. The slope of this ratio between income classes also corresponds to the difference of the cross-section marginal propensities to save of salary earners, wage earners and farm households.

The above is an analysis of family budget data in 1926. It is particularly interesting to compare it with the results of the postwar period. However, it is very difficult to compare the prewar and postwar saving patterns in terms of *real* disposable incomes classified by income classes, owing to the large discrepancy between the Laspeyres' and Paarsche's cost-of-living indexes. An accurate comparison of real incomes in 1926 and after the war would be difficult. As a substitute, we will use the relative incomes of various income classes relative to the (sampling) averages in the two periods.

In Fig. 11, the relative incomes in this sense are measured on the horizontal axis, and the ratios of deposits and insurance and annuity premiums as well as the ratios of deposits withdrawn and insurance and annuity proceeds to disposable incomes are measured on the vertical axis, respectively. As the coverage of the two surveys may be different, the relative incomes to the sampling averages will not always be an adequate basis for comparison, but the analysis made in Fig. 11 may suggest a broad outline. The comparison of prewar

Fig. 11. A Comparison of Prewar and Postwar Cross-section Relations of Changes in Deposits, *etc.* as % to Disposable Incomes

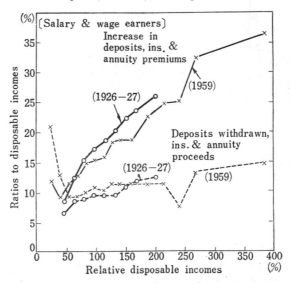

and postwar data in Fig. 11 suggests that in 1959 there was a recovery to the prewar level of the relations of positive saving flows or negative saving flows to disposable income. There is no significant difference in the prewar and postwar curves of negative saving flows, but there is a slight difference in the curves of the former. The latter difference, however, seems to be negligible, if the statistical errors and differences in concepts and methods in the basic data are taken into account.

Fig. 12, on the other hand, shows the three relations : 1) the ratios of debt increases and credit purchases, 2) the ratios of repayments, and 3) the ratios of increases in cash holdings, for the same two periods. In 1926–7, the ratio of debt increase and credit purchases and that of repayments were almost equal. Moreover, the ratio of

Fig. 12. A Comparison of Prewar and Postwar Cross-Section Relations of Debts, Repayments and Changes in Cash Holdings as % to Disposable Incomes

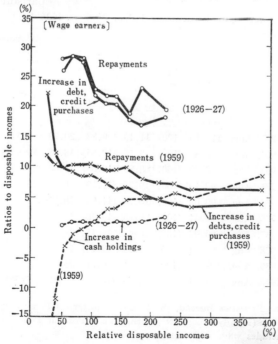

267

increase in cash holdings was almost zero. However, these relations are quite different in the postwar period. As we see in Fig. 12, there is a gap between the curve for repayments and that for debt increase and credit purchases. The curve for increases in cash holdings shows a rising tendency up to over the 8% point as we move to the higher income groups, and this is quite different from the prewar pattern. Although in the prewar period installment payment system did not yet prevail in its modern form, it was customary for even small retailers to sell their commodities on credit, and the period of repayment was much longer than that after the war, sometimes over six months or a year. This practice seems to have been more prevalent in the rural areas and more intensified during depressions. The above is an explanation why the ratios of debt increases and credit purchases (and also that of repayments) was higher in the prewar period.

Table 14. Prewar Saving Structure of Urban Workers, 1926–1940
—All cities—

	Disposable income		Deposits withdrawn, insurance & annuity proceeds		Deposits, insurance & annuity premiums		Increase in cash holdings and others	
	yen	%	yen	%	yen	%	yen	%
1926, Sept.-1927, Aug.	113.19	(100)	11.13	(9.83)	20.73	(18.31)	1.80	(1.59)
1931, Sept.-1932, Aug.	86.32	(100)	9.18	(10.63)	18.08	(20.95)	1.24	(1.44)
1932, Sept.-1933, Aug.	88.50	(100)	8.89	(10.05)	19.06	(21.54)	1.09	(1.22)
1933, Sept.-1934, Aug.	90.19	(100)	10.27	(11.39)	20.88	(23.15)	.83	(.92)
1934, Sept.-1935, Aug.	90.09	(100)	10.76	(11.94)	20.15	(22.37)	.83	(.92)
1935, Sept.-1936, Aug.	90.41	(100)	9.46	(10.46)	19.21	(21.25)	.73	(.81)
1936, Sept.-1937, Aug.	93.42	(100)	10.42	(11.15)	20.40	(21.84)	1.41	(1.51)
1937, Sept.-1938, Aug.	97.91	(100)	9.54	(9.74)	21.66	(22.12)	2.04	(2.08)
1938, Sept.-1939, Aug.	104.48	(100)	10.67	(10.21)	25.75	(24.65)	2.52	(2.41)
1939, Sept.-1940, Aug.	115.11	(100)	12.64	(10.98)	27.12	(23.56)	3.63	(3.15)

Source : The Statistics Bureau, the Prime Minister's Office, *Sengo Junen no Kakei* (Family Income & Expenditure in Postwar Ten Years), 1956.

Note : Includes wage and salary earners.

Before we go on, a few words on Fig. 11 should be added. Before 1959, the prewar and postwar gap in the ratios of deposits and insurance and annuity premiums were wider, and as time went on, this gap has been narrowed to the extent shown in Fig. 11.

The above analysis can be reformulated in time-series form by using the averages of the prewar urban worker family budget data, year by year. In Table 13, we see a relative stability in the ratio of deposits withdrawn and insurance and annuity proceeds around the 10% level, and in the ratio of increases of deposits and insurance and annuity premiums around the 20–24% level, although there are some small changes in the latter. The ratio of increase in cash holdings and others (including debts and repayments) reveals some changes, but the percentages themselves are very small. If we are entitled to assume that the increase in cash holdings is close to zero, then we may suppose that increases in debts and credit purchases had been offset year by year by repayments.

We have already taken up the postwar movements in Table 6.

Table 15. Comparison of Prewar and Postwar Saving Structures of Urban Workers

—All cities—

	Deposits withdrawn insurance & annuity proceeds	Deposits, insurance & annuity premiums	Increase in debt, and credit purchases	Repayments
1936, Sept.-1937, Aug.	11.15 %	21.84 %	16.47 %	16.35 %
1951	6.80	6.28	4.95	4.79
1952	6.25	8.43	4.57	3.42
1953	7.62	10.86	8.89	9.03
1954	7.80	11.92	9.01	13.25
1955	8.14	13.76	7.95	15.71
1956	8.74	15.57	7.86	10.88
1957	8.71	16.66	7.23	9.13
1958	9.20	17.36	7.13	9.37
1959	10.27	19.05	7.20	9.27

Note: See Source and notes as in Table 14.

269

However, in that table, the deposits and the repayments were summed, and then expressed as a ratio to disposable income. The same procedure was applied to the deposits withdrawn and increases in debts. Therefore, we have separated out deposits, deposits withdrawn, debts and repayments in Table 15 and made these ratios comparable for the prewar and postwar periods. It is noted that the ratio of deposits withdrawn, and insurance and annuity proceeds fell drastically once after the war, but gradually recovered to the prewar ratio in 1959, and the ratio of deposits and insurance and annuity premiums has also followed a similar course, but it was still a bit lower than the prewar ratio in 1959. However, the ratio of increases in debts and that of repayments are still very much lower, with the latter higher than the former.

8. Cross-Section Consumption Functions in the Earlier Prewar Period

Fairly large-scale family budget surveys were begun in 1926 by the Cabinet Statistics Bureau. Before that time there were only sporadic surveys, most of which were neither as extensive nor nationwide as the later surveys. Therefore, we must be satisfied with very broad and tentative analysis of the results of these earlier Taisho (1912–25) period surveys. Many of the family budget surveys are summarized in *Hompo Shakai Tokeiron* (Social Statistics in Japan) 1928, edited by the late Iwasaburo Takano, a statistician, and our studies depend mainly on his summarized data.

The first surveys from which we have computed cross-section consumption functions are those conducted by Dr. Takano himself, covering worker households in Tsukishima (southern section of Tokyo), and also of the households of elementary school teachers in and around Tokyo in 1919. The resulting income-consumption relations are shown in Table 16 and Fig. 13. In Fig. 13, we can see how much steeper the consumption curve for the teacher-households is than that of the Tsukishima worker's. However, an epidemic was then prevalent and this may partly account for the lower marginal

Table 16. Income-Consumption Relations from the Family Budget Survey by Dr. Takano, 1919

Income classes	Worker Households		Households of Elementary School Teachers	
	Income before tax	Consumption incl. tax	Income before tax	Consumption incl. tax
	yen	yen	yen	yen
under ¥49	39.816	47.602	46.557	51.708
¥ 50— 59	56.393	60.206	55.573	57.651
¥ 60— 69	63.575	63.923	66.591	73.497
¥ 70— 79	73.438	65.322	75.124	75.180
¥ 80— 89	88.720	75.050	84.980	83.953
¥ 90— 99	—	—	93.988	91.723
¥100—109	107.808	90.724	102.228	100.266
¥110—	138.498	127.334	133.627	141.819

Source: Iwasaburo Takano, ed., *Hompo Shakai Tokeiron* (Social Statistics in Japan), 1928, pp. 215-222.

Notes: Surveyed households number 40 for workers and 95 for teachers.

Fig. 13. Income-Consumption Curves Derived from the Data in Table 16

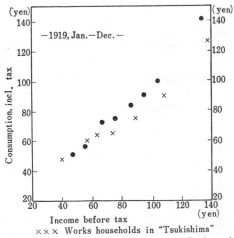

××× Works households in "Tsukishima"
●●● Households of elementary school teachers in and around Tokyo

propensity to consume of the Tsukishima workers (.5967 or .7706, see Table 20 in p. 275), notwithstanding the fact that the objective of the survey was the relatively lower-income classes. But another reason is that the marginal propensity to consume of salary earners is generally higher than that of wage earners.

Another fairly large-scale survey conducted in 1921–22, is that of the *Kyochokai* which covers twelve prefectures, and over 650 households. The results are shown in Table 17 and Fig. 14. The

Table 17. Income-Consumption Relation, *Report on Family Budget Survey*, by the Kyochokai
—1921, June–1922, May—

Income classes	Disposable income	Consumption expenditure	Number of surveyed households
under ¥50	yen 40.11	yen 41.10	8
¥ 51—100	73.56	68.22	192
¥101—150	107.72	96.61	253
¥151—200	146.03	126.07	114
¥201—250	181.03	157.36	56
¥251—300	213.53	182.59	23

Source: The Kyochokai, *Hokyuseikatsusha Shokko Seikei Chosa Hokoku* (Report on the Family Budget Survey of Salary and Wage Earners), 1925.

Fig. 14. Income-Consumption Curve Derived from the Data in Table 17

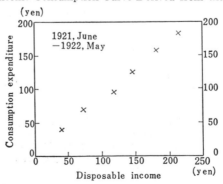

cross-section marginal propensity to consume is .8162, as indicated in Table 20.

Two other surveys are the Family Budget Surveys conducted by the Social Affairs Bureau of the Ministry of Home Affairs (1921) and by the Social Affairs Bureau of the Tokyo Prefecture (1922). The former covered households in several slum areas of Tokyo, and the latter middle class households in Tokyo Prefecture. The data and corresponding curves are shown in Table 18, Fig. 15, Table 19, and also in Fig. 16, respectively.

The results of the computations of inter-income class consumption functions are summarized in Table 20. Excluding Takano's survey for Tsukishima workers, the coefficients of the marginal propensity

Table 18. Income Consumption Relation, for Slum Families, *Family Budget Survey* of the Ministry of Home Affairs
—1921, Nov.—

Income classes	Income before tax	Consumption incl. tax
	yen	yen
under ¥20	27.36	27.48
¥ 21— 40	30.84	35.78
¥ 41— 50	43.89	42.22
¥ 51— 60	52.25	52.04
¥ 61— 70	61.75	59.50
¥ 71— 80	71.09	65.17
¥ 81— 90	78.28	73.59
¥ 91—100	85.12	78.09
¥101—120	100.47	89.48
¥121—150	116.87	103.25
¥151—	177.65	161.24

Source: I. Takano, *op. cit.*, pp. 222–223.

Notes: 1) Surveyed areas were Asahi-cho in Yotsuya-ku, Asakusa-cho in Asakusa-ku, and Motomura-cho and Sarue-cho in Fukagawa-ku, Tokyo City. Surveyed households numbered 497.

2) The objectives were families in slum, paying less than ¥5 per month rent, and engaged in unskilled occupations such as cart-pulling, odd jobs, *etc.*

273

Table 19. Income-Consumption Relation for Middle-Class Households, *Family Budget Survey* of the Social Affairs Bureau, Tokyo Prefecture
—1922, Nov.—

Income classes	Income before tax	Consumption incl. tax	Surveyed households
	yen	yen	
under ¥60	56.63	74.14	17
¥ 61— 80	71.94	80.02	214
¥ 81—100	90.34	97.66	251
¥101—120	109.42	118.68	194
¥121—150	134.71	137.69	152
¥151—200	169.95	176.05	127
¥201—220	216.79	214.58	52
¥251—300	263.53	244.39	11
¥301—350	313.97	296.42	5
¥351—	413.39	185.83	4

Source: I. Takano, *op. cit.*, pp. 233–237.
Note: Surveyed areas were Tokyo City and neighboring towns and villages.

Fig. 15. Income-Consumption Curve Derived from the Data in Table 18

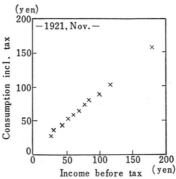

to consume range from .816 to .870, and are fairly stable. The Ministry of Home Affairs' Survey of slum families was focused on the lower income groups, while the Tokyo Prefecture Survey of middle classes covered the ¥300-and-over income class. Nevertheless, the cross-section marginal propensities to consume of both surveys

274

Fig. 16. Income-Consumption Curve Derived from the Data in Table 19

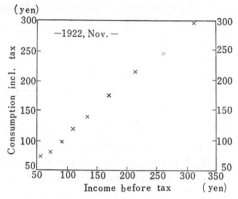

Table 20. Cross-Section Consumption Functions form Various Family Budget
Surveys in the Taisho Period

Surveys	Consumption functions	Remarks
1. Takano's survey for Tsukishima workers	$\begin{cases} C=24.399+.5967\,Y:R^2=.9764 \\ C=13.181+.7706\,Y:R^2=.9612 \end{cases}$	Excl. highest class Incl. all classes
2. Takano's survey for school teachers	$C=12.578+.8477\,Y:R^2=.9858$	Excl. highest class
3. Kyochokai's survey	$C=8.219+.8162\,Y:R^2=.9998$	Disposable income-consump. relation for salary & wage earners combined
4. M.H.A., survery for slum dwellers	$C=5.44+.8610\,Y:R^2=.9970$	
5. Tokyo pref.'s survey for middle classes	$C=21.88+.8707\,Y:R^2=.9970$	Excl. highest class

Note :   1)   Based on the data presented in Tables 16–18.

were similar, *i.e.*, .861 and .870. However, zero saving income derived from the consumption function of slum families, was ¥39.14, but the counter part income from the middle class survey was ¥169.22, showing a large difference. This may be due to the difference in the consumption standards of slum and middle-class groups. It is clearly impossible to compare the propensities to consume of the two groups in terms of absolute incomes, but a comparison in terms of relative incomes might be feasible. In this sense, the comparison of different classes would justify the relative income hypothesis.

We have already seen that the cross-section marginal propensity to consume for urban workers during the prewar Showa period (1926–1940) was less than .8, while in the latter Taisho period (1921–1926) various computations suggest marginal propensities to consume of over .8. We have established our hypothesis that the cross-section marginal propensity to consume will move up or down in the same direction as the business cycle. From this point of view, the fact that the cross-section marginal propensity to consume in the 1921 and 1922 recession was over .8, again seems to support our hypothesis.

The above analysis is mainly based on Dr. Takano's summary, but, after writing the above, there has come to light another important survey conducted in 1917 by the Ministry of Finance for taxation purposes. As this survey was entitled " The Survey of Tax Burdens ", its existence had remained unnoticed and even Dr. Takano's summary did not include it. However, Mr. Saburo Yamada, Graduate Student of Tokyo University, has worked on this survey, and I will summarized some of his results in Table 21.

As this survey centered around the relatively higher-income tax-paying groups, it cannot be compared with the results in Table 20. Nevertheless, this survey has merit in that the sample are extremely large and shows the consumption behavior of farmers, business proprietors, salary earners and rentiers in the earlier period. As can be theoretically expected, the marginal propensity to consume of farmers, business proprietors and rentiers (0.46–0.57) is less than that for salary earners (0.74). The marginal propensity to consume for salary earners (0.74) is exclusive of the highest income class, so that it may roughly be compared with the results for the later Taisho period and the prewar Showa period as far as the salary and wage earners are concerned. It is lower than that around 1921–22, (a period of falling prices), but close to the marginal propensity to consume in the early Showa period (a period of rising prices). Thus,

Table 21. S. Yamada's Computation of Cross-Section Consumption Functions Based on the Ministry of Finance, *The Survey of Tax Burdens*

	No. of surveyed households	Consumption function (1916)		Average propensity to consume
		Exponential	Linear (excl. highest class)	
Farmers	3,963	$C=7,564\,Y^{0.6696}$	$C=262+0.46\,Y$	59.0%
Business proprietors	3,349	$C=8,802\,Y^{0.6497}$	$C=284+0.47\,Y$	61.8
Government officials (Salary earners)	1,241	$C=2,202\,Y^{0.8676}$	$C=118+0.74\,Y$	83.3
Rentiers	238	$C=7,927\,Y^{0.6661}$	$C=201+0.57\,Y$	47.9

Source : The Ministry of Finance, The Bureau of Temporary Research, *Sozei-futan Chosho* (The Survey of Tax Burdens), September, 1917 ; taken from Saburo Yamada, " Gyoshubetsu Shohikansu no Keisoku " (A Measurement of the Consumption Function by Various Occupations), *Nogyo Keizai Kenkyu*, August 1961.

Note : As the survey is taxation data, the sample is biased toward the upper income classes ; this is especially true for the farmers, the survey being mainly confined to owner-farmers and land-owners.

we have additional evidence that the cross-section marginal propensity to consume moves inversely with the ups and downs of business cycles.

9. Intertemporal Shifts in the Cross-Section Saving Relations

Lastly, it will be appropriate here to review the intertemporal shifts in cross-section saving ratio-income relations, for these may clarify certain features of consumption-saving behavior in Japan. For instance, in the United States, there has been a gradual shift to the right of the cross-section saving ratio-real income curve, which means that the saving ratio corresponding to the same real income tends to decline secularly.   This is a mechanism through which the aggregate saving ratio in the economy maintains relative constancy

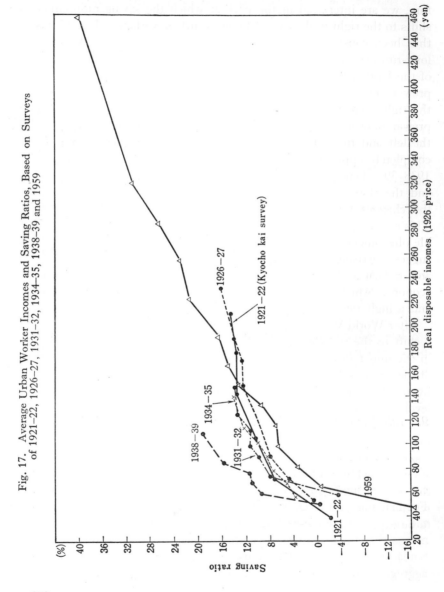

Fig. 17. Average Urban Worker Incomes and Saving Ratios, Based on Surveys of 1921–22, 1926–27, 1931–32, 1934–35, 1938–39 and 1959

278

over a long period in spite of the increase in real income.   Therefore, we are interested in the pace at which the saving-ratio curve shifts to the right in the case of Japanese urban workers.   Fig. 17 has thus been constructed notwithstanding the probable defects in the long-run price deflator.   It is interesting that in contrast to the case of the United States, the saving-ratio curve moves to the left in the prewar period.   Between 1921–22 and 1926–27, the curve shifts to the right, reflectiong the recession phase, but following that in the prewar Showa period (1931–32, 1934–35, and 1938–39), it shifts to the left and the main picture for the 1920–40 period seems to be completely opposite to that of the United States.   Even excluding 1938–39, when the saving-ratio curve moves to the left very sharply and the slope becomes more vertical owing to the war economy, the changes for 1920–35 entails no movement toward the right. This may be partly due to incomplet data, but is still a very remarkable phenomenon, in contrast to the United States experience.   This suggests a rising average saving ratio in urban worker households, and indicates the prevalance of the so-called " low pressure " economy, which in turn favors export expansion on the one hand, and a high rate of capital accumulation, on the other.

After World War II, the curve for 1959 shows that there occurred a shift to the right in the lower income classes, but the movement in the upper income classes was toward the left, and that the slope of the curve is more perpendicular than in 1931–35.   The estimates by the Economic Planning Agency of real per capita consumption level (1934–36=100) suggests that it surpassed the prewar level by 29% in 1959.   In this situation, it is to be noted that the saving ratio of the lower income classs declined and that of the higher income classes increased.

On the whole, the impression given by Fig. 17 is different from that for the United States.   The reason for this, together with the relatively higher saving ratio in the international comparison, remains to be explored in the next section.

10. The High Saving Ratio

So far, we have focussed our analysis mainly on the quantitative aspects of saving-income relations. However, one important analytical approach to the problem why the Japanese saving ratio is so high has not been taken up.

Of course, in a country like Japan, with an extraordinarily high growth rate, the saving ratio would also be very high. This may merely reflect the high investment ratio, because according to the Keynesian doctrine saving is a shadow of investment. It is fairly easy to see that corporate profit, and therefore corporate savings, will rise as a consequence of an investment boom, hence it is very clear that the investment is the cause and saving is the result, as far as the corporate investment and saving are concerned. In the same way, some of the investments of unincorporated firms in their factories or shops would also be represented directly in the savings in a physical form.

However, the above relation is not always valid as far as household saving is concerned. Why the saving ratio for *urban worker families* is also so high in Japan, as compared with other countries, would deserve our attention. According to the United States' family budget studies, the average saving ratio for urban worker alost been less than 10%, while in Sweden and the United Kingdom it is often less than 5%.[6] Therefore, it may be of interest to try to enumerate here the factors behind the high saving ratio even for urban worker families.

1) In Japan, the system of social security is not as advanced as in the Western countries. For instance, the ratio of the cost of social security to national income (for 1953–54) is only 6.7% in Japan, while it is 19.2% in the West Germany, 18.5% in France, 14.7% in Italy, and 10.7% in the United Kingdom.[7] If so, people must save more as a precaution against disease, unemployment and old age, than in other countries where social security is much more advanced.

6) For example, see M. Friedman, *op. cit.*, p. 41.
7) ILO, *The Cost of Social Security*, 1958.

2) The age composition of Japanese population is younger than that of the United States and the United Kingdom. According to Colin Clark, " Savings are generally accumulated by the young and decumulated by the old, so a rapidly growing population with a high proportion of young men should have a high rate of accumulation, an elderly population a low rate."[8] His data suggest that, in the pre-war period (about 1935–40), the proportion of the persons over 60 as percent of the persons 20–39 years old, was 41% in the Great Britain, 52% in France, 39% in Germany, and 32% in the United States, while it was only 26% in Japan. In the postwar period too, the proportion of the persons over 60 years old in the total population, is 29.5% in the United States (1955), 23.2% in the United Kingdom (1958), while it is only 8.3% in Japan (1960).

3) When two economies are compared, on the one hand, an economy like Japan which has a dual structure with an immensely unequal income distribution and, on the other, an advanced economy with much more equalized income distribution, it seems that the former economy may have a much higher saving ratio than the latter. This is because the saving ratios in lower income groups would not differ greatly, while in higher income groups the economy with more unequal income distribution might exhibit a higher saving ratio.

4) Especially in the postwar period, a drastic decrease in the liquid assets-income ratio should bring about a rising trend in the urban worker's saving ratio up to its peak of 15% in 1960, in order to overcome a postwar decline in the curve of liquid assets-income ratio, and to allow the latter to catch up to the normal line projected from the rising prewar trend of liquid assets-income ratio. Moreover, the shortage of residential housing made people desire acutely to save more in order to provide for the future building of their houses. Not only for house-building but also for the purchases of consumer durables, like television, refrigerators, *etc.*, the pressure to accumulate liquid savings seems to have been more intensified in the postwar period.

8) Colin Clark, *The Conditions of Economic Progress*, 2nd ed., London, 1951, p. 505.

5) In the recent postwar period, especially since 1955, the Japanese people, even the manual or salaried workers, have been aware of the relative advantage in investing their money in stocks rather than depositing them in banks. The Dow-Jones index of stock prices has continued to rise steeply, reflecting the particularly high economic growth, and there has been no tax burden for the capital gains arising from stock transactions. This has entailed not only the transformation of the savings structure towards increasing holdings of stock and other securities, but also the increase in the saving ratio itself.

6) We have already discussed the role of the increasing proportion of income represented by the transitory income component, such as bonuses *etc.*, in the rise of urban workers' saving ratio. This may naturally be an outcome of high economic growth, through the process that a rapid growth means a rise in profit and accordingly an increase in employee compensation in the form of bonuses, *etc.* If so, it seems to be interesting to see what the proportion of such temporary income components is in other countries. At present, I have not prepared any statistical data which might give us a clue through international comparison. It should be sufficient here to raise the untested hypothesis. If it is plausible to suppose that in an economy with higher rate of economic growth the proportion of employee compensation in transitory form would also be higher, the above hypothesis may be valid. But if it is appropriate hypothesis, then it becomes clear that even the high saving ratio of worker families is partly a reflection of the high investment ratio or of the high rate of economic growth.

7) Lastly, we must mention a residual factor not covered above. Eventually we approach a line, beyond which an objective analysis is impossible. This is the character of nations. I believe that the Japanese people is relatively more diligent and industrious, and more thrifty on an international standard. Why they are so is difficult to explain. But, we see the monthly instalment deposits which prevail even among the low income groups in Japan. This type of savings which were more predominant in the prewar period are evidently not treated a residual; rather consumption appears to be

treated as the residual. These savings are sometimes contractual as are in some kind of the postal savings, but it is to be noted that even if the savers have no contract they often plan regular savings without a contract. On this point, we lack objective evidence, but this difference in the character of nations (as to thriftiness) cannot be neglected.

CHAPTER 11

REAL AND MONEY INCOME MULTIPLIERS

1. A Dilemma in the Keynesian Dynamics

The most conspicuous feature of the prevailing trade cycle theories since Keynes' *General Theory*, is that trade cycles or economic fluctuations have been largely explained in terms of such an aggregate concept as *real* national income. Although Keynes himself did analyze the fluctuations by an indicator such as employment or national income in wage-terms, the post-Keynesian has customarily adopted the real-term concept. This tendency seems to be unavoidable to a degree, as far as the consumption function, a keystone of the Keynesian economics, is concerned.

Why must it be expressed in real terms? If we assume a linear form of consumption function, the consumption function *in money terms* which connects money consumption expenditure C and money national income Y, will be

$$C = a + bY \dots\dots\dots\dots\dots(1)$$

where a and b=constant. From this equation, we can drive

$$C/Y = b + a/Y \dots\dots\dots\dots(2)$$

in which is involved a false implication that a particular average propensity to consume will correspond to a given *money* income. However, provided that no money illusion exists among consumers, it will be more plausible to deal with the average propensity to consume as a particular function of *real* income $\left(\dfrac{Y}{P}\right)$, *i.e.*,

$$C/Y = \beta + \alpha \Big/ \left(\frac{Y}{P}\right)\dots\dots\dots\dots(2')$$

If we transform (2') into the following form,

$$\left(\frac{C}{P}\right) = a + \beta\left(\frac{Y}{P}\right) \quad \dots\dots\dots\dots(1')$$

the *real consumption function* will be obtained, which represents the ordinary Keynesian way of thinking.

Once the consumption function, the nucleus of the Keynesian economics, however, has been expressed in real terms, it will be natural to represent all other functions too in real terms. Thus the Keynesian economics could not but follow the way towards the *real output dynamics.*[1] Nevertheless, the multiplier process itself, even though derived from the real consumption function, is essentially a *monetary phenomenon*, because the multiplier sequence is nothing but a self-expanding process of monetary expenditures and even if changes in real output were not to move correspondingly, the price level would increase as if it were a variant in a more general sense of the multiplier process. Therefore, it is a serious contradiction that the consumption function is usually composed in real terms. Notwithstanding the fact that the 'multiplier rolling' is a monetary phenomenon, the consumption function, the computing origin of the above, is obliged to wear a *real* garment, in order to maintain the *stability* of the function. The trade cycle is now analyzed largely in terms of real output, in spite of the concurrent severe fluctuations of prices. The exposition of price fluctuations is treated as if it were a causally isolated phenomenon from the multiplier process, although both are actually interwoven with each other.

If output follows behind the effective demand faithfully like a shadow, and if the reversed Say's law that 'the demand creates its own supply' is valid, the Keynesian real output dynamics may

---

1) Cf. J. R. Hicks, *A Contribution to the Theory of the Trade Cycle*, 1950. As Hicks pointed out, the investment function, in addition to the consumption function, must be expressed in real terms, because the *acceleration principle* will be more conveniently developed in real terms than in wage terms. "For what that principle is concerned with is the effect of change in *output* on investment; it is not evident that a rise in output will have any different effect in this direction when it is due to increasing employment from what it will have when it is due to many of the various causes which can be grouped together as increasing productivity." (p. 8)

quite naturally be constructed on the basis of a real consumption function. The actuality, however, is extremely different. Formerly the Wicksellian analyzed the price fluctuation process as being caused by the investment-saving gap. Now the Keynesian Revolution elucidated that IS gap will promote a change in output. But *in fact*, the gap generates both fluctuations in prices and production.

Keynes, in Chapter 21 of his *General Theory*, deals with the problem how a change in monetary effective demand will be absorbed between price and output alterations. His analysis in terms of price and output elasticities, $e_0 \cdot e_p$, nevertheless, is not in harmoney with his theory of the multiplier. One of our major problems lies in this harmonization.

One dilemma in the Keynesian economics originates from the above-mentioned inconsistency between monetary multiplier and real consumption function, but his economics also faces another dilemma in the exposition of reality. As a matter of fact, during the inter-war period, in the United States and other countries, there occurred an extraordinary severe oscillations in production, and so far as that period is concerned, the real output approach is fairly realistic. But in prewar Japan or in Great Britain in the 19th century, the Juglar cycle of industrial production or real national income, lacks distinctness. Prices were rather more cyclical than production, and very frequently the Juglar cycles of production disappeared in its secular upward trend, still more so with reference to the Kondratieff long wave. We cannot find the Kondratieff waves clearly in the *level* of industrial production or real *GNP*. Nevertheless, sometimes we see economists who drawed the long waves in terms of the *level* of *GNP* with distinct ups and downs. This seems to be contradictory to the fact. But such is an example of Keynesian adherence to real output fluctuations.

It is one of the shortcomings of the present Keynesian dynamics that it fails to synthesize price fluctuations with those of output. Of course, we do not attempt to solve the whole problem here. We are merely satisfied to grasp a simple formulation of the inter-relation between multiplier and price changes.

2. Relation between Income Multiplier and Price Fluctuations

It has been generally assumed that the theory of multiplier is only valid within the economic sphere of a constant price level, or when the elasticity of production with reference to effective demand is always unity. In other words, it postulates the hypothetical case where the whole increment of effective demand is necessarily absorbed by production increases with the result of no price changes. Generally, it is called the theory of under-employment multiplier. In fact, however, prices usually fluctuate even in the stage of under-employment, and in the statistical determination of multiplier, such series as income, consumption, investment, and so on are often deflated by the index of the general price level.

The theoretical assumption of a constant price level is supposed to be abandoned when real-income multiplier is statistically computed, because if the assumption of a constant price level is an indispensable condition, its statistical computation is nonsense.

Although Keynes adopted the wage term, many post-Keynesians used the real term. Consequently we shall henceforward use the multiplier in real terms. When national income is expressed by Y, investment by I, savings by S, general price index by P, price elasticity with reference to money national income by e_p, and output elasticity with reference to Y by e_0 $(=1-e_p)$, we are able to construct the following relation between real-income multiplier

$$k_r \left[= d\left(\frac{Y}{P}\right) \middle/ d\left(\frac{I}{P}\right) \right]$$

and money-income multiplier $k_m[=dY/dI]$,

$$k_r = \frac{d\left(\frac{Y}{P}\right)}{d\left(\frac{I}{P}\right)} = \frac{\frac{dY}{P} - Y\frac{dP}{P^2}}{\frac{dI}{P} - I\frac{dP}{P^2}} = \frac{dY - Y\frac{dP}{P}}{dI - I\frac{dP}{P}} = \frac{1 - e_p}{\frac{dI}{dY} - \frac{I}{Y}e_p} = \frac{e_0}{\frac{1}{k_m} - \frac{S}{Y}e_p}$$

287

$$\therefore \quad \frac{k_r}{k_m} = e_0 + k_r e_p \frac{S}{Y} \quad \dots \dots \dots \dots \dots (3)$$

We call this *the fundamental equation of real-and money-income multipliers.* The meaning of this is as follows : The ratio of real to money income multilpier $\left(\dfrac{k_r}{k_m}\right)$ largely depends on the value of e_0, *i.e.,* upon the intensity of inflation, for the value of k_r is usually 2–3, S/Y the savings ratio 10–15 %, and e_p in normal times does not rise above 0.5, thus the product of the above three coefficients $k_r e_p \dfrac{S}{Y}$ is 0.1 or thereabout Therefore, $\dfrac{k_r}{k_m}$, is dominantly determined by the value of e_0.

As a matter of course, $1 = e_p + e_0$, because it can be derived by the total differential of the identity $Y = O \cdot P$, (where O is the physical output). Therefore the nearer e_0 is to zero, the closer e_p will be to unity, and the economic conditions will be inflationary. On the contrary, the nearer e_0 is to unity, the closer e_p will be to zero, and k_r will get close to k_m.

Consequently, the severer an inflation becomes, the closer e_0 will be to zero, with the consequence of the difference $k_m - k_r$ growing greater. Formerly, Richard and W. M. Stone computed the marginal propensity to consume and the multiplier with the reference to the six countries, *i.e.,* Germany, Great Britain, Netherlands, Poland, Sweden and America, but they used not k_r but k_m.[2] Although an international comparison of k_r is meaningful, that of k_m, may make little sense because even if the computed value of k_r should be equivalent between two countries, k_m in the more inflationary country would be relatively greater than that in the less inflationary country. Colin Clark once compared k_m from time series with k_r from budget studies,[3] utilizing Stone's results. This may also lack economic meaning.

2) Richard and W. M. Stone, " The Marginal Propensity to Consume and the Multiplier, A Statistical Investigation," *The Review of Economic Studies,* October 1938.
3) Colin Clark, *The Conditions of Economic Progress,* 1940, Second edition, Chapter 15.

The above is a formal relation between k_r, k_m and e_0, and, in a sense, the bridge between Keynes' multiplier theory and his $e_0 \cdot e_p$ theory. If the multiplier theory should be constructed on the assumption of constant price level Keynes' two theoretical apparatus could by no means be harmonized. However, if the multiplier is to be calculated by the *deflated* income-consumption data, they can be satisfactorily combined, though k_r in this case is not in a position causally to determine real national income relatively to an initially performed investment in money terms.

If the real consumption function is relatively stable, k_r will also be stable. As J. Duesenberry pointed out,[4] this may be a *fundamental relation*. On the contrary, the monetary consumption function or money income multiplier is a *derived relation*, because it is difficult to forecast how much prices will change in the forthcoming period, whereas it is comparatively conjecturable how much real consumption will change when a given real income changes. Therefore the money income multiplier as a derived relation depends upon the degree of price fluctuation when the real income multiplier, as a fundamental relation, is once determined.

In the fundamental equation (3), e_0 may be assumed to change in a volatile manner in each phase of business cycle.

If we assume $e_0 = 1$, and substitute it into (3), we obtain,

$$\frac{k_r}{k_m} = 1 \; ; \quad k_r = k_m$$

When the price level is perfectly stable, the money-income multiplier will coincide with the real-income multiplier.

But when $k_r = k_m$ to the contrary, is e_0 always 1? Surely such will be a special case, but not always, since the relation is not symmetrical or reversible. If we put $k_r = k_m$ into (3), remembering $e_0 = 1 - e_p$, we have

$$1 = \frac{S}{Y} k_r ; \quad \text{(since } k_r = k_m) \quad 1 = \frac{S}{Y} k_m$$

4) J. Duesenberry, *Income, Saving and the Theory of Consumer Behavior*, 1949, pp. 73–75.

$$\therefore \quad k_r = k_m = \frac{1}{S/Y}$$

Consequently when there is no intercrept in the two-dimensional diagram composed of S and Y, the condition $k_r = k_m$ will always be satisfied however much the price level changes.

The above, however, is too imaginary case. In fact, not only prices are variable, but also there cannot be supposed any two dimensional diagram without intercept with reference to S and Y. If we compute the values of k_r and k_m from the U.S. Department of Commerce national income data and the BLS consumer's price index 1929–40, we obtain the result $k_r = 2.8$ and $k_m = 3.5$. This coefficient k_r is not a genuine multiplier, since S and Y are not reduced to a *per capita* basis, but it will probably be adequate as a coefficient indicating the connection with the value $e_0 \cdot e_p$. If we further assume that $S/Y = 0.1$ and put these values into (3), e_0 thus derived indirectly becomes 0.72. On the other hand, e_0 in the United States surpasses 0.8 for 6 years and is below 0.8 for 5 years. For these periods, there are several years when S/Y is negative and S/Y actually fluctuated very violently. Therefore, if we put annually changing S/Y into (3), there will be established a clear consistent relation among k_r, k_m, e_0 and S/Y.

The multiplier under price fluctuations can be formally explained by the above formulation. But in the customary theory of multiplier, the assumption is generally made that before full employment prices do not entirely change ($e_0 = 1$) and only after full employment, the increase of effective demand will be wholly absorbed by price-rise ($e_p = 1$). Goodwin's procedure is one example.[5]

We are interested, then, in deriving the so-called full employment multiplier, *i.e.*, the money-income multiplier when $e_p = 1$. Substituting $e_p = 1$ into (3), we obtain

$$\frac{k_r}{k_m} = k_r \frac{S}{Y} \quad ; \quad k_m = \frac{Y}{S} = \frac{Y/P}{S/P}$$

5) R. M. Goodwin, "The Theory of Multiplier," in Harris ed., *The New Economics*, 1947, pp. 482–499.

In the form of the propensity to consume,

$$\frac{dC}{dY} = \frac{C}{Y} = \frac{C/P}{Y/P} = \frac{C_f}{Y_f}$$

where C_f and Y_f is full employment consumption and income respectively, and will be equivalent to C/P and Y/P at and after full employment, if, until full employment, a constant price level is maintained.

If we assume, in Fig. 1, that Y_f is the full employment income and real consumption schedule before full employment is eb, the monetary consumption function after full employment will be bd.

Fig. 1.   Goodwin's Case

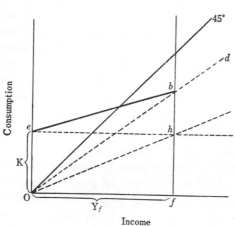

Income

This reveals that the ratio between real consumption and real income at the point $f(=C_f/Y_f)$ will remain unchanged, however nominally money income may be swelled.

As generally observed, the marginal propensity to consume after full employment bd is greater than that before full employment eb, and a slope of bd represents not only the marginal but also the average propensity to consume.

Goodwin's full employment multiplier[6] was formulated as,

6)   *Idem.*, p. 497.

$$\frac{1}{1-(a+K/Y_f)}$$

where a is the pre-full-employment marginal propensity to consume and K is the intercept of the real consumption function eb. Our result perfectly coincides with his formula, because, as the graph distinctly shows,

$$
\begin{array}{ccc}
bd & = & a & + K/Y_f \\
\| & & \| & \| \\
\dfrac{bhf}{Y_f} & = & \dfrac{bh}{Y_f} & + & \dfrac{hf}{Y_f}
\end{array}
$$

The above graph indicates the following interesting consequence. The closer the point where the consumption schedule intersects with the 45° line, approaches towards the full employment level f, the wider the distance bf becomes, with the inevitable result that the income-consumption ratio at full employment (ob) as well as the marginal propensity to consume (bd) becomes greater. As the slope bd becomes steeper, k_m after full employment grows greater. And just when the break-even point of income=consumption coincides with the full employment level, bd becomes the 45° line itself. This is the case of the marginal propensity to consume=1 and the money income multiplier=infinity, where the economy is at the verge of instability. Provided that private investment and government expenditures are added to this level of consumption, the inflationary price-wage spiral will necessarily begin. We can easily understand from the above exposition why in the post-war devastated countries where real income has greatly declined, the hyper-inflation was inevitable.

We must now recognize the hitherto postulated assumption that relative prices are invariable over time, *i.e.*, the parallel movement of the price level of investment goods and the general price level. But such an assumption, of course, is unrealistic. In this respect, J.R. Hicks has made the following suggestion. The value of real investment in terms of consumption goods, he says, is the multiplicand, to which the multiplier has to be applied. Thus, without any expansion in real investment in terms of investment goods, there will be an expansion in consumption, due to the multiplier effect, *merely as a result of the price rise.*[7] This is the Hicks' method of solution which he proposed as an inspection of ceiling. But the unparallel movement between investment goods prices and consumption goods prices occurs not only in the neighborhood of full employment, but also at the phase of recovery from depression. Consequently, his method contradicts his fundamental procedures of real output dynamics, especially with reference to this exposition of acceleration principle *in physical terms.* However, it is easy to see why he had no other course than choose that way. The essence of real income multiplier probably obliged him to do so.

As a matter of course, the multiplier is essentially monetary. Therefore the multiplier will lose its proper character if we pursue the truly real relation when relative prices change, but we shall proceed to follow the consequences of the real-income multiplier, remembering this limitation.

If we assume the general price level as P_y, the investment goods price level as P_i, then the real-income multiplier k_R which takes into consideration these two deflators becomes,

$$k_R = \frac{d\left(\dfrac{Y}{P_y}\right)}{d\left(\dfrac{I}{P_i}\right)} = \frac{\left(dY - Y\dfrac{dP_y}{P_y}\right)P_i}{\left(dI - I\dfrac{dP_i}{P_i}\right)P_y} = \frac{1 - e_p}{\left(1 - \dfrac{dP_i}{P_i}\Big/\dfrac{dI}{I}\right)} \cdot \frac{P_i}{P_y} \cdot \frac{dY}{dI}$$

If we assume the elasticities of investment goods prices and investment goods output with respect to monetary investment are I_p and I_0 respectively,

$$k_R = \frac{P_i}{P_y} \cdot \frac{e_0}{I_0} k_m \quad \ldots\ldots\ldots\ldots\ldots(4)$$

P_i and P_y, however, are in terms of index numbers and are unity respectively at the base point of time. Therefore we can neglect P_i/P_y. Then

$$\frac{k_R}{k_m} = \frac{e_0}{I_0} = \frac{\dfrac{dY}{Y} - \dfrac{dP_y}{P_y}}{\dfrac{dI}{I} - \dfrac{dP_i}{P_i}} \cdot \frac{\dfrac{dI}{I}}{\dfrac{dY}{Y}} \quad \ldots\ldots\ldots(5)$$

7) J. R. Hicks, *op. cit.*, p. 130.

It is evident that the ratio k_R/k_m will be determined, if the values of $\dfrac{dY}{Y}$ and $\dfrac{dI}{I}$ are given, solely by the relative variations of the two price levels. In this case the relative price will exert a dominant influence upon the gap of k_R and k_m.

Further if we assume $I_0 = 1$, *i.e.*, that in the investment goods industry, prices are constant, the real-income multiplier in this case $k_{\bar{R}}$ will be

$$k_{\bar{R}} = k_m e_0 \quad \dotfill (6)$$

This means that although the initial investment is instantaneously embodied in real capital equipment, $k_{\bar{R}}$ relative to k_m declines owing to the price-rise in other industries. This fact will happen even if the price-rise of investment goods is steeper than that of consumer's goods, since, while the investment will be embodied at every current price level in physical capital goods, the consumers will be in a position to purchase consumer's goods only after the lapse of a further price-rise. Keynes criticized the forced saving theory by his own new theory of multiplier,[8] but his criticism is inadequate because the multiplier process will ordinarily accompany a price-rise and evitably cause a time lag, thus enforcing upon the masses forced saving to some degree. The ratio $k_{\bar{R}}/k_m$, therefore might be an indicator of the degree of forced saving.

The equation (6) $k_{\bar{R}} = k_m e_0$ is valid when a price-rise does not occur in the investment goods industry, as above explained, but it may be used for another purpose, *i.e.*, when we are mainly concerned with the problem of the production effect of monetary investment or monetary government expenditures. Then, by multiplying the money income multiplier by e_0, we can estimate the proportion the monetary investment contributed to the rise in production as compared with the successive increase in money income.

The statistically computed multiplier we frequently come across, however, is not the money income multiplier k_m but the real income multiplier in the form of k_r. The next problem is how to derive $k_{\bar{R}}$ when k_r is known.

8) J. M. Keynes, *General Theory*, pp. 79–81.

By transforming (3)

$$k_m = \frac{k_r}{1 - e_p\left(1 - k_r \dfrac{S}{Y}\right)} \quad \dotfill (3')$$

and remembering the equation (6), we derive

$$k_R = \frac{k_r e_0}{1 - e_p\left(1 - k_r \dfrac{S}{Y}\right)} \quad \dotfill (7)$$

From this equation,

    if $e_0 = 1$ —— $k_{\bar{R}} = k_r = k_m$

    if $e_p = 1$ —— $k_{\bar{R}} = 0$

and, if for example $e_p = 0.3$, $\dfrac{S}{Y} = 0.1$ and $k_r = 2.8$, then $k_R = 2.5$. Consequently the ordinary real-income multiplier k_r is greater than *the production multiplier of monetary investment* $k_{\bar{R}}$ which is causally more significant. It is erroneous to think that monetary investment or government expenditures will yield its k_r times real income. By the equation (7), we should consider, instead, that its $k_{\bar{R}}$ times of real income would be generated. In this sense, the Keynesian theory of multiplier, has so far unconsciously given some illusion to economic students. It is not essential for the *ordinary* multiplier whether the multiplier process is an output expanding process or price-rise process, since the nucleus of the multiplier is substantially monetary.

3. Keynes' Mistake on the Theory of Price and Output Elasticities

Our simple attempt at harmonization of the multiplier theory, on the one hand, and the $e_o \cdot e_p$ theory, on the other hand, was developed in section 2. We intend, here, to digress from the main description, and to give a close inspection as to Keynes' own theory of price and output elasticities with respect to effective demand.[9] Present-day

9) I previously tackled this problem, in my book *Koyo to Chingin* (Employment and Wages), 1949, but there is another small essays in 1946, which first paid attention to the error in Keynes' $e_o \cdot e_p$ theory.

Keynesians are quite oblivious of Lord Keynes' brilliant Chapter 20, " The Employment Function " and Chapter 21 " The Theory of Prices," as if they were one of the " red herrings " of the General Theory, but it may be necessary to make the trade cycle theory a vivid picture of actuality by utilizing those chapters. In this section, however, we confine ourselves within the criticism of Keynes $e_o \cdot e_p$ analysis.

In the preceding section we defined $e_o \cdot e_p$ in money terms, *i.e.*,

$$e_o = \frac{dO}{O} \cdot \frac{Y}{dY} \text{ and } e_p = \frac{dP}{P} \cdot \frac{Y}{dY},$$

by the total differential of the identity $Y = O \cdot P$. Keynes, however, defines them in wage terms, *i.e.*,

$$e_o = \frac{dO}{O} \frac{Y_w}{dY_w}, \text{ and } e_p{}' = \frac{dP_w}{P_w} \cdot \frac{Y_w}{dY_w},$$

by the total differential of the identity

$$Y_w = O \cdot P_w, \text{ where } Y_w = \frac{Y}{W} \text{ and } P_w = \frac{P}{W}$$

and w is the money wage level. Henceforth, we shall use D and D_w in place of Y and Y_w, following Keynes' notations. Consequently, Keynes' first formula is

$$1 = e_o + e_p{}' \dots\dots\dots\dots\dots\dots(8)$$

$e_o = \frac{dO}{O} \frac{D_w}{dD_w}$ and $e_p{}' = \frac{dP_w}{P_w} \frac{D_w}{dD_w}$. This means the percentage change of the effective demand in wage terms will be absorbed by the percentage change of prices in wage terms and that of output $\left(i.e. \ \frac{dD_w}{D_w} = \frac{dP_w}{P_w} + \frac{dO}{O} \right)$. But the rise of P_w is equal to the decline of real wages $\frac{w}{P}$, and the decline of P_w to the rise of $\frac{W}{P}$. Now if we define $W_p = \frac{W}{P}$,

$$e_p{}' = -\frac{dW_p}{W_p} \Big/ \frac{dD_w}{D_w} \ \dots\dots\dots\dots(9)$$

because $\dfrac{dP_w}{P_w}\Big/\dfrac{dD_w}{D_w}=\left(\dfrac{dP}{P}-\dfrac{dW}{W}\right)\Big/\dfrac{dD_w}{D_w}=-\left(\dfrac{dW}{W}-\dfrac{dP}{P}\right)\Big/\dfrac{dD_w}{D_w}$

$=-\dfrac{dW_p}{W_p}\Big/\dfrac{dD_w}{D_w}$. $e_p{}'$ is now transformed into an indicator of real wage variation from that of price flexibility. Therefore, we can see nothing of the theory of prices in the equation (9). It may rather be a formula of decreasing returns in response to the rise of output or employment. It is quite natural that Keynes himself rewrites the notations in (8), before going from Chapter 20 " The Employment Function " to Chapter 21 " The Theory of Prices." But in order to express them in money terms, we may replace the equation (8) by the following equation.

$$1 = \dfrac{dO}{O}\Big/\dfrac{dD}{D} + \dfrac{dP}{P}\Big/\dfrac{dD}{D} \quad\ldots\ldots\ldots\ldots(10)$$

Strangely enough, Keynes obtains different formula in money terms,

$$1 = e_p + e_o(1-e_w) \quad\ldots\ldots\ldots\ldots\ldots(11)$$

where $e_p=\dfrac{dP}{P}\Big/\dfrac{dD}{D}$ and $e_w=\dfrac{dW}{W}\Big/\dfrac{dD}{D}$ according to his definition. The equations (10) and (11) clearly contradict. Which is correct? As will be noticed, e_p in this equation is not in money terms. By transforming (11), we derive

$$e_o = \dfrac{1-e_p}{1-e_w} = \dfrac{\dfrac{dD}{D}-\dfrac{dP}{P}}{\dfrac{dD}{D}-\dfrac{dW}{W}} = \dfrac{dO}{O}\Big/\dfrac{dD_w}{D_w}$$

Thus e_o in (11) is not $\dfrac{dO}{O}\Big/\dfrac{dD}{D}$ but $\dfrac{dO}{O}\Big/\dfrac{dD_w}{D_w}$ in the notations of Keynes, *i.e.*, in wage terms. Consequently, the equation (11) is expressed in mixed terms. Formally Keynes himself is right, because e_o is the same not only in (8) but also in (11). A few problems however, remain.

First, in Chapter 21, Section 6, he says " The condition $e_w=1$ means that the wage-unit in terms of money rises in the same proportion as the effective demand, since $e_w = \dfrac{DdW}{WdD}$; and the condition $e_o = 0$ means that output no longer shows any response to a further increase in effective demand, since $e_o = \dfrac{DdO}{OdD}$."[10] He clearly recognizes $e_o = \dfrac{DdO}{OdD}$, i.e., in money terms, if so, the equation (11) is mathematically erroneous. If we take $e_o = \dfrac{D_w dO}{OdD_a}$, the above verbal explanation becomes incorrect. At any rate he causes an unnecessary confusion.

The *second* problem is substantial, as against the formal dilemma in the first. The problem is why only e_o in (11) must be expressed in wage terms. In fact, e_o in wage terms cannot be compared with e_p or e_w in money terms on an equal footing. For instance, if there

period	1	2
D	100	110
P	100	109
O	100	101
W	100	109
D_w	100	101
P_w	100	100

occurs a price rise of 9%, a production increase of 1%, and 10% rise in effective demand, and further the parallel movement of wages and prices, then e_o in wage terms becomes 1, while e_o in money terms is 0.1. This is an astonishing difference. When e_o in wage terms ($=1$) is compared with e_p in money terms ($=0.9$), we cannot judge whether the economy is inflationary or not.

As already explained, e_o in wage terms $= \dfrac{1-e_p}{1-e_w}$ or $\dfrac{\dfrac{dO}{O} \Big/ \dfrac{dD}{D}}{1-e_w}$. From this we derive a few consequences.

10) J. M. Keynes, *op. cit.*, p. 304.

298

1. If $\dfrac{dP}{P} = \dfrac{dW}{W}$, $e_p = e_w$. $\therefore$ e_o in wage terms$=1$, except when $e_p = e_w = 1$. Therefore, except in the indeterminate case when the percentage change of production is zero, the parallel movement of prices and wages will always make e_o in wage terms$=1$, however severe the inflation may be.

2. When production is constant, $\dfrac{dO}{O} \Big/ \dfrac{dD}{D}$ is always zero. Therefore e_o in wage terms is always zero, except when $e_w = 1$. In the case when $\dfrac{dO}{O} = 0$, $\dfrac{dD}{D} = \dfrac{dP}{P}$, and $\dfrac{dP}{P} = \dfrac{dW}{W}$ (inflationary case), we have $e_p = 1$ and $e_o = 0$. But at the critical point when e_w is unity, e_o becomes indeterminate.

3. Mathematically the above formal argument may be possible. But, as an actual problem, the constancy of production and a 0.2% rise of production may be identified. On the other hand, it does not make any difference $\dfrac{dP}{P} = \dfrac{dW}{W}$ or $\dfrac{dP}{P} - \dfrac{dW}{W} = 0.2\%$. e_o in wage terms is thus a very delicate and unstable coefficient which may be unity or zero at random by an operation of raising or dropping fractions. Whereas the economy itself might be in a state of hyper-inflation, whether e_o is zero or unity. It is unrealistic that $\dfrac{dO}{O}$ becomes completely zero, but it may be more probable that the percentage increase in P and W is close to equivalence in hyper-infla-flation. Consequently, we shall not go too far in saying that e_o in wage terms is in the neighborhood of unity, since the difference between $\dfrac{dP}{P}$ ahd $\dfrac{dW}{W}$ may usually be negligible in true inflation, notwithstanding the trivial positive or negative changes in production.

4. Some Statistical Analysis

We shall now stop our theoretical consideration of the relation of real and money income multiplier, but attempt to supplement our article with some statistical, though preliminary, analysis.

Before analysing the Japanese economy, we shall dwell on the American economy. Since the postwar Consumption Function Controversy, we have many consumption functions computed in relation to the American economy, but they are usually personal consumption functions with personal disposable income as their major variable. Consequently they are probably inadequate as compared with those from which we derive a national-wide multiplier, because they do no take into consideration " business savings," as a leakage besides personal savings. For this reason, we shall prefer national income to disposable income as a determinant of consumption expenditure, thus composing two sorts of consumption functions, one in real terms, the other in money terms. Utilizing the Department of Commerce national income estimates and the BLS consumers' price index, the real consumption function would be (suffix r means real term)

1929–1940 and 1946–47 $C_r = 20.5 + 0.641\ Y_r$; $k_r = 2.786$
1941–1943 $C_r = 64.7 + 0.1254\ Y_r$; $k_r = 1.143$

On the other hand, in money consumption function, composed of national income and consumption expenditures in current prices, the marginal propensity to consume is 0.714 in the former period ($k_m = 3.5$) and 0.333 in the period 1941–44 ($k_m = 1.5$).

What are, then, computed values of $e_o \cdot e_p$? We have tried to draw Fig. 2, with NNP on the horizontal axis, and with a price level on the vertical axis, each measured in logarithms, in order to grasp the behavior of e_p graphically.[11] As is easily seen, the slope of the curve shows the elasticity e_p, because it represents $\dfrac{d \log P}{d \log D}$. The results are as follows. At the end of the First Great War, e_p becomes a relatively high value, showing a very flexible price responsiveness to the monetary effective demand (1920 = 0.795; 1921 = 0.735). On the contrary, during the period 1922–1929, the price level was extremely stable, notwithstanding the rise of American production, as if $e_p = 0$

11) The data is taken from S. Kuznets, *National Products since 1869*, 1946, pp. 55–56. The index of the price-level for final products is derived from a comparison of NNP in current prices with NNP in 1929 prices.

Fig. 2.   Effective Demand and Price Level in the United States

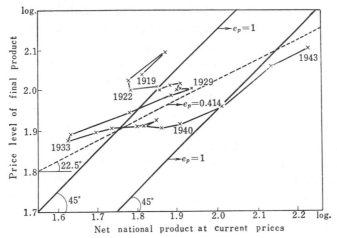

Note: Net National Product → from S. Kuznets, *National Product since 1899*

Price level of final product → $\dfrac{\text{NNP in current prices}}{\text{NNP in 1929 prices}}$

($1923=0.09$; $1929=-0.114$). Owing to the general increase in capacity output, and the invariable level of employment during this period, the bottlenecks, such as full employment and full capacity, did not come into view, which made possible the extraordinary high stability of the price level. Almost zero value of e_p shows not a stage of depression but a phase of high productivity enhanced by successive investments.

Next, in the recession from 1929–1933, we obtain $e_p=0.41$, and by a comparison of 1929 and 1932, $e_p=0.37$ is obtained. This exhibits the *asymmetry* of e_p between the prosperity and recession of business cycles. Such asymmetry reappears in the recovery phase of 1933–1940, causing a smoother slope of $e_p(=0.095)$ than in the recession. The reader will find *the Z-shaped behavior of price-effective demand curve* during one business cycle. This asymmetry is different from what Lord Keynes once pointed out. The asymmetry between Inflation and Deflation, pointed out by Keynes,[12] was the fact that

12)   J. M. Keynes, *op. cit.*, p. 291.

whilst a deflation of effective demand below the level required for full employment will diminish employment as well as prices, an inflation of it above this level will merely affect prices. But the fact that such inflation did not occur in 1920's, has made the Z-shape behavior of prices different from what Keynes once expected. After the Second World War, e_p becomes greater, 1941=0.418: 1942= 0.879; 1943=0.438. Such regularities of e_p during business cycles will be a first step not only in the synthesis of real and money income multiplier, but also in grasping in an organic manner the whole behavior of prices and output.

We can draw a similar type of graph (Fig. 3) also with reference to Japan. It is interesting that we again find the Z-*shape pattern* (*but tilting to the left*). The characteristics of price behavior in Japan lies in the very fact of this tilting. What causes this tilting? First cause is the secular upward trend of the price level since the Meiji era, second is the extraordinary downward flexibility of prices in the period 1920–1931, in spite of the still continuing rapid growth of

Fig. 3. Effective Demand and Price Level in Japan

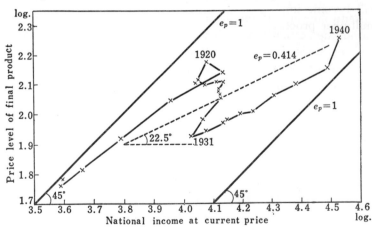

Note: National income → from K. Ohkawa and others, *The Growth Rate of the Japanese Economy since 1878*, Tokyo 1957. Price level of final product → the weighted average of wholesale price and cost of living indexes (with the weights of 3 : 7).

industrial production during the same period. The fluctuation of e_p is as follows. During the first World War, 1915–1920, $e_p = 0.843$. In the price-fall period, 1925–31, $e_p = 1.658$ (this is an abnormal case when prices and output exhibit an opposite movement). In the recovery phase 1931–36, e_p was 0.385. But in the war period 1936–39, e_p increased to 0.553. In 1940, e_p amounted to 2.564. From Fig. 3, we can see a steeper slope of e_p in Japan, as compared with the American economy. The tilted Z-shape pattern also shows the greater flexibility of the Japanese price level. These present a striking contrast with the American case (Fig. 2). These peculiarities are also the consequence of the almost cycle-weak rapid tempo of economic growth in Japan (especially with reference to the growth of the manufacturing industry).

Now what is the value of multiplier? Rigorously speaking, it is impossible to compute the value of multiplier without constructing a complete model, for not only investment but also government expenditure and exports will join in the multiplier repercussion as the multiplicand. Therefore, we will stop to do so, and should be satisfied merely to raise an analysis of price-behavior pattern, which will become important when the price changes in relation to the multiplier process is empirically taken up.

CHAPTER 12

THE MULTIPLIER AND THE MARGINAL
PROPENSITY TO IMPORT

The point to be developed here is very simple, but it concerns a problem long neglected and sometimes completely suppressed by economists.

Keynesian economics has developed remarkably since the emergence of the *General Theory*. However, theoretical models have usually been based upon the drastic assumption that the price level remains unchanged in the process of income expansion. The " real " cycle theories depending upon the interaction of multiplier and accelerator, for example, have been constructed on this assumption. On the other hand, the economics of inflation has been based on the assumption of constant output. The intermediate areas, in which both output and prices fluctuate have rarely been explored.[1] By assuming constancy of the price level, the usual type of anaysis has neglected the difference between the real-income multiplier and the money-income multiplier, or the effects of the elasticity of the price level with respect to effective demand (Keynes' e_p) upon the money-income multiplier. In addition, the influence of changes in the relative prices of imported goods upon the numerical value of the marginal propensity to import (or, say, the marginal " foreign leakage " ratio) has been assumed away in some of those attempts that have been made to analyze open systems.[2] In this article, we

1) In the preceding chapter, my analysis was restricted to a closed system and omitted foreign trade, but in this chapter, it is will be developed by including the effect of foreign trade.
2) Tse Chun Chang, *Cyclical Movements in the Balance of Payments*, Cambridge, Eng., 1951, esp. pp. 79–95 ; J. H. Adler, " United States Imports During the Interwar Period," *Am. Econ. Rev.*, June 1945, XXXV, pp. 418–30 ; Hans Neisser and Franco Modigliani, *National Incomes and International Trade*, Urbana 1953, Ch. 4, esp. p. 78 ; J. J. Polak, *An International Economic System*, Chicago, 1953, esp. Ch. 2, 3 and 8.

analyze the multiplier in an open system with foreign trade, taking into account changes in the general price level and in the relative prices of imported goods.

1. The Marginal Propensity to Import and the Leakage

As we are dealing with an open system, it may be convenient to examine, first, unrecognized characteristics of the marginal propensity to import. Before doing so, however, it is necessary to point out that there are three different ways of computing the marginal propensity to import: (1) the marginal propensity to import in *money* terms, dM/dY, (2) the marginal propensity to import in *real* terms,

$$d\left(\frac{M}{P}\right)\bigg/d\left(\frac{Y}{P}\right),$$

(3) the marginal propensity to import in *physical* terms,

$$d\left(\frac{M}{P_m}\right)\bigg/d\left(\frac{Y}{P}\right) = \frac{dm}{dY_r},$$

where M, m, and P_m denote the total value, quantity and unit-price of imported goods respectively, and Y, $Y_r (= Y/P)$ and P represent money and real national incomes and the general price index. The second propensity employs a common deflator and the third one different deflators. The distinction between the two is very important, as will be indicated later.

Suppose the relative prices of imported goods rise. Then, even if the ratio of the physical quantity of imports to real national income were to remain constant, the proportion of the " foreign leakage " would naturally increase.[3] We do not refer here to the problem of the effect of relative prices upon the quantity of imports. On the

3) Actually, when relative prices of imported goods rise and the terms of trade are adversely affected, real income may decline even if real output is constant. This is a supply-side effect, and for the convenience of our discussion we neglect it here. We may simply assume that this decline of real income is balanced by an increase due to other factors so that the ratio of physical imports to real income remains constant.

contrary, the effect to be emphasized here will be most conspicuous when the relative price-elasticity of import demand is equal to zero, for the alteration of the relative prices of imported goods will then be reflected perfectly proportionately in the change in the foreign-leakage ratio.

Nevertheless, in the ordinary statistical computation of the marginal propensity to import, the import quantity (the value of imports divided by the import-price index) is assumed to be a function of real national income (money national income divided by the general price index). This means that the derived marginal propensity to import leaves out of account the change in the foreign leakage ratio due to the change in the relative prices of imported goods. Therefore, it is not correct to think that this marginal propensity to import in *physical* terms, along with the marginal propensities to save and to tax as indicators of "home leakage," will determine the value of the multiplier.

Yet many statistical studies of the marginal propensity to import jump from this computation in physical terms to conjectures concerning the value of the multiplier. For example, Chang, Polak, Adler, Modigliani and Neisser all computed the marginal propensity to import in physical terms.[4] Polak and Chang went on to make conjectures as to the value of the multiplier. It is possible that they preferred to compute the marginal propensity to import in physical terms because they wished to derive import demand functions that would be stable. In this respect their computations did yield results that were superior to those of computations carried out in money terms (for instance, De Vegh's[5]), for even if the latter may sometimes get a higher correlation coefficient, it may be a spurious one.[6]

When the multiplier is calculated in real terms, as is often done, the marginal propensity to import must be expressed in a comparable

4) See footnote 2.
5) I. De Vegh, " Imports and Income in the United States and Canada," *Rev. Econ. Stat.*, Aug. 1941, XXIII, pp. 130–46.
6) Prices fluctuate very often in the same direction as changes in physical quantities, and thus the cyclical covariation of price and quantity series may entail an apparently high correlation between imports and national income in money terms, in spite of a possibly poor correlation of them in real or physical terms.

form; we should adopt the marginal propensity to import using a common deflator, for it would reflect adequately the ups and downs of the foreign-leakage ratio due to changes of the relative prices of imported goods. When we use different deflators, the marginal propensity to import may be more stable. However, when we use a common deflator, we take into account the effects of the relative changes of import prices on the propensity to import. Each method has its respective advantages, but studies have usually lost sight of the latter (economically more important) advantage and have employed the physical-terms method.

The ordinary marginal propensity to import in physical terms, ν, which Chang, Polak, *etc.*, used is derived from the following equation:

$$M/P_m = \mu + \nu(Y/P) \quad \dots\dots\dots\dots\dots(1)$$

where $\nu = dm/dY_r$. What is the difference between this and the marginal propensity to import using a common deflator

$$d\left(\frac{M}{P}\right)\Big/d\left(\frac{Y}{P}\right)?$$

The latter can be expressed as follows:

$$\frac{d\left(\frac{P_m m}{P}\right)}{d\left(\frac{Y}{P}\right)} = \frac{d\left(\frac{P_m}{P}\right)m + dm\left(\frac{P_m}{P}\right)}{dY_r}$$

$$= \frac{dm}{dY_r}\frac{P_m}{P}\left\{1 + \frac{d\left(\frac{P_m}{P}\right)}{\left(\frac{P_m}{P}\right)}\frac{m}{dm}\right\} \quad \dots\dots\dots\dots(2)$$

P_m/P is an index number, and it may take values different from unity, according as the real values m and Y_r in dm/dY_r are defined in terms of different base-periods. However if we start from the present instant of time when P_m/P is unity, P_m/P may be crossed out.[7] For

---

7) P_m/P also appears in the left-hand term of equation (2), but here an increment is involved, hence it could not be crossed out in this term.

since we are concerned with an infinitesimal change and since the difference between the base and the current point of time is extremely small, P_m/P may still be approximately equal to unity. Equation (2) would then be:

$$\frac{d\left(\dfrac{P_m m}{P}\right)}{d\left(\dfrac{Y}{P}\right)} = \frac{dm}{dY_r}\left\{1 + \frac{d\left(\dfrac{P_m}{P}\right)}{\dfrac{P_m}{P}} \frac{m}{dm}\right\}.$$

Thus, the marginal propensity to import in real terms depends not only upon the marginal propensity to import in physical terms ($= dm/dY_r$), but also upon the flexibility of the relative prices of imported goods with respect to the volume of imports. We must bear in mind that this flexibility is not the reciprocal of the price elasticity of import demand. It is merely an " observable " or *ex post* flexibility, as the mode of expansion of the equation indicates.

The differences between the above two coefficients are sometimes quite remarkable and very important in countries where the proportion of imports to national income is very large and annual fluctuations of the terms of trade are marked. If we neglect this fact and use the marginal propensity to import in physical terms for estimating the numerical value of the multiplier, the procedure will entail a serious theoretical bias ; for we then lack an indispensable ingredient in the construction of the multiplier. Furthermore, if an econometric model is constructed in physical terms the curious result may ensue that when the terms of trade become extremely favorable there will appear to be an import surplus measured in physical terms in spite of the actual occurrence of an export surplus measured in terms of current values.

For problems not involving exports and imports, different deflators are rarely used. For instance, in the case of the consumption or saving function, as a rule a common deflator is used. However, in the Klein-Goldberger econometric model, there arise the following discrepancies between the two concepts of the personal-saving ratio. In money terms, it is 5 per cent (1929), 4 per cent (1949), 8 per cent (1952) ; whereas in physical terms it is 7 per cent (1929), −1 per cent (1949), and 2 per cent (1952). These discrepancies are obviously due to the use of different deflators.[8]

Since the multiplier is a tool for analyzing the demand side of the economy, a common deflator should be used in computing it in order not to eliminate the effect of relative price changes upon the numerical value of the marginal leakage. In this respect, multiplier analysis is fundamentally different from input-output analysis which is a tool for analyzing the supply side. In the latter case, it might be very useful to make an intertemporal comparison of the physical production coefficients of various industries, by using different deflators.[9]

2. Algebraic Analysis of the Marginal Propensity to Import

After examining the characteristics of the marginal propensity to import as a marginal-leakage ratio, we move to an algebraic explanation of the implications of the marginal propensity to import in money and real terms. By doing this, we can make clearer the numerical relationship among the three kinds of marginal propensity to import when changes occur in the relative prices of imported goods and the intensity of inflation.

Let us start with the preliminary assumption that the marginal propensity to import in physical terms is stable. Transforming equation (1), we may write

$$M = \mu P_m + \nu P_m \frac{Y}{P}. \quad \ldots\ldots\ldots\ldots\ldots\ldots (1')$$

By differentiating this with respect to money national income, Y, we derive the marginal propensity to import in money terms,

8) L. R. Klein and A. S. Goldberger, *An Econometric Model of the United States, 1929–1972*, Amsterdam, 1955; Carl Christ, "Aggregative Econometric Models," *Am. Econ. Rev.*, June 1956, XLVI, pp. 385–408, esp. pp. 396–97. Christ correctly commented, "Thus their consumption function is fitted to a distorted set of data, from the point of consumption decision."
9) *Cf.* Richard Stone and S. J. Prais, "Systems of Aggregative Index Numbers and Their Compatibility," *Econ. Jour.*, Sept. 1952, LXII, pp. 565–83.

$$\frac{dM}{dY} = \nu P_m \left(\frac{P - Y\frac{dP}{dY}}{P^2} \right) = \nu \frac{P_m}{P}(1 - e_p) = \nu \frac{P_m}{P} e_o \quad (3)$$

where

$$e_p = \frac{dP}{dY}\frac{Y}{P}, \quad \text{and} \quad e_o = \frac{dY_r}{dY}\frac{Y}{Y_r},$$

the elasticity of the price level and of output with respect to effective demand respectively. As $Y = PY_r$, necessarily $e_o + e_p = 1$.[10]

The following important point now becomes evident. Even if the physical-terms marginal propensity to import ν has great stability, the marginal propensity to import in money terms will be variable according as P_m/P and e_o fluctuate. It would be a serious omission to be satisfied with the computation of ν alone.

If prices do not change, *i.e.*, $e_o = 1$, then

$$\frac{dM}{dY} = \nu \frac{P_m}{P}.$$

If the case were one of hyperinflation, *i.e.*, $e_o = 0$, then

$$\frac{dM}{dY} = 0.$$

This is because under the assumption of $e_o = 0$, an increase of money income will not induce any increase of real output, *i.e.*, Y/P is constant; and by equation (1), the quantity of imports will also be constant when Y/P is constant. Further P_m is also given as a parameter, so $m \times P_m = M$ is also invariant. This is why dM/dY will be zero when $e_o = 0$. This of course assumes away the possible intra- and intertemporal substitution through the relative price effect. For instance, when domestic inflation reduces P_m/P, there will occur a substitution of imported goods for domestic goods. To take account of this fact, our equation must be further extended. Let the relative

10) The first user of this formula was J. M. Keynes. However, he developed two formulas, one measuring Y and P in money terms and another measuring them in wage terms. That there is an algebraic mistake was shown in the previous chapter.

price effect be introduced in equation (1):

$$m = \mu + \nu Y_r - \xi\left(\frac{P_m}{P}\right) \quad \dots\dots\dots\dots(4)$$

where

$$\nu = \partial m / \partial Y_r \quad \text{and} \quad \xi = \partial m / \partial\left(\frac{P_m}{P}\right).$$

Multiplying both sides of the equation by P_m and differentiating with respect to Y, we get the marginal propensity to import in money terms:

$$\frac{d(mP_m)}{dY} = \nu\frac{P_m}{P}e_o + \frac{\dfrac{dP}{dY}\xi P_m{}^2}{P^2}$$

$$= \frac{P_m}{P}\left(\nu e_o + \xi P_m e_p \frac{1}{Y}\right)$$

$$= \frac{P_m}{P}\left(\nu e_o + \eta_m e_p \frac{m}{Y_r}\right) \quad \dots\dots\dots\dots(5)$$

where

$$\eta_m = \frac{\partial m}{\partial\left(\dfrac{P_m}{P}\right)}\frac{\left(\dfrac{P_m}{P}\right)}{m} = \xi\frac{\left(\dfrac{P_m}{P}\right)}{m},$$

i.e., the price elasticity of import demand.

If $e_p = 0$,

$$\frac{dM}{dY} = \nu\frac{P_m}{P},$$

and if $e_p = 1$, then

$$\frac{dM}{dY} = \eta_m\frac{P_m}{P}\frac{m}{Y_r} = \eta_m\frac{M}{Y}.$$

The fact that dM/dY depends on η_m indicates that dM/dY is affected by the degree of substitution of imported goods caused by the domestic inflation. Let us further assume that $e_p = 1$ and $\eta_m = 1$, then

$$\frac{dM}{dY} = \frac{P_m}{P}\frac{m}{Y} = \frac{M}{Y}.$$

This means the marginal propensity to import in money terms will then coincide with the average propensity to import. When $e_p=1$ and $\eta_m=0$,

$$\frac{dM}{dY} = 0.$$

We have so far analyzed the marginal propensity to import in money terms. This is useful when the multiplicand is an increment of monetary expenditure. However, when we want to use the real-income multiplier, the marginal propensity to import must be expressed in real terms (using a common deflator). Let us attempt this.

Multiplying both sides of (4) by P_m/P, and differentiating with respect to real income Y_r, we obtain the following equation.[11]

$$\frac{d\left(\frac{mP_m}{P}\right)}{dY_r} = \frac{P_m}{P}\left[\nu - \frac{e_p}{e_o}\left\{\nu + \left(\frac{\mu - 2\eta_m m}{Y_r}\right)\right\}\right] \quad \ldots\ldots(6)$$

If we assume in this equation that $e_p=0$, then

$$\frac{d\left(\frac{mP_m}{P}\right)}{dY_r} = \nu\frac{P_m}{P}.$$

If $e_p=0.5$,

$$\frac{d\left(\frac{mP_m}{P}\right)}{dY_r} = \frac{P_m}{P}\left(\frac{\mu - 2\eta_m m}{Y_r}\right).$$

And if $e_p=1$ (therefore $e_o=0$),

$$\frac{d\left(\frac{mP_m}{P}\right)}{dY_r} = \infty,$$

provided that the expression enclosed in { } <0. If the expression enclosed in { } >0, it will be $-\infty$. If $\eta_m=0$, it will be

11) As to the derivation of equation (6), see the Appendix I.

312

$$\frac{P_m}{P}\left(\nu-\frac{e_p}{e_o}\frac{m}{Y_r}\right),$$

because

$$\nu+\frac{\mu}{Y_r} = \frac{m}{Y_r}.$$

What I have shown in this section may be summarized as follows: If prices are constant, *i.e.*, $e_o=1$ and $e_p=0$, then P_m/P is also invariable, because P_m is given as a parameter. Therefore the coefficient, ξ or η_m, expressing the relative price effect do not affect the volume of imports. In this case, dM/dY, as well as

$$d\left(\frac{M}{Y}\right)\Big/d\left(\frac{Y}{P}\right), \quad \text{is equal to} \quad \nu\frac{P_m}{P},$$

i.e., it is identical to the marginal propensity to import in physical terms multiplied by the relative prices of imported goods. When the case is one of hyperinflation, *i.e.*, $e_o=0$, then the money-terms marginal propensity to import

$$\frac{dM}{dY} = \eta_m\frac{M}{Y}.$$

This means that in the hyperinflation dM/dY is zero when $\eta_m=0$, and that the larger the price elasticity of import demand η_m becomes, the greater the numerical value of dM/dY will be. And in the critical case where $\eta_m=1$, the marginal and the average propensities to import in money terms coincide with each other. Therefore, when $e_o=0$, the marginal propensity to import in money terms $\gtreqless$ the average propensity to import in money terms, according as $\eta_m\gtreqless1$. Since

$$dM/dY = \eta_m\frac{M}{Y}$$

in the case of $e_o=0$,

$$\eta_m = \frac{dM}{dY}\frac{Y}{M}.$$

And in the critical case where

$$\eta_m = 1, \quad \frac{dM}{dY}\frac{Y}{M} = 1.$$

The economic implication is clear. Since $e_o=0$, $dY/Y=dP/P$, and since P_m is constant, $dM/M=dm/m$. Further since P_m is a parameter,

$$dP/P = -d\left(\frac{P_m}{P}\right)\bigg/\left(\frac{P_m}{P}\right).$$

Therefore, when $e_o=0$,

$$\eta_m = \frac{dM}{dY}\frac{Y}{M} = \frac{dm}{dP}\frac{P}{m} = -\frac{dm}{d\left(\dfrac{P_m}{P}\right)}\frac{\left(\dfrac{P_m}{P}\right)}{m}.$$

However, when a relative price effect has to be taken into account, the results in the case of

$$d\left(\frac{M}{P}\right)\bigg/d\left(\frac{Y}{P}\right)$$

will be as follows: When $e_o=0$, $d(Y/P)$ will be zero. Therefore, the marginal propensity to import in real terms will be infinite. Intermediate cases where $1>e_o>0$ can be judged from equation (6), but the propensity in real terms appears to be more volatile than in money terms especially in semi-inflationary stages, for its numerical values range from ∞ (when $e_o=0$) to

$$\nu\frac{P_m}{P} \quad \text{(when } e_o = 1\text{)}.$$

Even on the assumption that the marginal propensity to import in physical terms is stable, it is clear that the marginal foreign-leakage ratio which is an ingredient of the multiplier is not always stable, depending on the instability of P_m/P, e_o and η_m.

3. Real- and Money-Income Multipliers Reconsidered

We have explained that even if the coefficient which has a statistical stability might be the marginal propensity to import in physical

314

terms, the coefficient measuring the marginal foreign leakage adequately as a component of the multiplier should be the marginal propensity to import either in real terms or in money terms, depending on whether we are concerned with the real- or money-income multiplier. In this section we consider the implications of the preceding analysis for the analysis of the multiplier in an open system.

As we are concerned here with the multiplier in an open system with foreign trade and public finance, we must also examine the other two marginal-leakage ratios—the marginal propensities to save and to tax—in order to complete our multiplier analysis. The marginal propensity to tax should naturally be in money terms, since the tax rates are applied to money incomes. The marginal propensity to save might more plausibly be defined in real terms, because the average propensity to consume or to save is regarded as a function of real income rather than money income.

For simplicity, we start from the simplest linear consumption function in real terms,

$$\frac{C}{P} = a + b\left(\frac{Y_d}{P}\right) \quad \ldots\ldots\ldots\ldots\ldots\ldots(7)$$

where C is money consumption expenditure, and Y_d is money personal disposal income. From this, we obtain

$$C = aP + bY_d. \quad \ldots\ldots\ldots\ldots\ldots\ldots(7')$$

Differentiating this with respect to Y_d, the marginal propensity to consume in money terms is computed:

$$\frac{dC}{dY_d} = \frac{dP}{dY_d}a + b = e_p\frac{aP}{Y_d} + b$$

$$= e_p\frac{aP}{Y_d} + (e_p + e_o)b = e_p\frac{C}{Y_d} + e_o b \quad \ldots\ldots(8)$$

where we assume that, approximately,

$$e_p = \frac{dP}{dY}\frac{Y}{P} = \frac{dP}{dY_d}\frac{Y_d}{P}.$$

When $e_p = 1$, we get

$$\frac{dC}{dY_d} = \frac{aP}{Y_d} + b = \frac{C}{Y_d}$$

and the full-employment multiplier in the closed system (Goodwin)[12] will be calculated from this. Goodwin's and our multiplier perfectly coincide in this case. When $e_p = 0$,

$$\frac{dC}{dY_d} = b,$$

and the ordinary underemployment multiplier will be obtained from this. Equation (8) covers both conceivable areas and also intermediate cases.[13] It is worth noticing that even if the marginal propensity to consume in real terms is constant, the marginal propensity to consume in money terms will be larger as the intensity of the price fluctuation becomes stronger. For this reason, an international comparison of the money-terms marginal propensities to consume and the money-income multipliers, once attempted by Richard and W. M. Stone, may make little sense.[14]

We denote here as A the various exogenous expenditures, such as government expenditure for goods and services G, private capital formation I, exports E, and other autonomous expenditures. We assume that imports M are siphoned off as a foreign leakage and that savings S and taxes T are absorbed as domestic leakages during the working out of the multiplier process. Then the money-income multiplier would be,

$$\frac{dY}{dA} = \frac{1}{1 - \frac{dC}{dY_d}\left(1 - \frac{dT}{dY}\right) + \frac{dM}{dY}} . \quad \dots\dots(9)$$

Representing dT/dY as t, and substituting equations (8) and (5) into (9), we obtain

12) R. M. Goodwin, " The Multiplier," in Seymour Harris, ed., *The New Economics*, New York, 1947, pp. 482–99.

13) For a comparison of the real- and money-income multipliers in a closed systems, see Appendix II.

14) R. and W. M. Stone, "The Marginal Propensity to Consume and the Multiplier, a Statistical Investigation," *Rev. Econ. Stud.*, Oct. 1938, VI, 1–24.

$$\frac{dY}{dA} = \frac{1}{1-\left(e_p\dfrac{C}{Y_d}+e_ob\right)(1-t)+\dfrac{P_m}{P}\left(\nu e_o+\eta_m e_p\dfrac{m}{Y_r}\right)}. \quad (10)$$

Here, b, t and ν are assumed to have stable values, and e_p, e_o and P_m/P are supposed to fluctuate according to the phases and conditions of the business cycle and balance of payments. However, since we cannot express their behavior mathematically, they are treated here as parameters. The elasticity η_m is a coefficient derived from a constant

$$-\xi = \partial m/\partial\left(\frac{P_m}{P}\right),$$

so it may change and be influenced by the alteration of P_m/P and m.

The main components of A, $i.e.$, G, I and E, consist furthermore of two parts, prices and quantities. Consequently, we can express them in this way, $G=gP_g$; $I=iP_i$; $E=eP_e$. g, i and e denote quantities, and P_g, P_i and P_e represent prices. It is very important to observe that not only increases in quantity but also mere price rises will be the multiplicands of multiplier expansion.

Furthermore, even in the case of the real-income multiplier

$$d\left(\frac{Y}{P}\right)\bigg/d\left(\frac{A}{P}\right),$$

the mere increases of relative prices (P_g/P, P_i/P and P_e/P) will entail the multiplier process in real terms. In other words, the changes of relative prices can be the multiplicand. This means that even when the amount of investment or of exports, deflated by its own price indexes, is invariant, it can bring about an increase of real income in so far as its value rises when deflated by the general price index. This fact was recognized, first, by Hicks,[15] in relation to the changes of P_i/P, and secondly by Polak,[16] in relation to the changes of P_e/P. However, in general, this point has not been taken into consideration, especially in econometrics.

In the case of the real-income multiplier, we should use b in

15) J. R. Hicks, *A Contribution to the Theory of the Trade Cycle*, Oxford, 1950, p. 130.
16) Polak, *ibid.*, pp. 22–23.

equation (7) as the marginal propensity to consume, and equation (6) as the marginal propensity to import. However, since the marginal propensity to tax was originally defined in money terms, it must be transformed into real terms. Assume a linear tax function,

$$T = tY - H \quad \dots\dots\dots\dots\dots\dots(11)$$

where t is the marginal propensity to tax and H is a constant. Dividing both sides by the price index P,

$$\frac{T}{P} = tY_r - \frac{H}{P} \quad \dots\dots\dots\dots\dots(11')$$

Differentiating this with respect to Y_r,

$$t^* = \frac{d\left(\dfrac{T}{P}\right)}{dY_r} = t - \frac{d\left(\dfrac{H}{P}\right)}{dY}\frac{dY}{dY_r} = t + \frac{e_p}{e_o}\frac{H}{Y}. \quad (12)$$

This t^* (the marginal propensity to tax in real terms) is supposed to be a component of the real-income multiplier. In equation (12), if $e_p = 0$, then $t^* = t$; if $e_p = 0.5$, then $t = t^* + H/Y$; and if $e_p = 1$, then $t^* = \infty$. This is because when $e_p = 1$, then $\Delta Y_r = 0$ by definition, whereas the tax in money terms will increase more speedily than money national income (consequently more than the price level too) under the restriction of equation (11). $\Delta(T/P)$ is positive, and, when this is compared with $\Delta Y_r = 0$, we have $t^* = \infty$.

As a formula for the real-income multiplier, we can derive an equation similar in form to equation (9),

$$\frac{dY_r}{dA_r} = \frac{1}{1 - dC_r/dY_r(1 - dT_r/dY_r) + dM_r/dY_r} \quad \dots(13)$$

where $A_r = A/P$, $C_r = C/P$, $Y_{dr} = Y_d/P$, $T_r = T/P$ and $M_r = M/P$. Substituting into this equation the coefficients in equations (7), (12) and (6), we have an equation for the real-income multiplier.

$$\frac{dY_r}{dA_r} = \frac{1}{1 - b\left(1 - t - \dfrac{e_p}{e_o}\dfrac{H}{Y}\right) + \dfrac{P_m}{P}\left[\nu - \dfrac{e_p}{e_0}\left\{\nu + \left(\dfrac{\mu - 2\eta_m m}{Y_r}\right)\right\}\right]}. \quad (14)$$

318

When $e_p=0$, the equation will be,

$$\frac{1}{1-b(1-t)+\dfrac{P_m}{P}\nu}.$$

This can also be derived by assuming $e_p=0$ in equation (10) for the money-income multiplier. However, in the world in which $e_p\neq0$, the real- and money-income multipliers may differ considerably from each other.

Thus post-Keynesian arguments have been too much simplified by assuming a world in which no change in prices occurs and no allowance is made for changes in the relative prices of imported goods as a factor bringing about fluctuations in the leakage. In making predictions for the economy, it becomes necessary to judge the magnitude of e_p, because the multiplier also depends upon e_p. Thus, results of predictions could considerably differ, according as prices in the future economy are anticipated as stable or inflationary.

4. Conclusion

It has not been our intention just to complicate the various formulas. The purpose of this article has been to clarify the role of absolute and relative price fluctuations during the multiplier process, to bring out thoroughly the limitations of existing econometric studies on the multiplier, and to attempt to consolidate the theory of the multiplier and the analysis of price fluctuations. Post-Keynesian economists seem to have become accustomed to arguments in real terms, and to " real " trade-cycle theories. However, except during the 1930's, the price cycle was more typical than the real cycle. The amendments of theory which I have proposed are particularly significant for countries in which the terms of trade are not constant and the ratios of imports to national income are comparatively large. In such countries, the ordinary type of computation of the marginal propensity to import will not serve as a useful tool for formulating economic policy nor for understanding the economy. I repeat that the points examined here are very simple, but, notwithstanding their importance, they have long been neglected by many economists.

APPENDIX

I. Equation (6) in the text can be derived as follows:
Starting from the following equation,

$$m = \mu + \nu Y_r - \xi\left(\frac{P_m}{P}\right) \quad\dots\dots\dots\dots(4)$$

and multiplying by P_m/P on both sides of (4),

$$\frac{mP_m}{P} = \mu\frac{P_m}{P} + \nu\frac{P_m}{P}Y_r - \xi\left(\frac{P_m}{P}\right)^2 \dots\dots\dots(4')$$

Differentiating this with respect to real income Y_r,

$$\frac{d\left(\frac{mP_m}{P}\right)}{dY_r} = \left[\frac{d\left(\mu\frac{P_m}{P}\right)}{dY} + \frac{d\left(\nu\frac{P_mY_r}{P}\right)}{dY} - \frac{d\left\{\xi\left(\frac{P_m}{P}\right)^2\right\}}{dY}\right]\frac{dY}{dY_r}.$$

Substituting the following results into the above,

$$\frac{d\left(\frac{\mu P_m}{P}\right)}{dY} = \frac{-\frac{dP}{dY}\mu P_m}{P^2} = \frac{-e_p\frac{\mu P_m}{Y}}{P};$$

$$\frac{d\left(\frac{\nu P_mY_r}{P}\right)}{dY} = \frac{P\frac{d(\nu P_mY_r)}{dY} - \frac{dP}{dY}\nu P_mY_r}{P^2} = \frac{\nu\frac{P_m}{P}e_o - e_p\nu\frac{P_m}{P}}{P};$$

$$\frac{d\left\{\xi\left(\frac{P_m}{P}\right)^2\right\}}{dY} = \frac{-\frac{d(P^2)}{dY}\xi P_m{}^2}{P^4} = -\frac{d(P^2)}{dP}\frac{dP}{dY}\frac{\xi P_m{}^2}{P^4}$$

$$= -2P\frac{dP}{dY}\frac{Y}{P}\frac{\xi P_m{}^2}{P^4}\frac{P}{Y} = -e_p\frac{2\xi\left(\frac{P_m}{P}\right)^2}{Y};$$

$$\frac{dY}{dY_r} = \frac{P}{e_o},$$

we obtain the following equation.

$$\frac{d\left(\dfrac{mP_m}{P}\right)}{dY_r} = \nu\frac{P_m}{P} - \frac{e_p}{e_o}\left\{\frac{\mu P_m}{Y} + \nu\frac{P_m}{P} - \frac{2\xi\left(\dfrac{P_m}{P}\right)^2}{Y_r}\right\}.$$

As the equation is still complicated for interpretation, we may simplify it by introducing the price elasticity of import demand,

$$\eta_m = \xi\frac{\left(\dfrac{P_m}{P}\right)}{m}.$$

$$\frac{d\left(\dfrac{mP_m}{P}\right)}{dY_r} = \frac{P_m}{P}\left[\nu - \frac{e_p}{e_o}\left\{\nu + \left(\frac{\mu - 2\eta_m m}{Y_r}\right)\right\}\right]. \quad \dots(6)$$

II.   Let us compare the real-income multiplier (k_r) and the money-income multiplier (k_m) under a closed system in which the influences of public finance and foreign trade are assumed away. As

$$k_r = \frac{1}{1-b}, \quad \text{and} \quad k_m = \frac{1}{1-b-e_p\dfrac{aP}{Y}},$$

$$\frac{k_r}{k_m} = \frac{(1-b) - \dfrac{aP}{Y}e_p}{(1-b)} = 1 - e_p\frac{aP}{Y}k_r. \quad \dots\dots\dots(a)$$

As it is a closed system, $Y = Y_d$. From equation (a), it follows that when $e_p = 0$, $k_r = k_m$, and when $e_p = 1$,

$$\frac{k_r}{k_m} = 1 - \frac{aP}{Y}k_r.$$

Since in general (in rigorous terms, if $S/Y > 0$),

$$\frac{aP}{Y}k_r < 1$$

k_m will be relatively larger than k_r according as e_p becomes larger. In the previous chapter a modification of equation (a),

$$\frac{k_r}{k_m} = e_o + e_p k_r\frac{S}{Y} \quad \dots\dots\dots\dots\dots(b)$$

was called the fundamental equation.

We assume, next, the Duesenberry saving function,

$$\frac{S_r}{Y_r} = \beta \frac{Y_r}{Y_{ro}} - a \qquad \text{(Duesenberry)}$$

where Y_{ro} is the highest real income in the previous peak and S_r is real savings. By multiplying both sides by PY_r, and differentiating this with respect to Y, we get

$$\frac{d(PS_r)}{dY} = \beta \frac{Y_r}{Y_{ro}}(1+e_o) - a. \quad \dots\dots\dots\dots(c)$$

This value ranges from

$$\left(\beta \frac{Y_r}{Y_{ro}} - a\right) \text{ when } e_o = 0 \text{ to } \left(2\beta \frac{Y_r}{Y_{ro}} - a\right)$$

when $e_o = 1$. The ratio between k_r and k_m in the case of the Duesenberry function is,

$$\frac{k_r}{k_m} = \frac{\beta \dfrac{Y_r}{Y_{ro}}(1+e_o) - a}{2\beta \dfrac{Y_r}{Y_{ro}} - a}. \quad \dots\dots\dots\dots(d)$$

If $e_o = 1$, then $k_m = k_r$.

Modigliani's saving function was,

$$\frac{S_r}{Y_r} = a^* + \beta^*\left(\frac{Y_r - Y_{ro}}{Y_r}\right). \qquad \text{(Modigliani)}$$

We merely note here the results of the computation:

$$\frac{d(PS_r)}{dY} = a^* + \beta^*\left(1 - e_p \frac{Y_{ro}}{Y_r}\right) \quad \dots\dots\dots\dots(e)$$

When $e_p = 0$,

$$\frac{d(PS_r)}{dY} = a^* + \beta^*.$$

When $e_p = 1$,

$$\frac{d(PS_r)}{dY} = a^* + \beta^*\left(\frac{Y_r - Y_{ro}}{Y_r}\right) = \frac{S_r}{Y_r}$$

III. Colin Clark, in a very helpful comment, points out that, in

322

the case of large countries (like the United Kingdom) whose imports represent a large fraction of the total supply, P_m may to some extent be a function of domestic money income Y. Although P_m is a parameter in my system, it now becomes a variable like P. Instead of my equation (3), he gets:

$$\frac{dM}{dY} = -\nu\frac{P_m}{P}(e_p - e_{pm}) + \nu\frac{P_m}{P} + \mu\frac{P_m}{Y}e_{pm} \quad \ldots\ldots(f)$$

where

$$e_{pm} = \frac{dP_m}{dY}\frac{Y}{P_m}.$$

If we assume $e_{pm}=0$, equation (f) equals my equation (3). His equation, however, can be simplified into a more interesting form:

$$\frac{dM}{dY} = \mu\frac{dP_m}{dY} + \nu\left(Y_r\frac{dP_m}{dY} + P_m\frac{dY_r}{dY}\right) = \nu\frac{P_m}{P}e_o + e_{pm}\frac{P_m}{P}\left(\frac{\mu}{Y_r} + \nu\right)$$

$$= \nu\frac{P_m}{P}e_o + e_{pm}\frac{M}{Y}. \ldots\ldots\ldots\ldots\ldots\ldots\ldots\ldots\ldots\ldots\ldots\ldots\ldots\ldots\ldots\ldots\ldots(g)$$

Then even if $e_o=0$, dM/dY may not be zero, when e_{pm} is larger than zero and M/Y is comparatively large.

CHAPTER 13

THE PRODUCTION FUNCTION IN PREWAR
MANUFACTURING

1. Introduction

Since the first empirical derivation of the Production Function in 1928, there have been accumulated a plenty of achievements by P. H. Douglas and others. *The Theory of Wages*, 1934 and "Are There Laws of Production?" *American Economic Review, March,* 1948, both written by P. H. Douglas, can be taken as two main summaries of the results of measurements hitherto accomplished.

In Japan, Prof. Ohkawa[1] has obtained a satisfactory results in respect to the computation of agricultural production function, but satisfactory computations are still lacking in relation to the manufacturing sector. This small article, rewritten from my work[2] published in 1949 in Japanese, aims to compute the cross-section production function for Japanese manufacturing. Reference should be made to the later work of the Institute of Economic Research of the Tōyō Bōseki (Oriental Cotton Spinning Company, Ltd.),[3] which attempts particularly to compute the Cobb-Douglas Function in the cotton spinning industry under the direction of Prof. Iemoto.[4]

While the statistical results have hitherto been accumulated in a considerable volume, there have arisen many animated controversies

1) Kazushi Ohkawa, *Shokuryo Keizai no Riron to Keisoku* (The Theory and Measurement of Food Economy), Tokyo, 1945.
2) M. Shinohara, *Koyo to Chingin* (Employment and Wages), Tokyo, 1949.
3) *The Relative Contribution of Labor and Capital to Production,*—On the Measurement of Douglas Function in relation to the Japanese Cotton Spinning Industry.
4) Hidetaro Iemoto, "Douglas Kansu Ikusei no Tameni" (To Defend the Douglas Production Function), *Riron Keizaigaku* (The Economic Studies Quarterly), Jan., 1951.

tions perfectly coincide not only with the rank of k in 1942, but also with the ranks of rates of alteration of k from 1936 to 1942.

6. Conclusion

The above results, as a matter of fact, were not tested by bunch maps. I believe some of the cases above computed may be statistically insignificant owing to multicollinearity. Consequently, it might be somewhat hasty to draw conclusions from our computed results.

However, anyone will confirm the long-run parallel between k and the relative share of labor and capital in the light of our analysis already concluded, notwithstanding the non-existence of a perfect coincidence. If I had been an enthusiastic Douglasian, I would have defended the theoretical validity of the Cobb-Douglas Function on the ground of those empirical findings, but I am not confident enough to do so.

Be that as it may, it is worth while to keep in mind that the relative shares of labor in Japanese manufactures were considerably lower than k computed. This fundamental fact may reflect not only the extremely monopolistic position of private enterprise as compared with the body of laborers, but also the special characteristics of the past Japanese economy in which the farm area, having a lower standard of living than the urban districts, supplied cheap labor to the latter. These circumstances enabled business firms to realize a high rate of capital accumulation, which fostered the prominent tempo of production expansion.

Other institutional factors than the marginal productivity would evidently have exerted a strong influence upon the distribution of income in Japan, but it cannot be denied that the influence of productivities of factors also was not negligible. This is a conclusion at which I have finally arrived as an optimistic Douglasian, but I am obliged to cast some doubts as to the statistical validity of these results.

(Whole Manufacturing) Statistical Data of *P, L, C*

Scale of factories by number of manual workers	(Unit)	5—10	10—15
1929 Value of gross products	million yen	620	306
Manual workers	thousand	198	92
H. P. in use of prime movers	thousand H. P	149	76
1930 Value of gross products	million yen	533	270
Manual workers	thousand	206	92
H. P. in use of prime movers	thousand H. P.	167	71
1931 Value of gross products	mlllion yen	506	249
Manual workers	thousand	211	94
H. P. in use of prime movers	thousand H. P.	169	74
1932 Value of gross products	million yen	550	275
Manual workers	thousand	220	99
H. P. in use of prime movers	thousand H. P.	169	77
1933 Value of gross products	million yen	591	326
Manual workers	thousand	232	108
H. P. in use of prime movers	thousand H. P.	173	81
1934 Value of gross products	million yen	651	380
Manual workers	thousand	254	122
H. P. in use of prime movers	thousand H. P.	183	87
1935 Value of gross products	million yen	665	396
Manual workers	thousand	258	134
H. P. in use of prime movers	thousand H. P.	186	92
1936 Value of gross products	million yen	714	422
Manual workers	thousand	263	150
H. P. in use of prime movers	thousand H. P.	176	101
1937 Value of gross products	million yen	1,004	554
Manual workers	thousand	317	165
H. P. in use of prime movers	thousand H. P.	247	125
1938 Value of gross products	million yen	1,183	666
Manual workers	thousand	322	172
H. P. in use of prime movers	thousand H. P.	271	131
1939 Value of gross products	million yen	1,752	1,045
Manual workers	thousand	437	252
H. P. in use of prime movers	thousand H. P.	296	177
1940 Value of gross products	million yen	2,158	1,148
Manual workers	thousand	451	237
H. P. in use of prime movers	thousand H. P.	328	180
1941 Value of gross products	million yen	2,264	1,342
Manual workers	thousand	388	219
H. P. in use of prime movers	thousand H. P.	345	202

Note: The above figures exclude the electricity and gas industries.

dix I.

Classified by Scale of Factories

15—30	30—50	50—100	100—200	200—500	500—1000	1000 over
660	583	879	888	1,376	884	1,542
186	147	193	190	247	206	360
178	163	212	471	1,174	709	1,322
528	468	711	703	976	774	982
180	139	194	190	244	189	240
151	139	212	458	863	718	886
499	439	610	616	822	679	740
175	139	186	172	239	195	233
146	136	191	327	626	731	800
564	511	694	701	949	750	974
194	152	192	190	234	189	256
145	141	183	321	547	527	718
660	643	853	870	1,277	1,009	1,626
212	168	209	200	267	209	267
158	150	203	327	615	474	847
773	711	926	865	1,378	1,136	2,449
250	189	233	217	258	230	403
185	163	221	340	669	569	1,548
913	804	1,047	1,147	1,559	1,360	2,924
273	210	255	238	283	244	465
202	166	238	451	816	545	1,903
966	958	1,103	1,196	1,852	1,472	3,484
305	242	262	246	313	256	547
209	188	269	467	835	730	2,298
1,305	1,198	1,383	1,541	2,356	1,870	5,118
325	255	263	260	344	275	723
241	210	280	626	945	735	3,266
1,581	1,487	1,659	1,802	2,735	2,094	6,403
341	276	274	291	375	303	852
267	250	538	636	1,019	947	3,488
2,161	1,840	2,140	2,155	3,235	2,387	8,080
430	316	314	311	411	331	971
336	297	347	518	1,281	1,172	3,760
2,476	2,075	2,428	2,340	3,388	2,727	8,363
429	304	324	305	405	348	1,027
353	303	408	523	1,371	1,356	4,340
2,935	2,173	2,774	2,436	3,714	3,131	11,271
415	275	319	276	400	312	1,306
432	351	521	711	1,310	1,167	4,772

Appendix II.

(Four particular industries) Statistical Data of P, L, C Classified by Scale of Factories

Scale of factories by number of manual workers		5—10	10—15	15—30	30—50	50—100	100—200	200—500	500—1000	1000 over
1931										
Textiles	P	115.2	56.6	142.4	118.6	181.8	185.5	296.0	374.7	455.9
	L	62.1	29.0	67.1	61.5	102.5	110.7	161.0	151.5	153.3
	C	26.0	11.3	31.5	26.2	42.2	52.9	120.5	180.9	396.5
Metals	P	34.0	16.7	39.3	36.1	45.8	61.0	59.0	70.0	69.5
	L	13.5	6.9	12.8	9.0	8.9	8.3	8.7	8.0	8.2
	C	10.8	6.3	14.2	14.1	18.6	37.9	65.4	72.4	68.2
Machinery and equipment	P	34.5	17.8	32.6	32.8	40.7	49.8	94.0	65.8	129.9
	L	19.7	9.0	15.2	12.4	13.1	13.5	18.1	16.0	41.6
	C	10.3	4.8	11.6	10.0	12.9	23.2	82.3	64.5	165.3
Chemicals	P	50.6	31.1	77.3	63.2	132.8	123.4	173.1	102.5	62.5
	L	8.1	5.2	12.8	11.7	18.4	14.7	21.4	11.0	19.2
	C	19.1	8.8	22.4	26.6	54.1	78.5	197.8	197.0	56.5
1934										
Textiles	P	142.9	89.8	212.2	191.5	264.8	267.7	377.0	566.4	1,055.5
	L	69.9	37.6	91.1	75.1	104.4	111.0	144.3	148.4	187.5
	C	30.7	16.6	39.2	31.1	43.8	41.5	82.9	183.7	362.8
Machinery and equipment	P	47.4	30.0	77.4	68.6	85.3	108.0	119.2	138.3	405.1
	L	28.6	15.4	30.9	23.8	26.1	25.0	29.2	29.4	106.2
	C	12.6	6.7	14.0	12.1	23.4	21.5	36.2	53.5	244.7
Chemicals	P	68.2	40.3	100.8	121.8	187.7	214.2	327.0	173.9	247.1
	L	10.2	6.5	16.2	17.1	23.1	22.2	26.1	19.0	51.9
	C	14.2	9.4	29.1	44.6	59.5	80.1	204.3	155.9	293.9
Textiles	P	148.0	104.0	258.3	242.0	302.3	323.6	503.0	660.2	1,113.4
	L	68.5	44.6	105.5	89.8	107.8	108.1	156.3	151.9	195.3
	C	32.2	19.3	45.4	38.8	51.8	59.6	115.5	241.8	495.7
Metals	P	54.4	46.4	135.9	139.1	120.6	157.8	230.3	217.6	1,106.8
	L	21.9	16.1	35.8	23.7	22.9	20.5	22.9	23.1	59.9
	C	14.5	10.9	27.8	29.0	34.9	38.9	84.4	128.1	764.3

Year	Industry										
1936	Machinery and equipment	P	56.0	42.5	100.2	104.8	130.4	134.4	238.6	207.7	701.8
		L	33.2	21.3	43.6	37.1	37.1	34.7	39.2	39.8	171.0
		C	15.9	9.3	20.0	18.8	25.9	29.4	41.2	63.3	374.9
	Chemicals	P	87.4	48.1	137.6	145.7	242.0	276.1	430.0	313.1	430.9
		L	11.2	7.1	20.4	20.1	25.6	26.1	37.6	28.2	97.2
		C	15.4	12.1	29.4	39.8	68.3	95.7	241.5	260.1	616.2
1939	Textiles	P	375.7	240.9	484.2	370.9	441.7	441.1	710.1	789.5	959.8
		L	120.2	69.7	125.3	89.9	95.2	102.0	151.8	153.8	159.4
		C	46.7	28.7	62.8	48.5	61.0	69.3	154.2	336.8	438.0
	Metals	P	157.2	122.2	304.8	301.6	255.2	282.9	472.1	520.6	3,164.3
		L	33.5	24.2	47.9	35.6	31.1	29.5	44.3	37.7	161.4
		C	28.6	23.2	53.4	51.0	48.1	65.6	140.9	218.3	1,323.2
	Machinery and equipment	P	177.6	149.2	372.8	370.7	445.7	425.2	571.1	475.7	2,604.1
		L	64.8	46.8	90.5	75.8	85.3	84.1	106.5	83.9	493.9
		C	37.3	27.5	55.7	55.8	60.6	75.4	105.1	97.3	758.5
	Chemicals	P	171.7	127.5	293.0	269.5	433.4	499.0	777.9	456.7	1,246.6
		L	23.2	16.7	30.6	27.6	31.7	38.8	54.0	37.0	137.5
		C	20.3	15.8	46.3	51.0	88.1	134.0	394.7	407.9	1,183.3
1942	Textiles	P	401.0	213.1	437.5	302.7	421.3	371.0	707.7	539.0	576.0
		L	89.6	47.2	88.6	59.0	76.3	68.1	124.8	90.8	90.8
		C	43.0	22.9	51.1	36.8	80.0	85.6	157.0	194.0	210.1
	Metals	P	190.6	143.8	361.8	274.0	335.9	288.4	536.7	624.1	4,276.7
		L	33.6	21.1	44.4	28.8	32.2	25.8	41.7	37.6	180.2
		C	44.4	28.3	69.0	60.3	75.7	80.8	183.5	173.5	2,114.1
	Machinery and equipment	P	319.2	227.5	633.2	586.6	730.3	692.3	991.0	1,164.3	5,237.5
		L	70.1	45.0	101.2	84.0	101.4	100.8	142.1	128.2	909.9
		C	49.5	33.1	83.1	79.3	110.8	112.1	175.7	184.1	1,350.4
	Chemicals	P	225.0	175.2	422.0	378.6	546.7	582.0	930.2	606.4	1,145.3
		L	21.8	15.5	32.7	26.1	36.0	34.9	49.2	38.6	118.3
		C	29.2	24.2	62.2	76.9	127.3	227.8	383.6	518.7	1,089.5

Notes: P = Value of gross products; L = Number of manual workers; C = Horse Power in use by prime movers.

Unit: P = million yen; L = thousand men; C = thousand H. P.

INDEX

Abramovitz, M., 176
Acceleration principle, 182
Adler, J. H., 304, 306
Age composition of agricultural working population, 143
Akamatsu, Kaname, 57

Balance of payments, 51–55, 83–84, 106
Bean, Louis H., 230
Bjerke, K., 132
Book-value, 135
Business cycle barometer, 153

Capacity-deficient economy, 111
Capacity-abundant economy, 111
Capacity-increasing coefficient, 112, 122–126
— three concepts of ∼ 133
Capital market, 19
Capital concentration, 19–23
Cash·deposit-national income ratio, 234
Chang, Tse Chun, 304, 306, 307
Christ, Carl, 309
Clark, Colin, 26, 65, 281, 288, 322
Cobb-Douglas function, 324
Commodity composition of trade, 55
Consumption function, 211–261, 270–283
real ∼ 285, 300, 315
∼ in money terms, 284
∼ in the earlier prewar period, 270–283
Consumption-saving pattern
— farmers' ∼ 211
— urban workers' ∼ 214
Cycle in the proportional composition, 161

Dependency on exports, 47–50
De Vegh, I, 306
Douglas, Paul H., 324

Downward rigidity in fixed investment, 156
Dual economy, 14, 23
Duesenberry, J., 211, 217, 289, 322
Durand, David, 325

Economic forecasting, 199–200
$e_o \cdot e_p$ theory, 289, 295
Efficiency-value, 135
Efficiency wage, 71
Expansionist policy of the Ikeda Cabinet, 138
Export function, 104
Export composition, 49
Exports-output ratios, 48
Export growth factors, 59–71
Export growth potentials, 28

Fisher, Irving, 232
Firestone, O. T., 132
Foreign leakage, 305
Friedman, Milton, 214
Friend, Irwin, 206, 207
Fujino, Shozaburo, 67
Full employment multiplier, 291
Fundamental equation of real- and money-income multipliers, 288, 321

Gilbert, Milton, 26, 37, 38
Gold embargo, 54
Gold standard, 83, 84
Goldberger, A. S., 309
Goto, Yonosuke, 110, 115, 186
Goto's effect, 186
Goodwin, R. M., 290, 316
Gross stock ratio, 137
Growth controversy, 110–147
Growth rates
international comparison, 4, 5, 7
∼ of transportation and electric power, 96
∼ of exports, 32, 43 46